Property and the Politics of
ENTITLEMENT

Property
and the
Politics
of
Entitlement

JOHN BRIGHAM

Temple University Press
Philadelphia

Temple University Press, Philadelphia 19122
Copyright © 1990 by Temple University. All rights reserved
Published 1990
Printed in the United States of America

The paper used in this publication meets the minimum
requirements of American National Standard for Information
Sciences—Permanence of Paper for Printed Library Materials,
ANSI Z39.48-1984 ∞

Library of Congress Cataloging-in-Publication Data
Brigham, John, 1945–
   Property and the politics of entitlement / John Brigham.
     p. cm.
   Includes bibliographical references.
   Includes index.
   ISBN 0-87722-715-2 (alk. paper)
   1. Right of property—United States. 2. Property—United States.
3. United States—Constitutional law. I. Title.
KF562.B75   1990
346.7304'2—dc20
[347.30642]   89-20568
                                                              CIP

SHEILA McCUSKER BRIGHAM

1945–1970

A sudden blow . . . wings beating still

Contents

ACKNOWLEDGMENTS ix

INTRODUCTION 3

I. Making Constitutional Sense 19
II. Taxes and Regulation 41
III. Double Standard Practices 65
IV. Wealth Discrimination 87
V. From Bias to Compensation 109
VI. The Giving Issue 131
VII. Policing the Constitution 157

CONCLUSION 179

NOTES 189

BIBLIOGRAPHY 195

INDEX 219

Acknowledgments

Before I studied constitutional law, I studied political theory. Like many of my colleagues, I spoke about property in the terms of political theorists such as John Locke and Karl Marx. After hearing me speculate on a rather abstract level for some time, my friend Neal Roberts suggested I look at law. The specifics, I believe that he thought, would be good for me. Of course, Neal didn't mean constitutional law—in the 1960s we didn't think one should look to the Constitution for insight into property. He meant "private law." I began to look at ways lawyers and judges spoke about property and became rather excited by what I found. The inquiry provided a context for the study of politics and a body of what we now call discursive practices. The inquiry has continued for about fifteen years, and I am, of course, grateful to Neal.

During most of the decade that I have been working on issues surrounding property and constitutional politics, I have participated in a group whose members once ambitiously referred to it as the Amherst Seminar on Legal Ideology and Legal Process. This group has heard presentations of my work on property and on the institutional life of the Supreme Court, and while it has been reasonably tolerant, it has also pushed me to draw out the implications of the work for the practice of law in less rarefied contexts. Thanks to the example and collegiality of Susan Silbey, Barbara Yngvesson, Austin Sarat, and particularly the work on legal consciousness among the working class

Acknowledgments

of Sally Merry (1990), this treatment moves in that direction. Jennifer Kates commented on parts of the manuscript, and interviewing in Holyoke, Massachusetts, was done with Doris Campos-Infantino.

Elements of the argument presented here and earlier versions have appeared in print. That there is a "sense" to property in the Constitution was an idea I discussed in *Polity* 16, no. 2 (Winter 1983). My work on property tax preferences was supported by a grant from the Lincoln Institute for Land Policy, Cambridge, Massachusetts. Initial formulations were presented at a seminar sponsored by Harvard University, and the results were published in Neal A. Roberts and H. James Brown, *Property Tax Preferences for Agricultural Land* (1980). I wrote about the California Coastal Commission in *Making Public Policy* (1979). The discussion in Chapter II draws on some of the material collected for that book by Michael Semler. I have been writing about institutional practices for some time, and a discussion of the Double Standard as an institutional practice was presented at the 1982 meeting of the Law and Society Association in Toronto. This paper was published in *Research in Law and Policy Studies* 1 (1987) and revised as part of a chapter in Michael McCann and Gerald Houseman, *Judging the Constitution* (1989).

My argument that the Constitution has a bearing on material discrimination was first presented at the 1984 meeting of the Western Political Science Association in Sacramento, California, and a revision was offered at the 1985 meeting of the American Political Science Association in Washington, D.C. *Law and Policy* 8, no. 2 (1986) generously published a further revision. Development of the "compensation" calculus went on throughout the life of the book. I benefited from the assistance of Timothy J. O'Neill, Christopher Pyle, Neal A. Roberts, Austin Sarat, and Miriam Whitney at various stages. I discussed the issues with the Amherst Seminar and appreciate participants' willingness to take up a line of inquiry a little outside the usual tradition. In addition, the editors at the *Journal of Law and Inequality* of the University of Minnesota Law School were probing in their questions and supportive in their concern about an equitable welfare policy in editing an earlier version of Chapter V.

The "giving" issue, as a focus of entitlement research, is the product of an interdisciplinary and cross-national study of land policy based at the Consortium for Research on North America, Harvard University. The idea was initially suggested to me by Jerry Milch, and the

Acknowledgments

project was run by Elliot J. Feldman. That research was published in Feldman and Milch, *Land Rites and Wrongs: The Management, Regulation and Use of Land in Canada and the United States* (1987), and editing was done by Michael A. Goldberg. The idea that discourse on entitlement is subject to professional policing was initially presented at the 1988 meeting of the American Political Science Association in Washington, D.C., where Martin Shapiro offered comments. A revision was given at the Law and Semiotics Roundtable in 1989, and commentary by Roberta Kevelson and Duncan Kennedy has been incorporated into Chapter VII.

This work draws on a continuing collaboration with Christine Harrington, which enlivens all of my research and has deepened my approach to law. We are engaged in a variety of projects and have moved well beyond disputes to share a common intellectual orientation, which has been presented in Europe and America as a critique of professional power in law. Here realism, not traditional formalism, is described as the structure through which power is wielded by modern legal professionals. Without Christine's insight and spirit in projects such as this—and some even bigger—my ideas on property would have remained outside the communities where ideas about interpretation of the Constitution are developed.

Property and the Politics of
ENTITLEMENT

Introduction

The Law of the Land (1989), a book by John Opie on law and America's farms, tells of an American landscape rationalized, cut up, and otherwise subjected to public policy by government land surveys. Opie begins with a story of colonial towns laid out so that people could live together with farm plots spreading from the houses and distributed in the lands. For the colonists, the boundaries would fall along natural demarcations: the streambeds, rock cliffs, and ravines that came with the territory. Against these practices, where the parameters of property were appropriated from nature, the founding generation commodified the land in more regular forms, the grids of the land surveyor, so that property could be transferred more easily, by reference to a piece of paper. The creation of property as tracts of land was a policy that opened up the Midwest and ultimately settled a continent.

Even in its most basic form, land, property is not a material thing. In conventional terms it is the relationship between people and the thing. In more careful analysis, the definition of that relationship in law creates the thing, that is makes some land a tract and that tract capable of being owned. Thus, property is a legal construction, and like all of them in America, it is ultimately governed by the Constitution. Property is addressed in the Fifth Amendment, with its protection against uncompensated "takings" and guarantee of due process. That relationship and what the American Constitution provides for property set the terms for the construction of property in law, at least what we are entitled to as property and how we are allowed to hold it.

Introduction

In earlier work (1978) I proposed that it is possible to understand the Constitution, like any body of living law, as a language. My inquiry was driven by the seeming naïveté in the positivism that prevailed until about that time. There was, in my experience of constitutional debates, a great deal more than stimuli and responses or inputs, throughputs, and outputs going on in constitutional politics. And, although constitutional scholarship was operating within this framework, most of the teaching handled doctrine in ways that made no sense given the research. I turned to language at a time when symbols were becoming more legitimate objects of study and when the frameworks of study were expanding. Thus, in *Constitutional Language* I hoped to establish that there was a sense to the Constitution and that, although there was room to maneuver, there were also constraints with such a system. Rather, the sense, the tradition, sets interpretive parameters, and the maneuvering takes place with reference to those parameters.

Here, I investigate various facets of property, from the land titles of dispossessed British loyalists to the Old Age Survivors Disability Benefits of today's Social Security recipients. My interest is in a particular facet of property that I refer to as "entitlement." The term, like property itself, has more technical and conventional meanings. Here, I use it to refer to the legitimate expectations people have about something that they believe to be rightfully and legally theirs. The legal part is important because it implies an orientation to the complex world of rights and duties, statutes, lawyers, and judges. It does not, however, imply or require that the claim be acknowledged by a judge or even a lawyer to be a legal claim. In politics, a legal claim does not depend for its status on a judicial determination that the claim is right (see Merry, 1990: ch. 3).

The consequences of the constitutional protection of property for a range of policy debates in America are described in the title as "the Politics of Entitlement." The intellectual progression in the text is from mandarin discourse—that is, judicial opinion—on the constitutional right to the vernacular, which ranges from Social Security claims to movement politics. The approach is political and epistemological. Some of the investigations focus on who creates the stuff called property, and they enable its treatment as a fundamental right. Some focus on related issues, such as tax and development policy. Other investigations here are more interpretive, and they attempt to show, by

Introduction

describing the practical limits on conventional talk about equality, how our definitions of other fundamental rights affect the way Americans deal with property. It is, then, the meaning of property as contested terrain that I have characterized as "the Politics of Entitlement."

Property has been marginalized in debates about the Constitution since 1937. Yet it has remained important in decisions by the Supreme Court on the meaning of clauses in the Constitution, and property has for a long time been at the heart of political theory in the West. The role of the so-called Double Standard in marginalizing talk of constitutional property is the subject of Chapter III, but here something of the great tradition of property-rights questions deserves note. For the theorist Gaetano Mosca, the principle characteristic of the Middle Ages might be understood in the rights of property. That period of absolutism was characterized, he believed, by a "confusion . . . which allowed the proprietor or owner of land to consider that he was invested with sovereign rights over the inhabitants of that land" (Mosca, 1972: 47). Early struggles over property in the United States were profoundly influenced by issues of property in people with roots in the Middle Ages. For John R. Commons—the great institutional economist, whose work *The Legal Foundations of Capitalism* (1924) is important in this book—450 years of struggle were required between the landlord and his tenants. Modern law, beginning with the Magna Carta, "transferred dominion from the will of the sovereign to the will of the tenant, by the simple device of making fixed and certain, in terms of money . . . the rents owed by the tenant to the monarch" (1924: 220). A personal quality remained in the nature of the law of property until the seventeenth century. Thus, steps out of the Middle Ages were evident in the law of property through conversion of "the personal relations of creditor and debtor" as equals into the "property relations of assets and liabilities" (1924: 250). This foundational move for modern liberty "consisted in inventing the transferability and survivorship of promises freed from the personality of the parties to the promise" (1924: 250). The move was, at the same time, a foundation for a new form of dependency, dependency on the market. The legal framework on which it rested was at the core of the modern constitutional system.[1]

Constitutional property in America is grounded in the Fifth Amendment protection, which states that "no person shall be deprived of life, liberty, or property, without due process of law; nor shall private property be taken for public use, without just compensation." Like the various descriptions of offices, such as judgeships, and understandings of institutions, such as courts, in the Constitution itself, this statement of basic property protection was not explained, though part of it[2] was applied to the states in the Fourteenth Amendment, passed by Congress in 1866 and ratified two years later. The basic meaning of property depended on a vast core of understandings in common and statutory law. Yet a special status has come to be accorded to constitutional protection, and consequently the practices that have developed around the minimal evocations in the Fifth Amendment have taken on heightened significance.

For Max Farrand, who chronicled the Constitutional Convention of 1787, "property was the main object of society" (1913: 541), and the centrality of the right was evident in the Federalist defenses of the new Constitution. Federalist no. 81, for instance, argues that no explicit protection is needed against the federal government because no incursions or "positive power over property" was granted. Yet, passage of the Bill of Rights is conventionally seen as a popular rejection of that view. Restrictions to safeguard property rights are evident in the general limitations on the new government's authority, as, for instance, contained in the separation of powers and in the particular restrictions imposed on both the states and the new government dealing with currencies and contracts (Beard, 1913: 179). After the Civil War, with the clear ascendancy of the federal government, contract was replaced by due process protection (Magrath, 1967: 108). Property under the Constitution began to shift from tangible things to the intangibles that now make its investigation so intriguing (Paul, 1969: 105).

Ignored for years, that constitutional protection became a focus of intense debate in the 1960s. Progressive interpreters extended due process guarantees to welfare recipients as an aspect of constitutional property protection (Reich, 1964; Sparer, 1968; Clune, 1975). Generally associated with the new left in law, this position always tottered precariously between a militant liberalism, with its concern for procedural due process protection, and more radical community-based socialisms that emphasized the legitimate claims of workers and the poor to equal protection. The extension of protection for what its proponents at the time called "new property" is now under attack from left liberals in the Critical Legal Studies Movement (Simon, 1985), for

Introduction

whom the assertion of rights in political struggles is problematic, and from social science liberals who are concerned about the implications of the property claim on strategic grounds (McCann, 1984).

On the other hand, the right wing in the legal academy has been intellectually provocative in its arguments that safeguards in the American Constitution's Takings Clause provide a basis for dismantling the welfare state (Paul, 1987; Epstein, 1985; Siegan, 1977). In his book *Takings*, the *enfant terrible* of the right in law, Professor Richard Epstein, argues for a much more restrictive reading of constitutional protection from eminent domain. As a brash and brilliant advocate in the tradition of the great and often equally reactionary common law jurists, Epstein reflects the outer fringe in the conservative design for the protection of wealth. With the reelection of Republicans, this kind of conservatism seems likely to advance, albeit at a slower rate than it did under Reagan. The economic advantage and the ideological clarity of this position, which allowed it to survive over years of isolation, maintain their hold with relative ease today.

This book reaches beyond the politics of constitutional property in its epistemological and sociological inquiries. In a sense, it approaches property from the top down. For instance, it is about constitutional property and pays what may seem like undue attention to high courts and the opinions they offer in support of their judgments. Here, I am in agreement with colleagues in the legal services community: *Goldberg v. Kelly* (1970) is a monumental decision, and the jurisprudence that it epitomizes is at the core of this study. But this book is also sensitive to the tragedy of letting particular decisions come to stand for bodies of thought, jurisprudential positions, indeed, constitutional practices that have much richer and more enduring foundations.

Thus, in another sense, the book moves from the past to the future of constitutional interpretation. That is, judicial opinions are treated as a place to begin in order to show how, in the end, the meaning of the Constitution is not a matter simply of judicial interpretation. This is done with attention to the practical import of decisions in a sociopolitical context. Whether through attention to the conservatives who dominate the present Supreme Court or by looking at the manipulation of the property tax in the name of reform, I am attentive to the importance of contexts for judicial decisions. Throughout, I emphasize that the creation of constitutional sense involves more than precedent and that the status of constitutional rights and practices lies

Introduction

well beyond the authority of particular institutions. I try and do this, in the end, with respect for the power of what I have termed the Cult of the Court.

My research on property began over a decade ago. Initially, it was a way of checking on the significance of Lockeian practices in American constitutional law. The question arose for me because, as a graduate student in the early 1970s, I became frustrated by the abstractions of political theorists who conventionally and persistently used the language of Locke in speaking of the property right in America but seldom established that this was the language of interpretation. At the same time, colleagues of mine more familiar with law were suggesting that the law of property, at least as it derived from the common law and was taught in American law schools, could not be captured by the abstract references to Lockeian individualism that political theorists were using. I was curious as to whether the language of Locke was really evident in the authoritative decisions made by appellate courts.

This investigation into the practices of property was a fruitful variation on reading texts. It grew into a body of research that addressed many of the critical factors in the politics surrounding the American Constitution in general and the contemporary status and characteristics of property as a fundamental right. Property, in all of its manifestations, has meant something technical, something different from folk conventions, for some time. Here, the sense of the concept that we are exploring is constitutional and thus removed again from even ordinary legal experience. The fundamental right guaranteed by the Constitution is one that is both more powerful and narrower than property generally. That is, constitutional property has a distinctive capacity that comes from its textual foundations.

Like the protection for privacy and expression in the Constitution, the protection for property has limited application, an important but narrow range of uses. Like the other two doctrines, property in the Constitution is affected by its textual neighbors, and it may be subject to developments in either of those rights more than to common law uses of the concept. The constitutional right is of recent origin, and 500 years of property talk in Anglo-American jurisprudence bears only tangentially on constitutional property. In fact, the recent history of constitutional protection for the rights of those with little power has had an impact on the nature of constitutional property that is unusual given the traditional association of property with the powerful.

Introduction

Recently, the work reported here has been able to draw from growing attention to the place of institutional, and by analogy doctrinal, life in political science and jurisprudence. Professor Rogers Smith (1987) of Yale's political science department has invoked the "new institutionalism" in a proposal for improving research on law, courts, and the judicial process. Quoting Professor Theda Skocpol, Smith suggests that public law scholars attend to the "dialectic of meaningful actions and structural determinants" in law. The seminal essay for practitioners and seekers after this new truth is by professors James March and Johan Olsen (1984). The essay heralded a return to institutional studies, while it claimed a new sophistication bred of social research over generations. The return meant an enlivened interest in the structures and conventions of courts, legislatures, and such. The sophistication would come from an enlightened social science where interpretation and validation might coexist. The article proposed a method that may institutionalize the postbehavioral striving of over a decade.[3]

This kind of scholarship applied to law, according to Smith's analysis, would allow for sensitive treatment of normative ideas—such as doctrines, professional ethics, or the authority of courts—as well as an empirical agenda that would presumably take us deeper into the world of the legal process. The project draws more directly on historical and sociological work than has been characteristic of positivist social science. This is especially true in comparism to judicial studies where a behavioral framework and quantification were the norm. The "new institutionalism" has antecedents in Marx and Weber and contemporary practitioners, such as Skocpol (1979) and Professor Stephen Skowronek (1982).[4] For the legal scholarship based in political science, the new method would enable scholars to transcend the schizoid positivism of traditional legal research, with its propensity to take institutions for granted often while developing elaborate schemes for quantification. The promise is for something both practical and informative.

Smith's call seemed to strike a chord. Although publication of the call in the professional journals is new, the movement has been under way for some time. Yet, however sensible, the orientation faces a challenge in law, where scholars are used to teaching behavior one moment and doctrine the next. Smith's article should stimulate some effort to lead public law scholarship out of a traditional wilderness where institutions are "givens" that exist to serve a plurality of interests. Smith says, for instance, that scholars must realize the limits to treating legal institutions "simply as epiphenomena of self-interested individual and group behavior" (1987: 91). The dialectic would involve "both the ways . . . institutions influenced the political actions in question, and the ways in which those actions altered relevant contextual structures or institutions" (1987: 91). This would be different, he asserts, because institutional life would not be "treated as simply the product of complexly interacting individual and group choices and actions" (1987: 92).

For Smith, there are two paths to the "new institutionalism," one from "Mainstream Political Science" and the other from "Historical and Sociological Determinism." In the first instance, rather than treat the "preferences and powers of political actors" as "exogenous 'givens,'" he would heed the critics of the late 1960s and 1970s and look harder for the "inarticulate, excluded, or systematically slighted" interests (1987: 92). He further acknowledges the limits of rational choice theory, which he notes has itself been conscious of the need to study institutions for their influence on choice. And the institutional project as Smith develops it draws on the "Crits" or Critical Legal Studies Movement in the legal academy. Although closely associated with a deterministic account of the play of interests through law, the movement is credited with a number of insights. Cited by Smith is Professor Robert Gordon (1984), who "insists that 'causal relations between changes in legal and social forms' are 'radically underdetermined'" (1987: 98). This enhanced picture of social forces should lead to rich description of influences on law and a fuller account of the legal terrain on which politics unfolds.

Given the conventional dualism between theory and empirical research, quite often we don't expect those who go into the field to be conversant with the latest theoretical fashion. Much less do we look for them to be making the applications. In practice, the theorist and the investigator leave each other alone. There is now considerable scholarship from political scientists who have aspired to the same goals described by Smith. Over the last twenty years, or since the limits of positivism first became evident, the studies have trickled into the stream of social research on courts. For me, articulation of problems with positivism in public law may be traced to the volume edited by Joel Grossman and Joseph Tanenhaus, *The Frontiers of Judi-*

Introduction

cial Research, published in 1968. Here two fathers of the movement for sociolegal research,[5] C. Herman Pritchett and Richard Schwartz, reflecting on that movement, argued that behavioral understandings had yet to explore fully the uniquely legal aspects of judging. Not long after this statement, the first generation of self-consciously structural and institutional studies began to address legal phenomena. This generation of work in public law included professors Isaac Balbus and Stuart Scheingold. Balbus's research on the urban riots of the 1960s pointed to "the dialectics of legal repression." This scholarship was anything but simple behavioralism. Scheingold developed an interest in law from studying international relations, but he too made a significant contribution to the field of public law in the mid-1970s by describing the myths surrounding rights as resources that could be mobilized in the political arena. This research showed an ideological dimension that is now widely recognized as a part of law (Amherst Seminar, 1988).

After these breakthroughs, the challenge was to fulfill the postbehavioral research prospects and not just describe the limits of behavioralism. Early in the decade, feminism brought attention to background attributes like sex and gender (Cook, 1978) and ideological ferment around doctrinal matters like equal protection (Goldstein, 1987; Baer, 1983). Interpretation also began to address the ideological nature of legal phenomena. Some of the work drew on the metaphor of language; other work extrapolated from language to constitutive norms in the culture; and in some hands the systems of symbol and meaning in law were most aptly captured by the ideological framework (O'Neill, 1981; Harris, 1982; Brigham, 1984a). While interest in dispute processing drew attention from judges, the activity produced sensitive readings concerning the nature of disputes so that scholars could speak of transformations that were the result of institutional action in the legal arena (Harrington, 1985b; Mather and Yngvesson, 1980; Felstiner et al., 1980).

More recently, issues from interpretation itself to the nature of the legal profession have transcended the stereotypical behavioralist or formalist analysis. Professor Michael McCann's work on comparable worth (1987) and Professor Kristin Bumiller's attention to rape and then to civil rights from a perspective informed by critical theory (1987) certainly deserve recognition as postbehavioral scholarship sensitive to the issues raised by the "new institutionalism." Here, the

Introduction

research is instructive. What McCann and Bumiller do with doctrinal materials as part of movement politics should be the story of public law, a story that would link law and policy in the context of constitutional interpretation. Thus, this work responds to contemporary scholarship on the conjunction of these three considerations—policy, doctrine, and jurisprudence. The coming together of these forces has not always been central to constitutional studies, but with the rise of a conservative jurisprudence, such as that offered by Professor Richard Epstein and Justice Antonin Scalia, the consequences of jurisprudence for doctrine and policy have become evident in their obvious impact on judicial selection.

The chapters that follow put the discussion of constitutional property in the context of present policy disputes and doctrinal issues. Political scientists didn't pay much attention to property fifteen years ago, particularly progressive political scientists. And, although language and discourse gained increasing momentum over those years, it was often in the service of an indeterminacy position that is distinctly not mine, so some of the things I have written just don't sit easily in the academy. Where I have written on the topic before,[6] I have reassessed the examples and extended the research to illuminate the arena I call "the politics of entitlement." The chapters are united by this common theme in constitutional property, with implications ranging from the philosophy of law and interpretation to questions of policy formation. The research is on law in context, what is mistakenly but suggestively known in some circles as "critical empiricism" (Trubek and Esser, 1989). The influence of bouts over this enterprise should be evident in the movement from mandarin discourses, primarily Supreme Court opinions, to the way people in the communities I have been studying talk about entitlement. This book looks to the root of the property right and a bias, particularly in contemporary applications, that reaches well beyond the traditional realm of constitutional interpretation (Brigham and Harrington, 1989).

Chapter I considers the proposition that there is a "sense" to Supreme Court decisions, a body of convention and knowledge that makes some things sound right, such as "racial discrimination violates the equal protection clause." Other things, such as "equal protection prohibits unreasonable searches," seem just a little off, at least to the ear of a conversant interpreter. This sense is a function of a number of considerations, perhaps the most important of which is the

Introduction

Court's past opinions. The chapter examines the Court's tradition concerning property claims and how the justices have settled them. The basic understanding of property seems to have remained stable over time, but new forms to which it applies have appeared in response to changing socioeconomic and political conditions. Property rights in titles, offices, grants, and franchises—among others—have been asserted and sustained. Thus, it is in the same sense, not some "new" sense, that statutory entitlements are property under the American Constitution.

Chapter II examines a tax break, use-value assessment for agricultural land that has increased in value. Here we take an opportunity to push into the statutory field where constitutional protection is less significant but where the basic determinations of how property will be treated are worked out. This policy developed in the 1970s and was instituted by most states. One of the things that becomes evident is that the environmental issues in which the policy is cloaked tend to mask the property interests that are served by this policy change. The chapter also looks at zoning and the transformation of prerogatives in land during a period of deregulation and conservative jurisprudence. The discussion offers a close look at property politics.

Chapter III looks at the well-known Double Standard as institutional practice. This is the announced reorientation of the Supreme Court, which is traced to the 1930s when the justices indicated their preference for intervention when an issue involved protection of political rights and withdrawal from the economic arena. Instead of treating the Double Standard simply as a legal norm, the chapter examines how this practice came to delineate the sort of issues that would be considered by the Supreme Court. Thus, the Double Standard is treated here as an institutional practice with implications for how Americans understand property as separate from civil liberties.

Chapter IV looks at a corollary element of constitutional discourse, the relationship of equal protection guarantees to discrimination based on economic need, or "means" discrimination. The discussion draws from the fact that constitutional "equal protection" has a technical meaning that orients legal thinking. Its roots are in *Plessy* v. *Ferguson* (1896) and the justification for separation of the races in schools, theaters, and other public places on the basis of a promise of material equality. *Brown* v. *Board of Education* (1954), in eliminating separation from constitutional protection also eliminated the consti-

Introduction

tutional promise of material equality. The approach to this ideology turns away from outcomes in order to get to the meanings, standards, and conceptual parameters that influence the application of constitutional discourse to discrimination against those with inadequate means.

Chapter V builds on what has gone before in establishing the utility of legitimate expectation as a conception of constitutional property and makes an argument for compensation when statutory entitlements are cut back. The idea is that when Social Security benefits are cut back—or, in the idiom of the Constitution, "taken"—those who have paid into the system should be compensated according to their legitimate expectation as to what they should receive. This chapter is followed by considerations that look at the protection for takings in reverse. Thus, in Chapter VI we look at how a comparative approach to development policy allows institutions to be isolated, that is, considered for their role in the policy process, where they exist in very similar cultures. The comparison is between Halifax, Nova Scotia, and Portland, Maine, and the issue is transfer of property from public to private hands. The analysis leads to a picture of the different traditions, one of relatively autonomous public administration and the other a policy process influenced by rights consciousness.

The book concludes with inquiry into constitutional vernaculars, an appropriate approach for this fundamental form of law. Rather than ending with the Supreme Court, the last chapter calls attention to the form of entitlement that is fundamental both because its subject is property and because it is part of our ordinary legal and political practice, the colloquial or vernacular Constitution. Very few claims will ever be subject to review by the Supreme Court. Even when it reviews matters that are constitutional because they are embedded in institutional practice, it is not at all clear that the Court can have much success dictating positions that are idiosyncratic and simply its own.

The result is a general treatment of constitutional property based on a model of legitimate expectation. The model is in the tradition of Professor Laurence Tribe's *American Constitutional Law* (1978, 1988), which introduced a number of ways for approaching the Constitution to the study of constitutional law. Legitimate expectation here draws on one of Tribe's models of constitutional adjudication. My treatment stretches the implications of the model and draws parallels with related frameworks, such as Staunton Lynd's claim for com-

Introduction

munity property rights (1984), which he developed in the struggles against shutdowns and plant closings in the steel mills. Here, the philosophical dimensions, such as the issue of "making sense" in matters of constitutional discourse; the comparative dimensions, such as the "giving issue" in Canada and the United States; impending policy areas, such as the discussion of tax policy; and the last chapter, which develops constitutional inquiry in ordinary social life, all carry the analysis beyond cases to practices in law.

In addition to establishing and using the expectation model, the book contains extended inquiry into how legal scholars approach law, with particular attention to political implications. The first chapter describes the construction of sensible discourses and meanings in the constitutional setting. Sense in the constitutional setting—including past opinions, the document itself, and possible interpretations—operates much as it does in language. Chapter III places policy in the context of understandings and processes by which property is situated in doctrinal and institutional life. Instead of treating the Double Standard as a myth, it is treated as an institutional practice that epitomizes the life of the law in many of its most significant aspects. Finally, in the last chapter, mandarin discourse and the vernacular are compared in order to show the constraints of realism and the politics in the idea that the law must be what the judges say it is. In the context of entitlement, from the discourse of constitutional property to interpretations announced in local welfare offices, approaches to law become central to the politics of legal authority.

The book is not all political philosophy. In a number of places claims are made and extensively argued that bear directly on the politics of entitlement. In Chapter II, a look at the basic processes of traditional entitlement in law as it is affected by tax policy and regulation shows changes in law while various interests remain the same. Here entitlement is sometimes less than might be expected, but institutional practice and policy formation amount to a significant dimension of how law is approached. Equal protection is turned upside down in order to challenge the nondiscrimination provisions and bring back lost promises of material equality. This is the chapter on wealth discrimination and the argument, although it will be hard to square with the ideological constraints of post–World War II liberalism, is linked to the legitimate aspirations of a growing number of black activists and progressive lawyers. In a similar vein, compensation for withdrawal

Introduction

of welfare benefits is presented as a reasonable elaboration of the doctrines of the "new property" and a pragmatic doctrinal strategy that would raise the level of debate over the vulnerability to budgetary cutbacks of those holding statutory entitlements. The policy consequences of the approach to entitlement practiced in this book also include attention to eminent domain and the "takings" protection, but from the other side. That is, rather than consider only the protection provided in the American Constitution for the individual when land is taken, I discuss public interests and situate them in the realm of entitlement. Here, the doctrine of public purposes has protected various interests, but the treatment suggests the limits of this approach when citizenship and polity are subjected to economistic logics that protect private interests but sneer at even the idea of a public interest.

Some recent collections and monographs raise the level of attention to property and economic issues in the American Constitution. Many, not surprisingly, have a conservative orientation. In the collection *Economic Liberties and the Judiciary* (Dorn and Manne, 1987), for instance, conservatives such as Antonin Scalia, Richard A. Epstein, Bernard H. Siegan, and Ellen Frankel Paul situate the property issue in what they call "the emergence of a new school of thought" (Kozinski, 1987), the conservative activism of the Law and Economics movement. This movement is known most for its model building on the foundation of neo-classical economic analysis. It has made a concerted effort to link common law institutions and conceptions to the rationalist skeleton, but it faces a challenge posed by a fundamentally different brand of conservatism, the natural right and natural justice framework of Leo Strauss and related believers.

By distinguishing kinds of conservatism, this book addresses the issues in both of the dominant strains in conservative thought. Both, I maintain, are grounded in practice. In the first place, I take pleasure in the Straussian belief that law does not just depend on what the judges say, but I have a great deal more respect than most of them for the bodies of thought that the judges have put out. On the other hand, I have an affinity for some of the suggestions made by contemporary economists with regard to such things as expropriation and some statutory entitlements, because economic analysis in these areas cuts against much liberal dogma. This makes the book more useful and I hope more intriguing than it might be if it were more clearly in one ideological camp. Yet, there will be little doubt that the articles

Introduction

offer a progressive reading of property that critically examines both traditional liberal and contemporary conservative biases.

The current interest in property stimulated by this scholarship and recent decisions of the Supreme Court require the sort of extended analysis this collection represents. And, since the realm of constitutional property has been ignored for nearly fifty years, there is certainly room for new conceptualizations such as those provided in the chapters that follow. Thus, this book appropriates some of that "room" with a provocative thesis: To treat constitutional property as a civil liberty and to recognize its centrality to the welfare state, property must be understood more democratically.

CHAPTER I

Making Constitutional Sense

Major holdings in the 1970s—that individuals have a constitutionally protected property right in licenses, franchises, and social-welfare benefits (*Goldberg* v. *Kelly*, 1970; *Goss* v. *Lopez*, 1975)—focused attention on property and what seemed to be a new class of beneficiaries. A conventional view is that this "new property" (Reich, 1964) differs from what has gone before because it comes from government. Proceeding from the presumption associated with John Locke that the source of property rights is labor, the market view generally loses track of its roots. The result is an understanding of property that has no rational foundations and amounts to greater solicitude for land owners (*Nollan* v. *California Coastal Comm.*, 1987) than welfare recipients (*Bowen* v. *Gilliard*, 1987) because the justices seem to identify more readily with the conditions of the former than the latter.

Judicial opinions provide a measure of whether property in statutory entitlement is indeed new or is consistent with a long tradition. The Supreme Court defines and applies rights through extrapolation from convention, from what the justices believe to be possible. These possibilities have been described as "the framework within which political thought and action proceed" (Shapiro, 1964: 39–44). Legal realism and behavioralism in the social sciences both helped to turn attention away from this framework. Consequently, it could be said that students of the judiciary in the late twentieth century nearly lost track of the "influences that operate toward uniformity" (Schwartz, 1969: 490).[1] Scholars turned from doctrine to the behavior of judges.

Yet, to have meaning among the community of lawyers and other judges, that behavior must be intelligible within the tradition; it must pay its dues by operating with familiar referents. Obviously, most of the time, the justices make sense; that is, they operate within a tradition of intelligible discourse.

However, *making* sense suggests creating the meanings as well as operating within them. The extent to which the justices are creative in the constitution of property is a central concern here that will be developed not only in this chapter but throughout the book. Here, for the sake of clarity, I will note that a shift in personnel or outcomes is not likely to affect the nature of a constitutional right as deeply embedded in discursive practices as property. In this regard, shifts such as the conservative swing on the Supreme Court that began to be felt in 1974 and gained momentum throughout the presidency of Ronald Reagan have not changed the sense of property in the Constitution. The orientation of the majority from the late 1980s has led to a conservative bias in decisions by the Court on the Constitution and on statutes. Such a bias is likely to be felt initially in the reach of the constitutional protection, and we see it in the claim by Justice William Rehnquist in *Arnett* v. *Kennedy* (1974) that social welfare or public employment entitlement holders "must take the bitter with the sweet" (152–54). This claim is discussed more fully in Chapter V. To focus attention on the emergence of the tradition of legitimate expectations here, in Chapter I, I note that the meanness of this position did not alter the sense of what property is under the Constitution. This distinction is of no consequence to those who are deprived of benefits or jobs, but it does figure rather heavily in laying out the politics of constitutional property.

The constitutional right to property is also examined here as a way of showing the operation of ideas as limits on behavior. It is in this way that law becomes relevant to judicial decision (Brigham, 1978). The concept of property has already been used to explore the ideological dimension of law. Karl Renner, a major figure in Marxist legal scholarship, viewed the concept of property as relatively stable and suggested that it was the social function of property that changed (Renner, 1969). The basic, normative concept of property, he argued, is precapitalist; that is, it is rooted in the law of feudal estates. It is the function that had been transformed from stipulating relations among things to governing relations among people (Vandevelde, 1980). Ren-

Making Constitutional Sense

ner added that the "peaceful enjoyment of one's own property has developed into draconian control of alien labor power" (Renner, 1969: 101). A comprehensive treatment of property along the lines suggested by Renner would require attention to the social function, and some of that is attempted in subsequent chapters. Here, we can see in a more limited way how Renner's analysis is supported by authoritative holdings in the Supreme Court. In decisions of the Court, the stability of the concept is evident, while the issues, reflecting shifts in the objects of legal conflict, undergo continuous change.

Some important scholarship on property as a social norm turns away from the Constitution altogether. This is the case in the legal histories of Professor Morton Horwitz. In works such as *The Transformation of American Law: 1780–1860* (1977), which won the Bancroft prize in American History for 1978, the turn is toward more typical or socially characteristic sources of law than those associated with the federal Constitution. This is in the spirit of contemporary legal historians who have generally felt that constitutional history has been characterized by "atypical 'great cases' "—that is, the *Dred Scott*s, the *Plessy*s, and the *Brown*s—and that these cases in particular and constitutional cases generally do not represent legal practices since they are "episodic" and "buttressed by a rhetorical tradition that is often an unreliable guide in the slower (and less conscious) process of legal change in America" (Horwitz, 1977: xii). Without falling prey to this error to which Horwitz and others have called our attention, there is insight to be gained into entitlement by attention to discourse around the Constitution.

The rhetorical tradition of authoritative commentary on the Constitution is, nevertheless, an important guide to national ideology. The work of the Court is not typical of law or legal practice. Yet, its opinions represent authoritative attempts to relate political as well as legal concepts to changing conditions. The result is an accommodation between issues and tradition. The contribution of the justices to a constitutional standard is explicit when they deal with Fifth Amendment protection. Sometimes property is beneath the surface as when "contract" linked "capitalism and constitutionalism" (Levy, 1957: 280). The opinions of the Supreme Court are instructive because they tell us how one branch of the government thinks about the Constitution. They are a running commentary on fundamental concepts, and they disclose ideological shift or continuity in the polity.

Making Constitutional Sense

Contemporary scholars have emphasized shifts in the concept of property. Horwitz (1977) reveals a change in the forms of property protected by law. The shift is from vested rights to development, from agricultural production to industry. The result is a change in the status of competing claims rather than a change in the concept's meaning. Another approach, that of C. B. Macpherson (1973), argues that property evolved from protecting status to protecting commodities and that it now protects expectation. Later he added that this interpretation links feudal status with the welfare state in a manner familiar to political theorists (Macpherson, 1978). The argument is similar to the classic scholarship of Sir Henry Maine (1883), institutional economist John R. Commons (1924), and to modern commentaries such as those of former law professor Charles Reich and the *Yale Law Journal* in a note by William Treanor (1985). These treatises, while provocative, have not taken a comprehensive view of the authoritative discourse on the subject. That remains to be undertaken here in the following study of what property has meant to the Supreme Court.

To understand the conventional opinions and creative emanations to be found in the Supreme Court's bouts with property, it is necessary to distinguish between the subjects protected and the concept that allows them to be considered property. The term "property," is often used imprecisely, even in legal writing. In this sense, property refers to what the right protects, land or security, rather than to the authority relation or dominion. However, it is historically accurate and legally appropriate to say that the form is distinct from the right. Throughout its history, the Court has been confronted with property rights in different things. Historic periods reflect changes in social, political, and economic relations, with protection shifting from grants to franchises and from compensable interests to entitlements. Each subject is related to the core concept. Issues that reached the Court during the nation's earlier stages of development reflected an unstable structure of authority. Expansion posed new questions, and contract was used to define rights in grants and monopolies. Later, traditional forms came under pressure, and the Court gave increasing attention to state regulatory power as a means of delineating the limits to possession and use. This was followed by issues of valuation and a transformation from possession to expectation as a basis for deciding whether a taking had occurred, a shift that helps make sense out of property claims for statutory entitlements.

Debts, Titles, and Offices

Fears about changes in authority over property were widespread during the Constitutional Convention (Beard, 1913) and the ratification debates (Treanor, 1985: 713). Many in the new republic feared that creating a strong federal government would take control over matters like legal tender, British debts, loyalist properties, state grants, and land titles (Warren, 1922: 190–91), which had traditionally been state responsibilities. These property questions dominated the Supreme Court's early dockets. The property rights involved government action: legal relations guaranteeing title, enforcing debts, and commissioning officeholders. Turning the focus from forms of property such as land or debt to the concept itself clarifies the importance of public authority. The most tangible aspect of property in these cases is likely to be a government document.

In one of their first opinions, *Georgia v. Brailsford* (1794), the justices addressed a debt due to a British subject and discussed the guarantees of possession. Relying on the law of nations and the treaty of peace, Chief Justice John Jay ruled that British debts could be revived after the war in spite of what the state of Georgia had legislated. Brailsford still had a right to recover his debt "the property of which had never in fact or law been taken" (415). Although it might have been hard to collect the debt itself, the "property" had not been transferred. Courts of the new nation also became deeply involved with admiralty cases determining possession and the legitimacy of claims at sea. In another early Supreme Court case, *Glass v. Sloop Betsy* (1794), the contest over property required that the jurisdiction of the new federal courts be settled. As Professor Sheldon Goldman reminds us, the overriding issue from the ratification of the Constitution until the Civil War had been the nature of the American Union, the power of the national government relative to that of the states (1981: 23). From such questions of jurisdictional authority, it was a small step to the matter of which parties had the best federal claim.

As early as 1796, protection of property by the Supreme Court began to have a constitutional foundation. *Ware v. Hylton* (1796) was argued before the Court by John Marshall, as attorney for the state of Virginia, just a few years before he was appointed Chief Justice. The issue was the status of the treaties that ended the Revolutionary War when their provisions conflicted with those of state law. The treaties had settled issues like confiscation of property during the war and the validity of prewar debts. *Ware* asserted the authority of the federal government over the states in preserving property with attention to the source of property limited to its legitimacy.

The principle of compensation to individuals when property is taken for public use, called the most "potent weapon used to further the process of redistribution from old to new property" (Horwitz, 1977: 63), is thought to have had little constitutional significance around the time of the Revolution. In his discussion of the period, Horwitz ignores the compensation provision in the United States Constitution. Yet, this provision played a significant role in some of the first Supreme Court cases. This period in the history of constitutional property is often ignored because it comes before the age of contracts. Soon after *Ware,* the Court turned to disputed inheritance in *Calder* v. *Bull* (1798) where legislation changing the status of a will was challenged on compensation, *ex post facto,* and various natural law grounds. Justice Samuel Chase's *seriatim* opinion dismisses the *ex post facto* claim arguing that such protection "was not considered, by the framers of the constitution, as extending to prohibit the depriving a citizen even of a vested right to property." He went on to develop the property right as a guarantee from the state: "The right, as well as the mode or manner of acquiring property, and of alienating or transferring, inheriting, or transmitting it, is conferred by society, is regulated by civil institution, and is always subject to the rules prescribed by positive law" (*Calder,* 1798: 394).

Thus, legal authority, not accumulation or labor, was the basis for property as the early Supreme Court justices expounded it. For Chase, a right is "the power to do certain actions; or to possess certain things, according to the law of the land" (1798: 394).

In the midst of the usual fare of common law and admiralty questions, a constitutional case came to the Court that reveals a little more about the relation between private expectation and the obligations of the state. Though ordinarily studied for other reasons, the holding in *Marbury* v. *Madison* (1803) supports expectations derived from official actions of the government. For John Marshall, the appointment process was completed when the Secretary of State signed the papers. The action of the appointing officer, rather than delivery of the disputed commissions, made Marbury a judge. The implication was that appointment according to the law, not the symbols of appointment, made the commission complete. The significance for constitutional property was that the holding derived a right from official action rather than anything tangible. Marshall cited Lord Mansfield, who had maintained that courts could intervene "whenever there is a right to execute an office, perform a service, or exercise a franchise (more especially if it be a matter of public concern, or attended with profit)" (1803: 168–69). Thus, the courts would back up rights according to status, which is more dependent on legal consistency than on human industry. These jurists contributed to the tradition of protection for legitimate expectation (which Chase had considered central to the "real" property right) as inherent in the law of the land.

Slavery was different from the other subjects of property protection treated in the early nineteenth century. In a revolutionary period ringing with the rhetoric of equality and freedom, property in people was a source of constant tension. The new government was built on a compromise that left slavery in place and protected property in slaves with many of the same instruments as those available for property in land and property as the obligation to pay a debt. The conflict over ownership of persons would not be settled until the Civil War, but the slave trade was doomed. By 1810, a Maryland law prohibiting the slave trade was brought to the Supreme Court. In this case, the Court held that the state could not grant freedom or deny property without an examination of the pertinent facts. The property right in these cases is still recognizable even where the form protected, slavery, is hard to comprehend.

Property cases before the Court in this period questioned insistently the authority of governments and the determinations delineated the emergent relations between the nation and the states. In 1805, the expansive powers that Hamilton had already claimed in support of a national bank were intimated in a decision that gave priority to debts owed to the United States. The issue again pitted federal against state power. As they had done in other cases, the justices demonstrated that the new government would preserve prior obligations (*U.S. v. Fisher*, 1805). In *Martin v. Hunter's Lessee* (1816), which concerned a dispute over title, the Supreme Court reasserted and further elaborated federal judicial authority over the state. Thus, the emergence of a national constitutional order was based, at least in part, on protection of property interests as a legitimate expectation.

Contracts and Grants

From about 1810 until the middle of the century, the constitutional protection of property grew in importance. Initially, the Supreme Court focused on expectation that was vested through state charters. Its decisions during the period place the Court, and consequently at least part of federal authority, on the side of limits to the promises a state may make. Early federal protection of property established the obligations of states to traditional entitlements such as those following title to land. Similar obligations appear later as constitutional protection under the Contract Clause. Here, the form of property, a contract, is the doctrinal ground for its protection. The obligations of the state changed during the early nineteenth century as expectation created by statute is evaluated with increased sensitivity to economic development.

The issue in *Fletcher* v. *Peck* (1810) was title to lands under a state grant. The form was similar to cases that arose immediately after ratification. Here contract became the basis for holding legislatures accountable. Chief Justice Marshall views the Constitution as protecting citizens "from the effects of those sudden and strong passions to which men are exposed" (138) and which may be expressed in legislation. He recognizes the injustice of holding property owners responsible where they did not "bear the stain" of an earlier fraud. Contract is thus interpreted as limiting state power. As in *Calder* v. *Bull*, the argument is supported by other prohibitions in the Constitution such as those applying to *ex post facto* laws and bills of attainder.

During this period, the interests protected as property began to change. A shift is evident by 1819 when the contract clause is held by the Supreme Court to protect the continued existence of a corporation. Special status for corporate bodies had been suggested before in the 1815 case of *Terrett* v. *Taylor*. In *Dartmouth College* v. *Woodward* (1819), charter-created rights were guaranteed by the Court. The result was a sort of "pure" property with expectation rather than possession of tangible things at the core. Adjudication under the contract clause does not directly address property; rather, the constitutional status of the right is enhanced by attention to its essence—a legitimate expectation or promise. In the same year that it protected Dartmouth College, the Court preserved traditional property interests where it found them threatened by "contract impairments" resulting from legislative action, and it declared a New York insolvency law unconstitutional (*Sturges* v. *Crownshield*, 1819). A few years later, the Court invalidated legislation that had nullified rents in land, holding that the Constitution covered "all contracts . . . whether between individuals or between a state and individuals" (*Green* v. *Biddle*, 1823: 92). This was a standard far more inclusive than the one the next century's civil rights revolution would produce. The early contract cases protected rights created by legislative action, and although *Gibbons* v. *Ogden* (1824) was not precisely a property case, its subject, a monopoly, was characteristic of the legislative grants of the period. In *Odgen* v. *Saunders* (1827), state laws were deemed applicable to insolvency as long as they were prospective, further indicating how the Constitution might be used to moderate the effects of legislation.

The interests protected as property began to change as the nineteenth century moved along. Laws began to favor economic development in judicial and legislative forums. This change was also reflected in Supreme Court decisions that took note of the public interest in fostering trade. Although, according to Justice Joseph Story, "the fundamental rights of personal liberty and private property should be held sacred" (*Wilkinson* v. *Leland*, 1829: 657), the justices found ways to honor sacred rights without losing track of practical economic considerations. Where divestiture alone was held not to offend the Constitution except when legislation might be faulted in some additional respect, the Court deferred to legislation that fostered growth at the expense of traditional interests (*Satterlee* v. *Matthewson*, 1829). In the Jacksonian period, the justices held that private benefits must be read narrowly when they are part of public grants (*Jackson* v. *Lamphire*, 1830), that evidence of the public's abandonment of prerogatives over property must be explicit in the law (*Providence Bank* v. *Billings*, 1830), and that public grants should be strictly construed (*U.S.* v. *Arredonda*, 1832). The Contract Clause was the doctrinal foundation of these decisions. Here, a shift from the old to emerging property interests was reflected in the interpretations. Consequently, public benefit began to override more traditional expectation and static relations.

Interest in economic expansion finds another expression in *Charles River Bridge* v. *Warren Bridge* (1837), where the claims on both sides derive from legislative grants. The property issue involves the prerogatives of the state over the property it creates. The justices show greater deference to the new grant than to the older one, as was characteristic of that time, and the opinion rings with enthusiasm for expansion. In *Charles River Bridge,* the holding is that an established charter to operate a toll bridge did not preclude Massachusetts from granting a competing authorization for a free bridge. Chief Justice Roger Brooke Taney ruled that "any ambiguity in the terms of the contract, must operate . . . in favor of the public" (341). The winning party represents development, but both sides derive their property claims from the government.

Thus, contract was the most adjudicated protection of property before the Civil War. Choice of a standard may have been influenced by the unavailability of Fifth Amendment protection for challenges to state statutes or it may have been that contract provisions were more flexible than property and thus most appropriate for a period of movement away from vested rights. Claims reflected controversy over "control of limited resources needed by others" (Commons, 1924: 6). Where tradition impeded development, the state was given an opportunity to enhance economic growth (*West River Bridge Co.* v. *Dix,* 1848). There was a marked insensitivity to old wealth as well as to wealth accumulated by labor (Hamilton, 1932: 864–80). The focus on contractual agreements, however, was not a radical transition from the legal status of debts, titles, and offices that had occupied the justices earlier. In the next period, development would continue to determine outcomes as the justices searched for viable boundaries to regulatory power.

Status and Franchise

After the Civil War, contests over the right of all citizens to equal treatment reached the Supreme Court as property issues. The constitutional right would delineate the range of valid legislation with greater attention to its impact on people. In protecting property, the emphasis shifted from contract to due process. For the first time, the Court considered which forms of property would receive constitutional protection. The impact of Fifth and Fourteenth Amendment due process on the conception of constitutional property was greater than that of contract adjudication, since "the contract clause, after all dealt only with contracts" (Magrath, 1967: 108). By the 1820s, "the principle of just compensation had won general acceptance" (Treanor, 1985: 714) providing a foundation for the shift from contract to property questions.

Given the treatment of expectation covered above, by 1856, in *Murray's Lessee* v. *Hoboken Land*, the Court could say that due process regulated the exercise of state power "according to some settled course of judicial proceedings." A disputed title evoked an eloquent statement in support of procedure. One year later, in *Dred Scott* v. *Sanford* (1857), a divided Court would strike down the Missouri Compromise as a deprivation of property, a violation of the slaveholder's due process. Although the war and the constitutional amendments that followed reversed the outcome, the decision did suggest a perverse judicial optimism about the capacity of due process protection. The Constitution was placed over an act of Congress only to have the substance of the act preserved by the war. Yet, another reading of due process was evident in the opinion. The importance of status created by the State appears in the dissents. According to Justice Benjamin R. Curtis, outlawing slavery did not violate constitutional property because "slavery . . . is created only by municipal law. . . . The Constitution refers to slaves as 'persons held to service in one state, under the laws thereof.' . . . Nothing can more clearly describe a status created by municipal law" (564). The legal status of people held the Court's attention as it did the nation's. As with other forms of property, political considerations influenced the legitimacy of the relevant expectation. Before the war, slaves were a commodity and the subject of legitimate property claims; afterward, their status as citizens would override claims of ownership. Property in status was in fact a claim of black Americans after the Civil War. By the end of this period, in *Plessy* v. *Ferguson* (1896), a person of color claimed a property right in passing as a white person. This was an attempt to block the emerging Jim Crow Society in the postwar South. Although unsuccessful, that property claim was a response to the Supreme Court, a guess as to what would move the Court to protect the rights of former slaves.

The Civil War Amendments and the early cases that came under them expanded the claims of businesses. Even where they were unsuccessful, they enlarged the discourse over the protection of property. The *Slaughter House Cases* in 1873 were brought by small butchers in New Orleans who were put out of business by a monopoly that the state had granted to the Crescent City Livestock Landing and

Slaughterhouse Company. The butchers claimed that the monopoly had denied them their property without due process. Dissenting justices treated property as a means toward wealth rather than as accumulated wealth. This was a shift, the importance of which was suggested by John R. Commons, who viewed the Court as divided between those who saw property as "use value" derived from tangible holdings like land and those who saw it as "exchange value" that meant some status or franchise that enabled one to make a living (1924: 11). The dissenters rested their opinions on an emerging form of property. Where the majority looked to the common law meaning with attention to possession and use, the minority considered the franchise to conduct a business as property. For Justice Nash H. Swayne, "property is everything which has exchangeable value" (*Slaughter House Cases*, 1873: 124–30). It was not simply possession in the physical sense, but the capacity to produce wealth that would be considered property. Justice Joseph P. Bradley relied on customary arrangements in order to establish that, "a law which prohibits a large class of citizens from adopting a lawful employment, or from following a lawful employment previously adopted, does deprive them of liberty as well as property without due process of law" (1873: 111–24). Although it did not save the disgruntled butchers, the idea that "their occupation is their property" did emerge from the case.

Early takings cases precede the recognition of intangible forms of constitutional property and establish the parameters, under the Fifth Amendment, for legislative action affecting individual possession. In *Munn* v. *Illinois* (1876) the Court ruled that property was not taken without a deprivation of title and possession and that revenues could be regulated for the public good. A balance between taking and policing appears in *Mugler* v. *Kansas* (1887), where Justice John Marshall Harlan's opinion, marking the beginning of compensation law in the constitutional setting, "pits exercises of the police power for which compensation is not compelled with 'takings' which require compensation" (Sax, 1971: 149). Harlan's analysis begins with the observation "that all property in this country is held under the implied obligation that the owner's use of it shall not be injurious to the community" (665). An exercise of the police power would not cost the state; eminent domain would.

Professional status and franchise or business rights expanded as subjects of property protection during the period of entrepreneurial capitalism. And, as professional associations were gaining strength during the same period, professional status emerged as a property interest. This expansive protection set new limits on the exercise of legislative power. In 1888 the right to practice medicine (*Dent* v. *Virginia*, 1888) and in 1897 "the right to pursue a calling" (*Allgeyer* v. *Louisiana*, 1897: 583) were brought under the constitutional umbrella. In the later case, a Louisiana statute prohibiting foreign insurance companies from doing business within the State was held to be in violation of the Fourteenth Amendment as a deprivation of the right "to be free in the enjoyment of all (one's) faculties" (589). Subsequent cases supported the right of aliens to earn a living and the right of lawyers to practice their craft. The conjunction of liberty and property is essential to the dramatic elevation of corporate prerogatives by the end of this period. The outcomes shift away from legislative prerogatives while the concept of protected interests remains much the same even as new forms are accommodated. Deference to legislative determinations becomes characteristic of adjudication from *West Coast Hotel* v. *Parrish* (1937), near the end of the Great Depression, to the present (*Andrus* v. *Allard*, 1980), almost. But *fin de siècle* adjudication had already fostered the determination of what constituted a legitimate property interest for which the government would have to offer compensation.

Compensable Interests

Constitutional guidelines for expropriation developed late in American history. Until about the end of the nineteenth century, the federal government was more actively disposing of property than acquiring it. After the Civil War, the reach of the Constitution extended to meet increasing interests in economic development. Expropriation led to an adjudication of legitimate interests based on "settled expectation." According to Laurence Tribe, the model that resulted restrains public authority on the grounds that "certain settled expectations . . . should be secure against governmental disruption, at least without appropriate compensation" (Tribe, 1978: 456). Determining when disruption of an expectation has occurred and then its value has become the constitutional standard for protection of property rights.

Prior to 1875, the national government had been initiating condemnation proceedings in state courts and under state law. When it expropriated land for postal sites in 1875, Justice William Strong observed that "this power of the Federal government has not heretofore been exercised adversely" (*Kohl* v. *U.S.*). In dissent, Justice Stephen J. Field expressed his preference for federal abstention. A few years later, the majority position was reinforced and eminent domain was described as an "attribute of sovereignty" (*Boom* v. *Patterson*, 1879). Its subsequent exercise under federal law caused the valuation of property to become a facet of constitutional law. The constitutional standard develops to such a point that in *Chicago, Minn. & St. Paul R.R.* v. *Minnesota* in 1890, protected property became something to exchange rather than simply to use. The extent of gain a property owner may legitimately expect and the emphasis on intangibles mature in the emerging regulatory state. According to John R. Commons, this sensitive calculus developed as the federal government sought to expand the tax base beyond physical property (1924: 182). In 1893, a franchise to take tolls was protected by the Supreme Court from uncompensated takings on the ground that it was "as much a vested right of property as the ownership of tangible property" (*Monongahela* v. *U.S.*, 1893).

For the next fifty years, the Court continued to confront cases which called for a determination as to when a "taking" had occurred or when individual interests were sufficiently compromised so as to require compensation. This period contributed the requirement that property may not be taken for private, rather than for public use. The definition of public use was often rather generous to private interests while the requirement demanded at least a sensible claim that the public would get some use out of the expropriated property. Decisions in the period also delineated spheres, such as navigable streams in which governmental taking did not apply. As the interests became less tangible, more attention was paid to the point at which a taking occurred. Thus, property set the parameters of the police power.

The actual calculus by which interests would be figured remained in dispute until 1922 when Justice Oliver Wendell Holmes presented the opinion in *Pennsylvania Coal* v. *Mahon*. The case involved a situation in which a coal mine had been dug on land to which a mining company had subsurface rights. Mahon, whose house was threatened, had tried to stop the tunneling by invoking a state statute prohibiting such activity. In holding for the mining company, Holmes bypassed contract considerations that might have stemmed from the mining easement on Mahon's land and relied on the compensation clause. He described property as a "bundle of rights," a notion derived from common law property. This metaphor clarified the balance Harlan had struck between governmental takings and the police power. Holmes emphasized the "danger of forgetting that a strong public desire to improve the public condition is not enough to warrant achieving the desire by a shorter cut than the constitutional way of paying for the change" (1922: 416). Holmes provided a metaphorical guide for adjudicating interests in property that smoothed the transition from regulation to "taking."

In subsequent cases, the Supreme Court accepted the government's contention that it had only a minimal obligation to compensate property owners according to possible gains in the market. In 1924, it held in *Mitchell* v. *U.S.* that business losses caused by condemnation would not be compensated and, a year later, in *U.S.* v. *River Rouge Imp. Co.*, that damages due to public work could be balanced against gains where compensation was at issue. For the next twenty years, compensable interests in lost opportunities were limited. The government had established its authority due perhaps to what Justice Robert Jackson would later call, in *U.S.* v. *Willow River Power Co.* the unexceptional fact that "rights, property or otherwise, which are absolute against all the world are certainly rare" (1944: 499).

Although property rights were not absolutes, it did become established doctrine that compensation was required under the Fifth Amendment, even when the government did not legally take possession. On this foundation, the Court intensified the process of adjudicating expectation. The standard, "equitable principles of fairness," was announced by Justice Hugo Black in *U.S.* v. *Commodities Corp.* (1950) where the War Department had requisitioned a quantity of black pepper and set a ceiling price below the market. The pepper merchant claimed the loss of profits as a deprivation of property. Black held that the provider was not entitled to a value based on "speculation." Justice Felix Frankfurter was similarly unsympathetic, noting that, "just compensation . . . has a way of attracting far flung contentions" (1950: 133). On the other hand, as property interests came to be evaluated, often successfully, in terms of exchange, regulation of use, as in the case of open housing legislation, also intensified (*Jones* v.

Mayer, 1968). Under the Constitution, the issue had become which private expectations were legitimate, given governmental interest in the public welfare. While the Constitution does require that losses "be borne as part of the common lot," it does not, as Black said in the 1950 commodities case, protect all profits that "might be realized in the distant future."

Penn. Central Trans. Co. v. *New York City* (1978) indicates how much the expectation standard has matured under the compensation rubric. The issue that came before the Supreme Court was whether New York's restrictions on the development of historic landmarks, as applied to the Grand Central Terminal, constituted a "taking" in violation of the Fifth and Fourteenth Amendments. Justice William Brennan, writing for the majority, admitted an inability to determine when "economic injuries caused by public action must be compensated by the Government." His finding was that challenges may be dismissed when government action does not interfere with "interests ... sufficiently bound up with the reasonable expectation of the claimant to constitute 'property' for Fifth Amendment purposes" (104). The corporation would have been able to claim a governmental taking if it could have shown deprivation of a reasonable expectation.

Property came under the compensation rubric after the regulatory power of the federal government had been established. With the "bundle of rights" metaphor, and an emerging federal authority, the Takings Clause became a means for evaluating new forms of property. However, the tradition has remained that states, in most instances, and the federal legislature in its share, have authority to define property (*Pruneyard Shopping Center* v. *Robins*, 1980; *San Diego Gas & Electric* v. *San Diego*, 1981). The result has been a standard of legitimate or settled expectation that delineated the prerogatives of private ownership and made reasonable profit a protected interest under the Fifth Amendment (Kramer, 1989). These developments link statutory entitlements to property under the Constitution.

Statutory Entitlements

As far back as *Marbury* v. *Madison* and maybe even further, the Supreme Court recognized that actions by the government create binding obligations. The nature of these obligations has, obviously, changed over the last century and a half. It is not surprising that in the middle of the Depression, the Court acknowledged that "property . . . reasonably may be construed to include obligations, rights, and other intangibles as well as personal things" (*Fidelity Deposit* v. *Arens*, 1933). A personal interest in intangibles is thus the foundation for the property right in welfare benefits. But, like other expectations, the granted benefit arrived at the bench because of obligations taken on by the government, in this case, the obligations associated with the rise of the welfare state (Jones, 1958: 143–56).

Reflecting regulation and new governmental responsibility, "property" provided the basis for a growing number of claims by the middle of the twentieth century. Initial arguments for property in entitlements were made with reference to Social Security. The Court first held the Social Security Act to be constitutional, and later considered the extent to which the benefits would be treated as "settled expectation." In 1960, *Flemming* v. *Nestor* reached the Court over a denial of Social Security benefits following deportation. The outcome is less important here than the judicial willingness to hear the claim. In the area of government employment, where the first challenges had appeared, interests formerly treated as privileges began to be considered rights in the 1960s. In 1961, the Court held that deprivation of expected benefits, in this case public employment, required unusually important government need to outweigh the right to a prior hearing (*Cafeteria Workers* v. *McElroy*, 1961). A few years later, Charles Reich argued that statutory entitlements were "the new property" inasmuch as the welfare state had altered the status of individuals. Although the right was not new (Cotterrell, 1986), its use in this context would replace the tradition of minimally regulated denial, suspension, and revocation of benefits like unemployment compensation, public assistance, and old age insurance. The right would not establish a general entitlement to certain benefits. Rather, it required the government to continue benefits already awarded (Van Alstyne, 1977: 445–83).

Statutory entitlement as property was the basis on which welfare benefits were protected in *Goldberg* v. *Kelly* (1970). In his majority opinion, Justice Brennan noted: "It may be realistic today to regard welfare entitlements as more like 'property' than a 'gratuity.' Much of the existing wealth in this country takes the form of rights which do not fall within traditional common law concepts of property" (262).

Brennan based his position on similar rights relating to unemployment compensation, tax exemption, and public employment. Thus, property in statutory entitlements was not just a claim that made some sense. It had become authoritative by a vote of the Supreme Court. The success of this development is evident in the plea by Gerald Gunther that the status of civil right be directed back to old-fashioned property. Denying the dichotomy between property and noneconomic rights, he sought support from Justice Stewart's observation in *Lynch* v. *Household Finance Corp.* (1972) that "property does not have rights, people have rights." This claim was made in an effort to enhance constitutional protection for a home or a savings account by associating it with "established" rights to travel and to continued welfare benefits. Expanded protection for the poor would now seem to be associated with diminution of "real" property rights. At the very least, it is clear that the Court's more recent attitude toward property is very different from the one it expressed when it described the poor as a "moral pestilence" in the 1937 case, *City of New York* v. *Miln* (Simon, 1985; Melnick, 1986).[2]

In the case of a college teacher, entitlement as property was amplified as an interest in continued employment derived from an "understanding fostered by the college administration." Here, Justice Potter Stewart acknowledged a prior grant of tenure to be a property right, and the Court held that "property denotes a broad range of interests that are secured by 'existing rules or understandings,'" and that "a person's interest in a benefit is a 'property' interest for due-process purposes if there are such rules or mutually explicit understandings that support his claim of entitlement to the benefits" (*Perry* v. *Sinderman,* 1971; *Board of Regents* v. *Roth,* 1971). Subsequent opinions have emphasized that "property interests are not created by the Constitution; rather . . . by existing rules or understandings that stem from an independent source such as state law" (*Bishop* v. *Wood,* 1976). In *Goss* v. *Lopez* (1975), the Court held such understandings to have been present when high school students were suspended from their classes without a hearing. Justice Byron White linked his reasoning to property in observing that "appellees plainly had legitimate claims of entitlement to a public education" (573). As with other forms, property here came from statutory guarantees. The deprivation was held to be substantial, and concern that the holding would damage the educational process was held to be outweighed by the importance of the entitlement. While termination of federal disability benefits was allowed without a prior hearing in *Mathews* v. *Eldridge* (1976), thus signaling the beginning of the end of the period of progressive interpretation, the Court acknowledged that its decisions had accorded government benefits "a statutorily created property interest protected by the Fifth Amendment."

By the mid 1970s, statutory property claims began to be less successful (*Arnett*, 1974; see also Chapter V). Appeals that failed included a foster family desiring to remain intact, a state prisoner being transferred, and a medical student who claimed to have been unjustly dismissed from school.[3] In *Board of Curators* v. *Horowitz* (1978), Justice Rehnquist maintained that Horowitz would have to establish the interest in her seat at the medical school as property "recognized by Missouri state law" in order to claim a constitutional deprivation. In this case, a deprivation of liberty seemed to the claimant to be the stronger basis for invoking due process guarantees. The year before, however, a related entitlement claim was successful. In *Memphis Light, Gas and Water* v. *Craft* (1977), the utility company had claimed an absolute right to discontinue service when bills had not been paid. The Supreme Court, however, recognized an exception when the bill was the subject of a genuine dispute. The company was liable for damages if the dispute turned out to be legitimate, and state protection against termination, except for cause, amounted to a property interest the Court was willing to recognize.

Seven years later, after Justice Stewart had been replaced by Justice Sandra Day O'Connor, the Court upheld a job-related property interest associated with the rights of the handicapped. In *Logan* v. *Zimmerman Brush Co.* (1982), Justice Harry Blackmun boldly restated the definition of property as "an individual entitlement grounded in state law" and ruled in favor of a shipping clerk with a short leg who claimed that he "had been unlawfully terminated because of his physical handicap." The protected property was a species Blackmun traced back to *Mullane* v. *Central Hanover Bank and Trust Co.* (1950), in which case the "cause" (or course) of action had been provided by the Fair Employment Practices Act, and the Court held that Logan was not to be denied access to its protection. Reference was also made to *Societe Internationale* v. *Rogers* (1958), in an opinion that rang with a new enthusiasm for protection of constitutional property, albeit, not without an expression of concern by Justices Lewis Powell and William

Rehnquist. Perhaps even more to the point was Justice White's opinion in *Cleveland Board of Education* v. *Loudermill* (1985), where he explicitly rejected the Rehnquist position on "the bitter and the sweet" (541).

In a case dealing with the right to due process in parole hearings, *Board of Pardons* v. *Allen* (1987), Justice O'Connor added to the conceptual range of entitlement in dissent from a decision resting due process on Montana law providing that parole was not "an award of clemency." "In my view," she said, "the distinction between an 'entitlement' and a mere 'expectancy' must necessarily depend on the degree to which the decisionmakers' discretion is constrained by law" (1987: 383). Her opinion draws attention to statutory limits on the "discretion of the decisionmakers." Two years later, in another prison case, the justices examined the due process implications governing denial of visitation in prison (*Kentucky Department of Corrections* v. *Thompson*, 1989). Here, Justice Blackmun relied on the concept of a "substantive predicate" to characterize the interest protected by due process. By this he meant the standards at law that "guide the State's decisionmakers" (see also *Connecticut Board of Pardons* v. *Dumschat*, 1981; *Hewitt* v. *Helms*, 1983). The majority in these decisions found an interest but did not consider the government's action so arbitrary as to have denied due process.

Returning to the issues of employment status that had been raised in *Loudermill*, the Supreme Court gave extensive treatment to the reach of statutory mandates that cover business in *Brock* v. *Roadway Express, Inc.* (1987). The case involved a federal statute that protects truck drivers from being fired for refusing to operate an unsafe vehicle by providing for reinstatement after an OSHA investigation and on the order of the Secretary of Labor. Roadway Express contended they had not been afforded an opportunity for informed participation in the OSHA investigation. In this case, both parties in the initial deprivation are private, presenting an unusual situation. The holding finds that the trucking company has no right to a formal hearing prior to reinstatement of an employee, but company representatives must have an opportunity for informed participation. Here, employment in the trucking industry is afforded special protection. The opinions in the case raise the possibility that economic interests against arbitrary governments may now reach into the marketplace (Rakoff, 1987), at least in certain circumstances.

These debates continue as part of a sensible discourse. The success of these claims is not the issue here. Rather, we have shown that the concept of property, operative over nearly two hundred years of constitutional adjudication, continues to be applied to new forms. Welfare benefits, like other forms of property, reflect public policies. Judicial attitudes shift with the political currents of the day. These attitudes affect the status, not the form, of property before the Supreme Court. As forms emerge, they acquire meaning as property because they can be associated with the sense of the concept.

Conclusion

Constitutional property has always been more dependent on government than conventional understanding would have us believe. When federal judges and justices adjudicate property rights, their holdings become the law of the land. The federal government, resulting from the Constitution of 1787, maintained property relations as they had existed under the Crown. The Supreme Court had been only minimally concerned with how property is acquired. One is hard put to find any special sensitivity, much less preoccupation, with the Lockeian notion of a person having created property through "the Labor of his body and the work of his hands." Karl Marx articulated the more modern perspective on the subject when he wrote that "the railways do not 'actually' belong to the shareholders, but to the statutes" (Edelman, 1979). Property claims that have made their way to the Court characteristically involve expectation derived from the promises or obligations of the state. Consequently, applying the right to welfare benefits and forms of employment makes sense in the constitutional setting. It is odd to call entitlements "new" property since they have the attributes of the old.

The property protected by the Constitution, like property generally, is "a system of authority established by government," and, as with any right, it "depends on the promise of government" (Lindblom, 1979: 8). When the courts rule on property, the decision involves a dominion one may lawfully exercise and its application in a particular situation. In constitutional history, the "things" to which the right is applied have changed, as have the doctrinal standards. The nature of the dominion, however, has not changed much at all. The society that allowed slaveholding made choices that seem wrong to us, but the way they were enforced should be comprehensible. The continuity in the meaning of the concept, despite shifts in the subject of its protection, is a key to constitutional property.

The justices may ramble, but constitutional decisions must be intelligible; they have to make sense to be understood. This is evident from the way the concept of property has been presented. Disagreement with an outcome may lead us to treat it as nonsense (Kairys, 1982). However, even *Dred Scott* v. *Sanford*, that deepest of wounds, had a coherence with the tradition of interpretation that should caution us against calling it irrational. Appeals are framed in terms of a tradition that, in the case of property, amounts to settled or legitimate expectation, dominion under law. This is constitutional property. It has taken the form of title, contract, grants, compensable interest, and statutory entitlement. It is a minimal standard to hold that constitutional decisions must avoid nonsense since we expect so much more. Yet, this constraint gives significance to tradition. The subjects of these rights change, but the change takes place incrementally on the basis of what makes sense. The creative element is manipulation of what is given: the constitutional text and past interpretations. This is the source of sense; the justices work with it, they do not make it.

CHAPTER II

Taxes and Regulation

In the United States, legitimate expectations under the Constitution are determined in a process that seems particularly subject to fashion. Certain policies may be in vogue one year but not the next. At one point, drugs, drug testing, or drug pushers are the issue; at another, it may be the homeless. This heightens a feeling of minimal connection between policy issues and governing institutions, yet policy is inevitably subject to the conventions through which it may be expressed. These conventions transform fashionable issues into law or leave the issues to pass from the scene. In the United States, basic conventions such as property taxation and land use regulation determine the nature of entitlement. This chapter's discussion of these two conventions, governing property in land, broadens consideration of entitlement and places constitutional property in context.

Two case studies of land policy are examined here, a statutory property tax break for farms and open-space land, and protection of the California coast by a massive land use planning scheme introduced through the initiative mechanism. The property tax break came into vogue from 1957 through the 1970s and is still on the books of most states for occasional use. During this period, over forty states decided to tax certain property owners on the basis of assessed valuations representing the use rather than the market for their land. It is, without some compelling explanation, curious that these tax preferences swept the country in less than twenty years. The Coastal Commission in California was more unique, but the same environmental schemes were reflected at the national level and the power to limit the use of property through zoning has become a basic constraint on property in land. Both stories are part of the dynamics of entitlement and provide a foundation for understanding the statutory bases of constitutional property.

Tax Preferences

The property tax, to some an "unjustifiable relic of the Middle Ages" (Seligman, 1895) is one of the oldest forms of taxation. Although it is an important source of local revenue, it is subject to perennial controversy and considerable confusion (Hale, 1985). In an essay published after the rage for preferential assessment had all but run its course, Glenn Fisher proposed that "honesty forces us to admit that changes in the property tax system have been slow and not always in the direction recommended by those who have made impartial studies of the tax" (Fisher, 1976: 5). The thesis in this chapter is that preferential assessment policies have developed rapidly and that, contrary to the perception of some writers, the "impartial studies" have often covered up the protection of traditional property interests. The introduction of preferential assessment is a story of protection for entitlement that drives developments in policy.

When one examines influences on the policy process at the state level, distinct facets are difficult to discern because of the limited context in which each statute is passed. Specifically, it is difficult to see the weight of new ideas relative to established interests. If we turn from the rationales to the conditions affecting policy, we find the states making taxation decisions on the basis of de facto preferences for farmland, traditionally maintained along with many other extra-legal tax preferences. The change in policy is best understood as a consequence of the movement for 100 percent valuation of property, which was itself stimulated by the growth of state aid and the effort to equalize local expenditures. Although occasionally acknowledged (Hagman, 1964: 637), these factors have not been systematically put forth to explain the new tax preferences. Since these preferences reflect shifts in tax policy that often preserve the status quo, it is not surprising that they fail to achieve their purported land-use objectives

Taxes and Regulation

(CEQ, 1976; Gustafson and Wallace, 1975; Gloudemans, 1974). Thus, to evaluate public policy proposals, I look not at what is said, but to the conventions that determine how we think about policy.

My analysis proceeds from the factors at the base of the policy process. Although infused with predispositions like the desire for suburban life, material change in the uses made of property establishes the basis for policy analysis. Material change presents the policymaker with the conditions on which policy must be evaluated. To understand policy, the ideological treatment given to policies—the rationales that support them—is not enough, but neither can it be ignored. Policy formation involves a response to social, economic, and legal factors that become institutionalized.

The Status Quo Ante

The most obvious factors bearing on preferential treatment for farmland are the population shift to the suburbs and the extraordinary increase in the per capita consumption of land for residential use. From the early 1950s to the mid 1970s, population shifts transformed the landscape and altered the social and economic environment under which people lived. Metropolitan growth during this period converted approximately 22,000 square miles of land from rural to urban uses. The rate at which land was being consumed increased from 30 acres per thousand new residents prior to the Second World War to 200 acres for the same number of new suburban residents in the postwar period (Brown and Roberts, 1978). The loss of farmland, 22 million acres from 1954 through 1959 (Barlowe, 1967: 92), underscores the intensity with which the agricultural establishment has turned to agricultural preservation, but the rising value of urban fringe land is also essential in explaining the rise of tax preference schemes.

Until relatively recently, a variety of de facto tax preferences existed for farms and homes (Netzer, 1968). Some, termed "assessment lag" (Paul, 1975), stemmed directly from increases in land values at the urban fringe. When land increases in value, it comes to be assessed at a diminishing percentage of its market price because the assessment lags behind the market. Thus, the pace of reassessment, combined with rising value, leads to a tax base that is out of sync with the market. Professor Marion Clawson has pointed out that frequency of reassessment must be considered in determining the tax costs on suburban land in a rising market (Clawson, 1971: 122; see also Engle, 1973).

De facto preferences depend on partial assessment. This characteristic of property tax administration has been called "one of the strangest characteristics of the property tax, and its most striking departure from the standard of market value" (Bonbright, 1937: 497). In his classic work, James Bonbright suggested that misinformed taxpayers associate a larger valuation with a larger tax and are not as contentious about the tax if they believe it is based on something less than their property is worth (1937: 498). "Farmers and homeowners are frequently the beneficiaries of these extralegal assessment practices" (Shannon, 1973: 30). Farms increasing in value not only received the benefits of "assessment lag" but generally received favored treatment in the local political environment that controlled the property tax. Local assessors often sought to lighten their constituents' burden at the expense of the other localities. This practice of partial valuation continued in the face of constitutional provisions for uniformity and equality in taxation and numerous court decisions, from early in the century right down to the present, that acknowledged the inequalities resulting from less than full valuation (*Fletcher Paper* v. *City of Alpena*, 1910; *Greene* v. *Louisville*, 1917; *Allegheny Pittsburgh Coal* v. *Webster County*, 1989). In fact, the practice probably increased with efforts to distribute wealth to poorer communities.

States and Equalization

Against this backdrop, another change operated to create the environment for statutory preferences, state involvement in local funding. The redistributive intent of these policies was a change that would transform the politics of assessment. State "intergovernmental transfers" increased dramatically after the Second World War (Maxwell and Aronson, 1977: 85). The disparities in the tax base between school districts began to be evident after the Second World War, due in large measure to the constitutional foundations of equal protection as applied to education. Concern about equality in education led to efforts to ameliorate the differential. In Texas, this was achieved through the Texas Minimum Foundation School Program, which was similar to those in other states. This program operated under a formula for distributing school aid in proportion to need. By the early 1970s, the program accounted for nearly half the total educational expenditures in Texas.

This effort to equalize state aid produced a far greater sensitivity to local assessments than existed previously. Although litigation examining the state effort on the basis of equal protection did not come until the 1970s (*Serrano v. Priest*, 1971; *San Antonio v. Rodriguez*, 1973), the major cases reveal the ongoing efforts to equalize state funding for education. In the case from San Antonio, Texas, the equalization effort was the basis for turning back a challenge to the inequities in funding different school districts in Texas (see Chapter IV).

At the same time that state involvement in local funding began to increase, the administration of the property tax began to be called into question. Both partial assessment and interdistrict disparities came under fire from the National Tax Association and state governments. This resulted in attention to the state equalization function and the way it was being administered. Commentators in a period of growing attention to equal protection were generally optimistic about the future of tax equity while critical of past practice, and a major equalizing effort was deemed necessary in light of the increased reliance on state funding (Yale, 1958). This prepared the foundation for equality of assessment, which in turn spawned statutory tax preferences.

Uniform Valuation

New standards for assessing property at mid century relied on market value as a guide to equality in taxation. These reform movements assumed that state governments would be the prime movers in rehabilitating the property tax (Maxwell and Aronson, 1977: 6). In the end, with a series of decisions beginning in the late 1950s, it was the courts that dropped a "nuclear bomb on the 100-year tradition of fractional and inequitable assessments" (Becker, 1969: 36). The trend since the late 1950s has been toward litigation that either ordered full market valuation or required uniformity within a taxing district. The cases reviewed local inequalities and equalized statewide or interdistrict inequalities.

Prior to this movement, review had been nearly impossible unless an individual assessment exceeded market value. In *Hamm* v. *State*, the Minnesota Supreme Court held taxation of some property owners at a higher percentage of market value to be a denial of the equal protection clause of the Fourteenth Amendment to the United States Constitution and a violation of the uniformity provision of the Minnesota Constitution (1959: 653). In these decisions and some new ones, courts began to order reassessment on the basis of full or market value as the best standard of equality. New York's Court of Appeals required statewide 100 percent valuation in *Hellerstein* v. *Assessor of Islip* (1975). The challenge to partial assessment had been dismissed in the lower courts, although state law provided that "all real property in each assessing unit shall be assessed in the full value thereof" (1975: 280). "Full valuation" had been required in the state since 1826. The custom of fractional assessment, however, was very old too (Kilmer, 1961: 210). The Court of Appeals ruled that the practice of partial assessment would have to be overturned in conformity with concern for equity of the property tax. With this decision, New York became one of the last states to require 100 percent valuation.

Preferential assessment for farmland emerged as a tax reform because court orders beginning in the 1960s had a greater impact than earlier decisions that had asserted a statutory obligation to equalization. In Massachusetts, during the five years prior to *Bettigole* v. *Assessors* (1961), only thirty-two of 351 communities revaluated. In a similar period following the decision, 177 of the communities in the state revaluated (Paul, 1975). The change is most clearly represented in suits filed by communities against state administrations (*Sudbury* v. *Comm. of Corps. and Taxation*, 1973). The claims were based on the loss of state aid that would go to towns that underassessed themselves. In Massachusetts, where full valuation had been required in various cities for over a decade, the *Sudbury* decision ordered the State Tax Commission to enforce the constitutional requirement of full-value assessment for all 351 cities and towns in the state.

Thus, state supervision over the property valuation process, whether involving inter- or intradistrict discrimination, created a new environment for the property tax. It emphasized uniformity of assessment in practice consistent with statutory requirements and brought about an obligation for periodic assessment that was particularly burdensome to owners of property that was increasing in value.[1] The response was often for ad hoc informal preferences, but eventually a movement for statutory preferences emerged, the most successful being that for agricultural land.

Valuation and Legislation

Unlike the land-conversion and open-space rationales publicly identified with tax reform, uniform valuation antedates the environmental movement and thus provides an important independent variable covering the entire period of legislative change. In New Jersey, uniform valuation and statutory tax preferences for farmland followed a case brought by Olivia Switz, who forced court-ordered 100 percent valuation in 1957. Following her initial success, the property tax for farmers in New Jersey went from $5 below the per capita national average to $222 above the average (Hagman, 1964: 638). The state legislature then passed a special preference for farmers. In Maryland, the imposition of full-value assessment in Montgomery County provided the impetus for the first use-value preference for agricultural land (Hagman, 1964: 637–38). A study of the preference in Connecticut described the farmer as having little or nothing to worry about until his property was faced with market valuation (CEQ, 1976). New Jersey, Maryland, and Connecticut were among the first to pass the preference legislation. Prima facie evidence thus exists for interpreting these preferences as having been sought where large landowners were faced with reassessment and the loss of de facto tax preferences.

The basis of support in Massachusetts during the early years was the agricultural community. The Massachusetts Farm Bureau began its efforts to change the law on agricultural land assessment in 1958, following the change undertaken by Maryland. This was prior to the first 100 percent valuation case in Massachusetts. The law emerged from the district in which the state's land-grant college and agricultural extension headquarters resided. It was ultimately necessary in 1969 to pass a state constitutional amendment making tax preferences legal. In 1973, relatively late in the movement for statutory preferences, the Massachusetts House of Representatives voted 218 to 10 in favor. The legislation had become overwhelmingly popular. A year later, the legislature defeated a statutory proposal that would have implemented earlier court decisions requiring full-value assessment.

The California Land Conservation Act of 1965, known as the

Williamson Act (Banta, 1980), was preceded by earlier preference legislation in that state. Although deemed unsuccessful, the Agricultural Assessment Act of 1957 provided tax preferences on the basis of zoning and represented early state policy that sought to induce farmers to retain their land. The intense pressure of land conservation joined with a strong agricultural industry explains experimentation with preferences that preceded the Maryland case, the earliest generally recorded. In California, property tax reform came in the mid-1960s (Revenue and Tax Code, sec. 401, 1966) coinciding with the Williamson Act, but subsequent to the earlier statutory preferences. The reforms in California, like those in some other states, provided for a fixed percentage of market value as the basis for assessment.

States required to revaluate early, such as Florida, and states where there was evident fear of the mandate, such as Maryland, passed preference legislation early as well. States that appear to have been surprised by the Court decision—such as Connecticut, New Jersey, and Minnesota—took a few more years to get the preferential legislation on the books. New York passed the preference prior to being forced to 100 percent valuation. But in this case, by the time the decision had been handed down in 1975, the movement for some farm preference had enough momentum to stimulate legislation. It thus transcended the original factors by which it can most readily be explained.

Thus, the introduction of statutory tax preferences has been characterized by interest group success in maintaining the status quo—not because the farms that would be affected were paying more than their share but because they were paying less. This makes the movement to uniform assessments at full market value the most important factor during the period under study in explaining preferential assessment and the interest group activity that supported change in the law. Yet there are interesting demographic differences that affected the rate at which states accepted the new assessment scheme.

Other Determinants

The point at which a state passed the preference for farmland during the last twenty years is also directly related to the significance of agriculture, the per capita property tax, and the amount of urban growth in the state. These are conditions that increase legislative sensitivity to this policy throughout the period and provide the basis for policy response to changes in the valuation of property. They all heighten the significance of full valuation and help explain why this policy change is not directly related to a state's propensity to be innovative in other policy fields.

The first ten states to pass the legislation[2] had strong agricultural interests and more dramatic urban population growth than the rest of the nation. They averaged $760 million in the value of farm products in 1964, the center of the period under study, against a national average per state of $705 million (Census, 1977: 679). They averaged 26.35 percent in the change toward a metropolitan population between 1960 and 1970 against the national average of 17.10 percent (Census, 1977: 17). Growth, by pushing up land prices, activated the agricultural community to maintain use-value assessment. Of the eight states that had not passed a preference by 1975,[3] the average value of farm production for 1964 was $673 million, and the change in metropolitan population was 13.37 percent from 1960 to 1970. The population shift is lower than that of the nation and half what it is for the states instituting the preference early. In examining the characteristics of the property tax itself, the most significant factor is that none of the nine states with the lowest per capita property tax in the country[4] passed legislation before the last decade of the period under study, and five of the nine are among the eight states that did not pass the legislation at all. In addition, four of the first seven states to pass the legislation ranked at the time in the top ten in their reliance on the property tax (Phares, 1973: 67).

Political scientists experimenting with "the diffusion of innovation" framework for studying agendas (Gray, 1973; Savage, 1978; Walker, 1969), focus on the propensity of states to make policy changes as a function of their institutional and political cultures. The more recent contributions provide a rough test for the adoption of legislation. Savage developed a scale of innovation using 181 policy measures and ranked states for three periods in American history (1978: 216–17).[5] Of the ten states passing the preference in its first decade, only three —California, Oregon and Indiana—ranked at the top of the innovation scale. Of the eight states that had not legislated a preference by 1975, three fell into the lowest decile on innovation: Alabama, Georgia, and Mississippi. Although none of the "most innovative" states failed to pass the preference and none of the "least innovative" passed it early, the generally low correlation of tax preference legislation with innovation for individual states lends support to the thesis that this legislation preserves the status quo.

Research and Rationales

As a social phenomenon, the rise and implementation of use-value assessment has at its core the protection of agricultural interests. In this context, it has been viewed as both a necessary measure to preserve the economic viability of farming (Engel, 1975) and as a classic case of special interest legislation (Stocker, 1976). Early commentary even from the agricultural establishment in Washington was not entirely favorable to the legislation as a means of keeping land in farming (Stocker, 1961). Yet, in nearly every state that passed the legislation, research describing its virtues was carried out by the extension service and experiment station network. This research proposed that use-value taxation was preferable to public ownership and other forms of regulation (Engel, 1975). Conducted first by the Department of Agriculture and then by the extension service in each state, the research was influential in getting the legislation adopted and was linked to public concern for open space only in the studies that came after the environmental movement had gotten under way and the tax preference had been widely institutionalized (Nelson, 1977: 215).

All of the forty-two states that had passed preference legislation by 1975 included a preference for agriculture, while only eighteen included forests, thirteen brought in open space, and only eight had offered the tax benefit to recreation areas. The various preferences were primarily farmers' statutes.[6] As farm rather than environmental legislation, the preferences have served the interests of speculators. Speculators have benefited from statutes that could not have been passed with their interests in the forefront. One way to gauge the influence of speculators and developers is to compare the bills that are particularly advantageous to them with those that are less favorable. In 1975, only eight states[7] had pure preferential assessment without additional eligibility requirements other than that the land be in a stipulated use. Of these, only Arizona and Indiana combined agriculture with significant urban growth. The political culture of Arizona has been very susceptible to the interests of speculators (Brown and Roberts, 1978). From the experience of California, we see the extensive use of the preferences for the benefit of speculators and large landholders (Fellmeth, 1973; Wagenseil, 1970). Thus, the legislation is best characterized in terms of farmer and speculator interests rather than those of environmentalists and planners.

The early studies coming from the agricultural research establishment did not assess the influence that the tax preference was likely to have on the behavior of farmers. Cost-benefit analysis of this sort did not come until after the legislation had been passed, and it reflects an environmental interest rather than those of agriculture. Farmers and their advocates didn't need to worry about costs and seemed disinclined to assess effectiveness, but the preferences were supported by environmentalists and planners who accepted the agricultural research that presented the statutes as a means of preserving farmland. These groups did not add their research capacity to assessment of the preferences until after the laws had been passed. By that point, disenchantment with the mechanism had begun to be evident from these quarters. In an evaluation done for the Council on Environmental Quality in 1976, the authors proposed that "while differential taxation was promoted under the slogan, 'Save Our Open Space,' preservation of open space was not the real concern of the farm and timber interests who were the major forces seeking the legislation" (CEQ, 1976: 236).

Farm interests provided the impetus and environmentalists joined in, perhaps naively. Environmentalism, although it generated widespread attention two-thirds of the way through the period of legislation, was markedly immature compared to the longstanding and highly institutionalized interests of agriculture. The environmental movement was just beginning to be a major political force by 1970, when it was confronted with the already activated preferential-assessment bandwagon coming out of the agricultural research establishment. Environmentalists may have been overly eager for a victory and thus willing to accept the intuitively correct, albeit superficial, claims for a relationship between tax preferences and the preservation of farmland and open space.

Once environmentally conscious research began to probe these tax preferences, the results were far more critical. In particular, conservation groups evaluated who benefited and the extent to which the preferences affected decisions about whether to stay in farming. Some of the most critical studies examined one of the most restrictive statutes. Professor Harris Wagenseil pointed out that "only 6.4% of the land under contract in the Williamson Act was located less than three miles from cities" (1970: 190). According to his assessment, those close to the cities, and hence the most likely to face development pressure, chose not to tie up their land. He concluded that there was no reason to believe that use-value assessment "will be the major tool in the curbing of urban scatteration and the preservation of open space" (1970: 192). A Ralph Nader study a few years later confirmed these findings for California, reporting that within a three-mile radius of the cities, less than 5 percent of the land was under contract (Fellmeth, 1973: 41). Large-scale developers and landholders can plan decades ahead and have thus been able to "use the Act for land which is not scheduled for immediate development" (CEQ, 1976: 293).

Conclusion

The limitations of tax preferences in fulfilling land-use objectives have stimulated a new set of rationales that rely on continued optimism. Tax preferences are seen as "at best . . . a holding action which may buy some time to develop alternative public land resource management methods" (Engel, 1975: 222). The preference schemes, however, offer marginal improvement in the welfare of the farmer against extraordinary advantage that may be gained by turning farmland into house sites.

In policy analysis, one is alerted to the limits of ideological rationales when the goals most generally stated seem not to be served and when all the research that was done in support of the schemes fails to show what subsequently turns out to be "obvious" limitations (see Coughlin, 1980; Ladd, 1980). The pervasiveness of tax preference legislation indicates the need for a material explanation that is sensitive to ideological rationales for their capacity to gain acceptance in the political sphere. The data presented here call attention to the dependence of policy change on economic factors not evident in the ideological positions. If factors like economic interests or legal change are adequately depicted, the results of legislation should be less surprising.

Taxes and Regulation

Success in passing the preferences may well be the key to their failure to contribute to the goals that were generally expected. If meaningful regulation of land use was to become national public policy, the idea of preserving farmland and open space through preferential taxation would become an artifact of the failure of interest group pluralism to carry out a planning function, and this failure may also be indicative of the way the statutory basis for the law of property is determined by economic interests.

Coastal Regulation

In 1972 an alliance of citizen groups successfully established a governmental priority. The priority was land-use planning for preservation of the aesthetic and recreational qualities of the California coastal region. The effort to establish this priority utilized the provision in California for popular lawmaking through an initiative. The planning mechanism consisted of the California Coastal Commission and a number of regional commissions, which sought to institutionalize the wishes of the citizens through a "Constitution for the Coast." The commissions have become the sites for struggle over coastal preservation with the state commission taking repeated cuts to its budget from Republican Governor George Deukmejian (*Los Angeles Times*, 1988a) and challenges to local boards being brought before the United States Supreme Court (*Nollan v. California Coastal Comm.*, 1987).

As background for this effort to protect the California coast, it is useful to understand the ways in which beliefs structure the consideration of public policy. Beliefs operate on the substance of debate, and, in their institutional form, they set the framework for political activity. Knowledge of the shared language and the nature of expectation in American society is essential to an understanding of American politics, since political life is shaped and characterized by these traditions. It is widely held that neither ethnic background nor blood makes an American. Instead, it is the rules delineating the political game that are the essential elements of group political life. The beliefs that serve this function constitute ideologies.

Ideologies are usually acquired in childhood, but they can also be adopted through a concerted effort to assimilate the traditions of a

Taxes and Regulation

chosen society. Ideologies are important, because what people believe and what they accept as appropriate influence the way in which policy is made. In the present case, a group of conservationists advocated an interpretation of the public interest that confronted a basic tenet of America's ideology. Americans have traditionally believed that it is their right to possess land for their own use, to claim state support for keeping possession, and to control and manipulate without encumbrance pieces of land acquired under the procedures stipulated by law. According to the liberal theories that stand as the forerunners of America's political ideology, which I examined in Chapter I, the right to property emerged from a right to the fruits of one's labor. For generations of Americans, that right has meant that the state will ensure possession of land that one owns. Along with ownership and possession has come the right to use the land with only minimal interference from the state. The proponents of the Coastal Initiative in California significantly expanded the extent to which the state might interfere with the use of land on the Pacific Coast.

But property rights have never meant that citizens may choose to engage in any sort of conduct on land that they own. There have always been important limits to the use of property. The limits range from the obvious prohibition against engaging in illegal practices to traditional zoning controls stipulating that acceptable uses of land may depend on where the land lies (see *Euclid v. Ambler Realty Co.*, 1926). In its final plan, the California Coastal Commission linked the parameters it set on use to a tradition of limited use, explicitly stating the tradition of limited property rights, especially as applied to social and ecological concerns. The following passage is from the final plan, submitted to the California legislature in December of 1975.

> The property rights of a landowner are not absolute. Rights can and do change over time, and the rapid urbanization of the United States during the 20th century has led increasingly to restrictions on the use of private property—restrictions held by the courts to be constitutional. For example, the U.S. Supreme Court held 25 years ago that property owners could not create an enforceable agreement requiring racial discrimination in the future sale of their land. For many years, laws have prohibited the use of property in a way that would result in health hazards or noxious effects on the public at large. And local zoning laws have been upheld by the courts since 1926.

Taxes and Regulation

In this document, a history of entitlement in land is presented in support of a new regulation, a history that holds the legitimate interests of the public to be an inevitable limitation on use of land.

A Constitution for the Coast

Public concern in California during the 1970s was moving away from the individual interest represented by a radical libertarian claim about the meaning of property rights to the common stake that people have in the earth's resources, which were being recognized as limited with a new sense of urgency. The ecology movement had led to increasing interest in land use, and it sought to increase the limitations placed on private interests. In the process, the nature of entitlement became the center of debate. The ecology and conservation movement clashed with some landowners and the interests that supported change in the uses made of land—real estate developers, utilities, and oil companies. This clash of interests, and the fundamental differences in social values that are implicit in it, characterized the electoral struggle over passage of the California Coastal Initiative of 1974. Powerful but threatened interests organized an appeal to the sanctity of rights and the privileges of property. The alliance behind the initiative presented a challenge to these interests and their interpretation of where tradition lay.

In democratic theory, the people, of course, are sovereign. But, in America, governments operate under a variety of institutional structures rather than by direct expression of opinion. One characteristic of these structures is the existence of multiple levels of government. The states traditionally retain all power not delegated to the national government. The localities have the power to conduct their own affairs within the bounds set down by the states. Local governments are legally creations of the states and their power is derived from state grants of authority. The states themselves, since they have a legal status that predates the national government's, operate under their own authority except where the national government has become involved. Although state and local power has been eroding in favor of the national government ever since the ratification of the Constitution in 1789, substantial powers remain at those levels of government. The states are still responsible for most of the law under which we live.

Taxes and Regulation

The state determines family law, the law for business enterprises, and the rules and regulations governing most areas of human conduct. The criminal law is overwhelmingly state law; until the last few decades, it was almost entirely so. The states delegate the authority they have in these matters to local governments under the provisions for "home rule." Schooling, police and fire protection, and issues related to the development of land have traditionally been local responsibilities.

Restrictions on the use of land have been carried out for the last fifty years through the power to "zone," or determine what sorts of activities are most appropriate in what parts of cities and town (*Euclid*, 1926). Most of this regulation has been concerned with conformity to adjacent land uses and with requirements for public improvements such as streets, sewers, and drainage. For the most part, local regulation has placed limits on the use of land only to the extent that these limits serve the interest of both local government and developers in growth. Municipalities get most of their revenue from the property tax. Since development increases property values, it has been in the interest of local government to develop vacant land into a tax-generating resource. Local regulation has also been relatively ineffective because it is focused on a limited area and is, therefore, less likely to be receptive to interests and values that transcend the region. Preservation of the California coastline is such a value.

By the late 1960s, the role of the state and regional institutions in meeting environmental quality and public health goals had begun to grow. The Coastal Initiative was exemplary because it created regional authorities with a mandate to protect the coastline from development. Central to the plan proposed and shepherded through the initiative process was the creation of an agency with regional authority. The agency would also make a plan that would serve the public interest. Here, the new value—coastal preservation—dictated the necessity for something more than the traditional local government role, since it was believed that localities had not adequately protected this value in the past. The concerns of this faction in local government were evident in this statement from the California Association of County Supervisors:

> We do not support the creation of new commissions, governments, boards, authorities or what have you to implement land use decisions at a local level. There is more than enough government right now to do the

Taxes and Regulation

job that needs to be done. Government may need more resources, authority, technology, experience or wisdom; but the people of California do not need more government.

The Coastal Commission chose, in its final proposal, to recommend phasing out the regional commissions after the local governments had submitted land-use plans that were consistent with the statewide plan. The state commission would retain the power to review all local decisions. The parties that supported the original proposal were not totally satisfied with the elimination of the regional commissions, as is evident in the report on the preliminary plan by the Planning and Conservation League.

Problems in many different policy areas that have been prominent nationally in the last few years have revealed the inability of existing governments to solve important issues because of jurisdictional limits. In many cases, the solutions that may be appropriate do not fit into the established governmental setup. New York City's government, for instance, claims that the city's tremendous welfare burden is not a local but rather a national responsibility. The debates on busing for racial integration have focused on the fact that our governing units often do not have authority to handle the problems that ultimately affect them. Planning for regional needs, and development of policy-making capacities consistent with regional needs, is an aspect of the politics of property that required a move beyond the established structures.

Organizations are not limited to one set of policy tools, and some political institutions are capable of creating new mechanisms. In this case, the route was the initiative petition. In an article in the *Sierra Club Bulletin*, Norman Sanders (1973: 10–13) wrote of oil drilling, land-fill pollution, harbor dredging, and a number of other travesties, which he contended local governments were incapable of handling because they had an interest in a broad tax base. It was federal legislation in the form of the Coastal Zone Management Act of 1972 that set the initiative process in motion. Here "a system of reward, rather than punishment," was used to assist states in managing natural resources. One requirement was a comprehensive plan. One issue referred to specifically by Sanders was limited access for the public. He pointed out that in California before the initiative that there were only about 263 miles of the 1,072 mile coastline that were accessible to the general public. The bill that was to change that was Proposition 20.

Taxes and Regulation

In one form or another, the initiative is in use in twenty states, most of which are in the western part of the country. The process requires 5–10 percent of the electorate indicate a desire for a proposal to be put on the ballot. It was a product of the Progressive Movement that swept through the western states soon after many had been admitted to the union. Here, relatively strong interest group activity and weak political parties laid the foundation. In the case of the Coastal Initiative, legislative reform had failed a number of times. According to Assemblyman Alan Sieroty from Los Angeles, the death of a tough regulatory measure in the Senate Natural Resources and Wildlife Committee on July 24, 1972, was "the legislature's last chance." The measure that went to the people in November was to create a California Coastal Zone Conservation Commission and six regional commissions to establish guidelines and issue permits for residential, commercial, and industrial development on the coast.

The first step required for the initiative was what activist Janet Adams called obtaining "a 'good government' seal of approval to certify that the proposed initiative was constitutional and fiscally responsible" (Brigham, 1977: 366). This was a determination to be made by the Secretary of State, the Attorney General, the Legislative Analyst, and the Director of Finance. Then the signatures had to be gathered and validated by 130 days before the election. Adams described one immediate impact of the strict rules for collecting signatures. Since the petitions could only contain signatures of registered voters and be obtained by a registered voter in the county of residence for both, beaches were out as a source of signatures. The petition drive required 16,000 signatures a day for thirty days, and the voting precinct of each signature had to be correctly recorded. The alliance behind the initiative filed its petitions in June with the clerks in forty-seven counties. Although it lost 12 percent—names that were invalidated because the signature was illegible, the name had been changed by marriage, or the voter had moved—the total number of acceptable signatures was 418,000, enough to qualify.

As a highly political process to make new law and declare a regulatory interest in coastal land, the initiative faced the same opposition once it had qualified that had kept similar proposals from becoming legislation. A coalition of interests hired the San Francisco public relations firm of Whitaker and Baxter to conduct a "No on 20" campaign. The strategy is evident in posters that screamed: "Don't let them lock up your coast. Vote No on 20" and "Conservation Yes, Confiscation No. Vote No on 20." In addition, a lawsuit was filed claiming an adverse impact on a nightclub far up the Sacramento River due to alleged ambiguous language in the initiative. Although supporters had to respond to a show-cause complaint, Proposition 20 remained on the ballot. The Whitaker and Baxter advertising campaign may have backfired. Even the governor at the time, Ronald Reagan, appeared to find it confusing. One institutional advantage was that state law required lists of campaign contributions to be made public before the election. The disclosure showed that land developers Deane and Deane and the Irvine Company had given $50,000 apiece: Standard Oil, $30,000; Bechtel, $25,000; and Union Oil, $10,000 to the "No on 20" fund. And, if that wasn't enough, Doris Day, Charlton Heston, and Lloyd Bridges came out in support of the initiative.

Regulating Coastal Land

Like the United States Constitution, which set up a strong central government uniting the American colonies after the revolution, the Coastal Initiative instituted a "constitution" to unify and regulate land along the Pacific. By establishing a public interest in "the coastal zone," a new planning authority was created with a mandate to preserve the California coast analogous to the federal plan two hundred years before. The commissions created by the Coastal Initiative had responsibility for granting interim permits for coastal development during a planning period. In the first two years, the applications for permits totaled 11,501. About 8 percent of these were denied. The initial processes also included preparing a plan "for the long range conservation and management of the natural resources of the coastal zone." This plan emerged from the permit process and was submitted to the legislature in December 1975.

The final plan gave some responsibility back to the local governments, but it was limited by a new emphasis on administration that substituted rules and guidelines for political bodies making political decisions. This faith in the expert has become a central part of the regulatory process and is essential to understanding entitlement relative to land. It's not that there is no politics in these arenas, rather that the politics is played out in the context of expertise and administration. Joseph E. Bodovitz, the first Executive Director of the California Coastal Zone Conservation Commission, was a planner, and in early remarks on the commission's charge, he argued that "we already know more about the coastal zone than we've thus far been willing to act upon" (Brigham, 1977: 388). He spoke of the great potential for landslides and earthquakes in certain areas as a way of encouraging citizens to support implementation of the comprehensive plan, and he drew on the image of *The Quiet Revolution in Land Use Control*, a book by attorneys Fred Bosselman and David Callies, which chronicled successes in environmental protection through innovative land use controls.

According to Bosselman and Callies, the "single predominant cause of the quiet revolution . . . is a subtle but significant change in our very concept of the term 'land'" (Brigham, 1977: 390). Here, it is said that "we are drawing away from the 19th century idea that the land's only function is to enable its owner to make money." For conservationists, land is described as a resource rather than a commodity, but the implication of the revolution in this analysis is that land is both a resource and a commodity. Land is widely traded on the market, and it is widely restricted from trade. Land is one of the precious commodities that we now understand requires a mechanism more sensitive than the nineteenth-century market. Not just in land, of course, and not just with regard to the environment but in the constitutional setting, we see that restriction on entitlement is a facet of American life. Under the American Constitution, property of many kinds has been subject to regulation.

But, there was also attention to public involvement and the expression of preferences in the zoning process. The mechanism is the permit process with public hearings on proposals. As the comprehensive plan was being produced, the permit process allowed a level of "amateur" participation somewhat unusual in American politics (Fleischmann, 1989). It may well have been the confidence derived from a mandate and an orientation to ecological concerns that led to creation of such a Jeffersonian institution. Still, debates are carried out in terms of tradeoffs with environmental concerns threatened by development and subordinate considerations, such as the threat power generation poses to clean air. For instance, in a hearing on expansion of the Encina Power Plant by the San Diego Gas and Electric Company, the League of Women Voters of San Diego opposed expansion of the

Taxes and Regulation

plant. They pointed out the influence the existing plants already had on air quality and submitted a statement on peak-load pricing alternatives prepared by a Professor of Engineering Sciences at the University of California, San Diego (Brigham, 1977: 394–95). The League stood against the County Board of Supervisors, which expressed concern about the adequacy of power for emergency situations and the propriety of superceding the authority of local jurisdictions, in this case the city and the county.

The final plan, the "Constitution for the Coast," included calls to provide public access; preserve wetlands, agricultural lands, and coastal streams; prevent "any significant degradation of coastal air quality" and encourage public transportation, concern for areas of high scenic value, and an aspiration that the public eventually own a strip of land paralleling the coast. Through the 1980s the state commission evaluated local coastal plans in comparison to the state plan and supervised enforcement of local decisions. In the late 1980s, the Commission Chair Michael Wornum carried on a running battle with Governor Deukmejian over these continued enforcement efforts and the funding for them (*Los Angeles Times*, 1988a). And, the Commission successfully withstood efforts by the U.S. Commerce Department under the Reagan administration to restrict its authority over offshore oil drilling (*Los Angeles Times*, 1988b). The dispute involved state authority under the federal Coastal Zone Management Act, which was initially established in 1977 as another manifestation of environmental concerns.

The Nollan Case

James and Marilyn Nollan owned a beachfront lot in Ventura County, California, between Los Angeles and Santa Barbara. A quarter-mile north of their property was Faria County Park, described as "an oceanside public park with a public beach and recreation area." Another public beach area, known as "the Cove" to locals, was 1,800 feet south of their lot. Under California law, the mean high tide line determined the oceanside boundary of the property. The beach from that point to the sea belonged to the public, as a matter of history and law.

The Nollans originally leased the property and a small bungalow, 20 by 25 feet, with an option to purchase conditioned on a plan to demolish the bungalow and replace it. To do this under the Coastal Zone Initiative—which had become California Public Resources Code §§30106, 30212, and 30600—the Nollans were required to obtain a coastal development permit from the California Coastal Commission. They submitted a plan for a three bedroom house in February 1982 and requested a permit. They were told that the permit had been recommended subject to their granting of a public easement to pass across a portion of their property between the mean high tide boundary and a seawall that marked the beginning of the beach portion of their property. This easement was proposed in the interest of making it easier for the public to move between the park and the cove.

Following a court order overruling its initial decision, the Commission held a public hearing, made factual findings and reaffirmed its imposition of the condition for an easement. The Commission found that the new house would increase blockage of the view of the ocean, thus contributing to the development of "a 'wall' of residential structures." The Nollans filed a supplemental petition for a writ of "administrative mandamus" in which they argued that the access condition violated the Takings Clause of the Fifth Amendment. The Superior Court in the county agreed with the Nollans, but the Court of Appeals reversed the decision finding in favor of the Coastal Commission and the restrictions it had imposed.

In *Nollan v. California Coastal Comm.*, decided June 26, 1987, by the United States Supreme Court, Justice Antonin Scalia wrote the majority opinion. He reviewed the ruling of the California Court of Appeals and held the easement to be a governmental taking of private property. In his argument, Scalia did not begin with the statute that created the Coastal Commission, or with the exigencies of beach overcrowding, as might have been the case if he was talking about welfare policy (*Bowen v. Gilliard*, 1987). Instead he began: "James and Marilyn Nollan . . . [who] own a beachfront lot . . . [and] a small bungalow . . . [that] had fallen into disrepair" (683). It's hard not to feel sorry for the Nollans (discussed more fully in the last chapter of this book), but we don't really learn much about them from the opinion. The characterization is of a couple who wanted to build a bigger house and needed the rules changed in order to do it. The rule makers, in this case the creatures of a relatively young process of regulating property, wanted something in return in the interest of protecting the Pacific Coast.

The tone of the opinion in *Nollan* is evident in the seriousness of the property analysis by the majority. There is little confusion about the meaning of the property right here. It is the liberals in dissent who venture into more humanistic territory. Scalia asserts that requiring an easement with nothing else to complicate things would most certainly be expropriating property. He spends most of his opinion on the matter of the specific, rather complicated situation before the Court. Here the standard is that "a use restriction may constitute a 'taking' if not reasonably necessary to the effectuation of a substantial government purpose" (687). Thus, the majority opinion relies on the practice around the Takings Clause holding that regulation must "substantially advance" the "legitimate state interest" sought (688).

The dissenters would have made the standard a rational relation test, the one traditionally applied in economic cases. Justices Brennan and Marshall held that the proper standard for reviewing the permit was dictated by the tradition of police powers. It was whether the state could rationally have decided that the measure adopted might achieve the state's objective. Under this standard they felt the required easement was easily justified. Blackmun held that the easement was adequately related to the governmental interest in providing public access to the beach. He placed the development of the Nollan's property in the context of general development along the shoreline. Then, as a valid exercise of the police power, it did not diminish any "investment-backed expectations." This case may be beyond the present boundaries of settled doctrine in the application of the Takings Clause to land use regulations. However, since *San Diego Gas & Electric* v. *San Diego* (1981), where Justice Brennan held, "After all, if a policeman must know the Constitution, then why not a planner?" The new activism in property has been clear. That query helps explain why Brennan and Marshall joined the majority in *First English Church* v. *County of Los Angeles* (1987). Judicial doctrine has swung toward property.

Although the Court did not challenge the "will of the people" in their decision to pass the coastal initiative, the justices in Washington certainly limited the authority of the agency the people created (see also, Symons, 1988). This case dealt a severe blow to the tradition of teaching that zoning boards had extraordinary authority to place restrictions on the use of land (see Chapter VII). We hear, in fact, that the decisions in *Nollan* and *First English* are already enhancing the rhetoric of property owners before zoning boards (Fischel, 1988: 1599). Yet, the decision may still have a limited effect in the context of traditional authority to zone where experts dominate the process (Plotkin, 1987). Ultimately, the reach of the decision will depend on the capacity of a popular mandate and public interests to resist the conservative influence of the federal courts (Paul, 1987b). In each case, the one thing that has become obvious is that property has returned as a subject of intense constitutional struggle.

These two areas of land policy, taxation and zoning, represent the regulation of old property. The property tax was imposed at least in part due to the view that increases in the value of property were not "earned" and could be siphoned off for the government with little consequence for the economy. Tax policy took on other dimensions as concern for equity and open space came together to produce a tax plan with less consequence for either of the precipitating concerns than many expected. The regulation of the California coast is a dramatic form of zoning, and as such it calls attention to public authority over land. However, a split decision of the Supreme Court reveals rather extraordinary deference to the holders of traditional entitlements in property. This orientation of the federal judiciary in the last decades of the twentieth century must be kept in mind as we consider the case of contemporary property. The concerns evident here for property as an autonomous sphere—recognition that wealth is generated by property and solicitude for the interests of those who would trade on this wealth—are essential foundations for assessing the bearing of constitutional property on entitlement in the modern state.

CHAPTER III

Double Standard Practices

More than fifty years ago, Justice Harlan Fiske Stone announced in *United States v. Carolene Products Co.* (1938): "There may be narrower scope for operation of the presumption of constitutionality when legislation appears on its face to be within a specific prohibition of the Constitution . . . [or] restricts those political processes which can ordinarily be expected to bring about repeal of undesirable legislation . . . [or is] directed at particular religions or national or racial minorities." Ever since, doctrinal and conceptual developments concerning the constitutional property right have been difficult to discern because of a judicial practice known as the Double Standard. This standard has held that the Supreme Court should monitor legislative action on fundamental political rights while avoiding review of economic rights. Political rights were taken to be things like the right to vote and the right to free expression, while economic rights incorporated the old liberty of contract protection and other creative uses of constitutional due process. Property, viewed as an economic right, has been subjected to this standard.

Thus, property has gotten little systematic attention from the Supreme Court or academic court watchers for half a century. Those who depend on the Court for a discussion of fundamental rights or to ground their own analyses of constitutional property have been left to wander aimlessly, except for a few cautionary comments (McCloskey, 1962; Shapiro, 1978; Funston, 1975). The Double Standard, though often discussed and widely recognized, may profitably be examined here in terms of its institutional significance (Smith, 1987) and because the standard appears to be changing (Shapiro, 1986: 94). We see this change and are beginning to acknowledge that recent decisions about the economy and some provocative property cases have altered the relationship between the Court and the Constitution. The justices are deciding more visible economic cases and this coincides with an ideological shift on the Supreme Court, where President Ronald Reagan and Attorney General Edwin Meese appointed a significant group of relatively young and quite conservative judges. Institutionally, changes on the Court appear to presage a shift from the Double Standard, perhaps to a new basis for judicial authority.

Because of these developments, there is reason to suspect that the Court is renewing its interest in economic matters as when it protected the powerful in the guise of a now-discredited orientation to economic rights. The shift will probably not appear exactly like the earlier version, but it will, no doubt, bear some relation. Once the ultimate vested right, property is sensitive to changes in constitutional jurisprudence, and it seems to promote particularly significant doctrinal developments. This chapter will examine constitutional property, particularly the contemporary institutional and political manifestations of a conservative economic policy reminiscent of the "*Lochner* era," represented by *Lochner* v. *New York* (1905), a conservative period in American jurisprudence when federal judges and justices ruled against progressive social legislation dealing with issues such as working conditions and the distribution of wealth. The consequence appears to be a new standard, perhaps even a new Double Standard, in which institutional decisions about property are removed from the domain of civil rights and cast into the market. The chapter concludes with a description of how this will affect constitutional politics.

Double Standard

The Double Standard is a practice that has come to delineate the boundary between Court and Constitution, that is, this standard sets the terms on which the justices deal with constitutional questions. The practice calls for deferring to legislative bodies when the Court reviews a law passed by Congress or a state legislature on economic

Double Standard Practices

matters such as those the Court learned to be wary of during the New Deal struggles. It involves claims arising from state efforts to aid workers, children, and consumers against corporate interests, or what Professor Martin Shapiro, in an apt turn of phrase, called "Republican" property (Shapiro, 1986: 94). According to the Double Standard, when faced with state regulation over this sort of economic interest, the justices merely have to ask that there be a reasonable basis for the law. The Court, since 1937, as a matter of convention has justified its more probing attention to noneconomic issues as necessary when the political process has been clogged up. This has amounted to the latest claim by the justices for an institutional distinctiveness in American government (Brigham, 1987).

Although the practice may be described in various ways, its meaning and institutional implications have been pretty clear to observers of the Supreme Court. According to Henry Abraham, "what the post-1937 judiciary did was to assume as constitutional all legislation in the proprietarian sector . . . but to regard with a suspicious eye legislative and executive experimentation with other basic freedoms" (Abraham, 1982: 15; see also Abraham, 1975), that is, those associated with the Bill of Rights. To constitutional scholar and resource to Supreme Court nominees Gerald Gunther,[1] "the modern Court has turned away due process challenges to economic regulation with a broad 'hands off' approach. . . . Only on a few occasions have some Justices expressed doubts about the Court's stance of extreme deference to economic regulation" (1980: 540). These observers, the justices, and others knowledgeable in the lore of the institution have given the practice significance.

The practice of deferring on economic questions as a basis for judicial review was a consequence of the New Deal struggle over the orientation of the Supreme Court. Retreating from a perceived strict supervision of the economy in *West Coast Hotel* v. *Parrish* in 1937, Justice Owen Roberts, the exemplar of a disposition in jurisprudence we have come to term mechanical, switched his vote and saved the Court from institutional reconstruction (Caldeira, 1987). The decision upheld a Washington state minimum wage law for women and children. This stance by the justices was the first time, following the Roosevelt threat, that the Supreme Court upheld such a statute and, as the chronicle of the emerging standard goes, "Gradually the Court embarked upon a policy of paying close attention to any legislative and executive attempt to curb basic rights and liberties in the 'noneconomic' sphere."

The standard took shape in *U.S.* v. *Carolene Products Co.* This 1938 case contained Justice Stone's crucial footnote 4, which would later be used to support intensified judicial supervision of noneconomic public policy. The Stone note claimed a special justification for judicial intervention where (a) legislation appears on its face to be within a specific prohibition of the Constitution; (b) legislation "restricts those political processes which can ordinarily be expected to bring about repeal of undesirable legislation," such as voting or political assembly; and (c) legislation is prejudicial to discrete and insular minorities.

Professor Robert G. McCloskey, in one of the first attempts to examine the standard and a particularly influential commentary for political science scholarship on the Supreme Court, said that later decisions such as *Day-Brite Lighting* v. *Missouri* (1952) and *Williamson* v. *Lee Optical* (1955) made it "pellucid" that no claim of a deprivation in the domain of substantive economic rights would be sustained by the Supreme Court (McCloskey, 1962: 38). The Court never repudiated jurisdiction over economic questions in clear and unequivocal terms, and McCloskey described the process as ad hoc and believed that it "set unforeseen limits" on constitutional adjudication (McCloskey, 1962: 34). Rather, the justices of the liberal Courts from Roosevelt to Warren's built a basis for interpretation and judicial review out of a footnote. McCloskey subjected the doctrine of economic due process, which had been buried by the Double Standard, to an "exhumation and reburial." He wrote of this standard: "It seems to have been a kind of reflex, arising out of indignation against the excesses of the Old Court, and resting on the vague, uncritical idea that 'personal rights' are 'O.K.' but economic rights are 'Not O.K.'" (McCloskey, 1962: 54). The standard is clearly linked to state interventions that limited the prerogatives of corporate powers. While the pre-1937 Court had intervened vigorously in struggles over early twentieth century regulation, the Court after 1937 is described by James Willard Hurst, the dean of American legal historians, as practically withdrawing "from the function of judicial review affecting statutory regulation of private market dealing" (Hurst, 1980–81: 456).

The distinction between economic and political matters carried by the Double Standard fits well with the basic proposition of modern liberalism. This standard is the institutional commitment to an old distinction. However strained its logic and forced the distinction may be when describing fundamental rights that quite often have economic correlates, such as the right to counsel or an abortion, the Court has relied on a distinction between politics and economics and thus offered a form of interpretation basic to liberal thought. In this and other manifestations—such as our distinction between law and markets, state and society, or even public and private—the distinction between politics and economics has become a characteristic of constitutional thought (Funston, 1975).

In this sense, the institutional practice of a Double Standard is a specific manifestation of a larger cultural phenomena, and like that aspect of the culture, this standard structures political practice. Back in 1937, and later in 1987, we heard the claim that the Constitution, read with the proper institutional gaze, can hold back the tides of arbitrary politics and subjective interest. Yet, the American experience has been that politics is the most significant factor influencing the emergence of such practices and that the practices in turn become an influence on politics. Civil rights in the age of the Double Standard expanded right up to the economic boundary (Chapter IV) but seldom crossed it.

The federal courts "as an engine of liberal social policy reform" (Grossman, 1987: 249–59), for all their intrusions into the political realm (Morgan, 1984), seldom pushed beyond the liberal wall of moderate political reform. The judges have become entangled with school committees, as in Boston, and they have occasionally dictated to budget officers, as they did in Michigan, but the intrusion has been characterized by respect for the liberal standard protecting economic interests without quite taking them into account. While there have been redistributive effects of these interventions, such as equalization standards for school districts with different economic resources, the real pressure for redistribution has always been from outside the courts. We saw this with the poor people's movements of the 1960s and 1970s, and we see it today in labor's struggle to establish community property interests in the workplace (Piven and Cloward, 1977; Lynd, 1984; Sparer, 1984).

The nature of this process is not revealed by the study of precedent, impact, or behavior but requires attention to the communities that constitute institutions—in this case the Court and the Constitution. The institutional perspective on the Double Standard, that is under review here, ties interpretation to communities. Some of the focus necessarily shifts to the communities behind the text to understand emerging standards with differential class benefits. Communitarian concerns are also the measure of an expanded property right based on legitimate or reasonable expectations.

Students of the American Constitution have learned to be realists when addressing judicial decisions and now, in an age of interpretation, we aspire to understand more about the significance of communities in determining what it makes sense for judges to say. We know that judges learned the law's codes and rituals as lawyers first. Although his breakfast may determine a judge's tolerance or disposition, nothing that he eats can determine the parameters of sensible discourse. For this you need communities, groups who know the issues and can contribute to the debates. These communities, in turn, are influenced by the ways they come to address political issues and describe political interests. The meaning of property is an issue seriously contested by communities around the law. Conversely, we are beginning to think more carefully about the significance for communities of what judges say (Fish, 1980; Fiss, 1982). It is not enough to acknowledge the world outside the authority of the state; we need to know the extent to which the law is actually autonomous and the extent to which the state reaches in to influence choices that might seem to be beyond the reach of the law, such as political strategies in the feminist antipornography movement. In this sense, we can suspect that the meaning of property as it comes to be interpreted in the appellate courts will have some impact on how movements talk about property.

The practice of the Double Standard and the widespread conception that the Supreme Court withdrew from the arena of economic matters missed some important developments over the last half century and left the community of interpretation in the civil liberties field out of the practice that defined those developments for constitutional property. In this period, a jurisprudence arose around the Takings Clause of the Fifth Amendment. This jurisprudence, although it had significant implications for civil liberties, was seldom considered to be an aspect of that important realm. Under the takings provisions, property rights continued to be protected by the courts as an exception to the Double Standard until they could draw support from some of the recent developments in the civil liberties field. But, one effect of the Double Standard, noted by political scientists, has been to prevent these developments from being incorporated into constitutional jurisprudence. That is, those who have collected the opinions and commented on the doctrines—such as Professors Gerald Gunther, Henry Abraham, and Sheldon Goldman—have generally deferred to the institutional practice as outlined in Stone's footnote 4. In most constitutional law texts, there is no section on property. The issue, where it is treated, is considered a matter of substantive due process (Goldman, 1986). Here, we review some of the tradition in constitutional property with an eye to assessing how it has developed since the New Deal.

Old Property under the Constitution

As we discussed in Chapter I, mechanisms to protect economic interests appear throughout the Constitution. While the focus in that initial chapter was on the Supreme Court and what property became under interpretations of the various constitutional rubrics announced by that Court, as commentators in the last two hundred years have pointed out, there was considerable material of economic significance undertaken by the founding generation with which the Court could work (see Wright, 1938; Magrath, 1967). Article I of the Constitution establishes federal power to regulate commerce, coin money, and punish pirates while limiting state power to "impair the obligation of contract." Article IV guarantees a republican form of government while Article VI provides for payment of debts against the United States.

The term property, however, is used in early versions of the Constitution only in the Fifth Amendment, which provides that no citizen shall "be deprived of life, liberty, or property without due process of law; nor shall private property be taken for public use without just compensation." The early Supreme Court protected economic interests without developing the meaning of constitutional property by referring to the various other constitutional provisions. In the 1810 case of *Fletcher* v. *Peck*, a case which involved fraudulent land sales by a state legislature and the implications for innocent secondary purchasers, Chief Justice John Marshall relied on the Contract Clause to prevent governmental whim from denying the legitimate expectations of innocent purchasers. Before the Civil War, with slavery casting an ominous shadow, interests that ranged from status in the community (*Marbury* v. *Madison*, 1803) to franchises to conduct business (*Gibbons* v. *Ogden*, 1824) constituted contested forms of property.

Due process protection emerged after the Civil War when property began to be viewed in terms of its value in the market (exchange value) rather than for its utility (or use) value (Commons, 1924: 11; Brigham, 1984b). This right was much more appropriate to an expanding industrial order, and the Fifth and Fourteenth Amendments became the key to constitutional protection for property. Thus, before judicial attention turned away from regulation of the economy in 1937, a conception of constitutional property had developed, which remained significant for a very long period due to the limited number of constitutional pronouncements on economic issues over the last fifty years.

As mentioned, Justice Holmes set a conceptual framework for property in the modern Constitution, like he did for so many other aspects of constitutional law. In the 1922 case, *Pennsylvania Coal* v. *Mahon* (see Chapter I), he protected the subsurface rights of mining companies by overturning legislation against "subsidence," the destruction of homes by mining tunnels. He did this by giving new life to the Fifth Amendment's Compensation Clause through the traditional "bundle of rights" in the common law definition of property. This framework protected constitutional property by modifying the compensation provision to allow property to be protected even though full legal title to the property did not change hands. The Pennsylvania statute, the Court held, had taken mine property. Since 1922, Holmes' concept of a "bundle" has called attention to the intangible rights in property and has provided the framework for a movement away from things and toward expectation in the fashion identified by C. B. Macpherson in his influential "Political Theory of Property" (1973).

Takings jurisprudence, during the half century reign of the Double Standard, found fewer opportunities for judicial intervention and has only recently begun to find a place in a larger discussion of constitutional law. In his treatise on constitutional law, Laurence Tribe described the protection of the Fifth Amendment's Takings Clause in terms of a model of "settled expectations," a distinctive form of constitutional adjudication. To Laurence Tribe, the Constitution places "restraints on government power" that vest rights in property on the

Double Standard Practices

grounds "that certain settled expectations . . . should be secure against governmental disruption, at least without appropriate compensation" (1978: 256). A review of Supreme Court decisions since 1789, such as that in Chapter I, reveals that constitutional protection of property depends on expectations that have been settled, legitimated, or are in some fashion reasonable—as through a title, grant, or body of understandings—rather than mere possession of tangible things.

Adjudication of expropriation questions is often concerned with what the state owes the property owner for appropriation or restriction of uses—what constitutes adequate compensation (Dunham, 1962: 65–66). Interest by the Supreme Court in these questions during the last decade is one manifestation of a growing orientation to economic issues. The contemporary doctrine of legitimate expectation—as developed in *Penn. Central Trans. Co. v. New York City* (1978), a case involving restrictions imposed by the city on buildings that had been designated historic landmarks—placed the dispute in constitutional terms as whether the restrictions constituted a governmental taking. The Court was unable to provide a formula for compensation (Brigham, 1988a). As I noted, the message was that although Takings Clause violations are traditionally found where there has been a "physical invasion" by government, the more appropriate understanding is that a governmental taking is an interference with "reasonable expectation." Thus, reasonable expectation was Fifth Amendment property. The Court held that Penn. Central would not lose sufficient profits to constitute a violation of an expectation that the company could legitimately have.

Commenting on the 1983 Supreme Court term, Judge Frank Easterbrook, a Reagan conservative, could say that the major cases, *Hawaii Housing Authority v. Midkiff* and *Ruckelshaus v. Monsanto Co.*, responded to the Double Standard by placing takings largely outside the realm of judicial review in that they treated "governmental expropriation of property as simply another form of socio economic regulation" (1984: 226). But, it may have been that the more significant consequence was that the Court and the commentators took a close look at a very political expropriation case in *Hawaii* while relying on the more modern standard of civil libertarian deference to private over public in *Ruckelshaus*, a case which dealt with disclosure of trade secrets by the EPA in the process of reviewing health and safety issues. The Hawaiian case, a large scale redistribution of title to end the concentration of land in the islands, was upheld by the Supreme Court. Thus, the practice of the Double Standard still appears in constitutional discourse even as the justices display an evident interest in matters economic.

New Property under the Constitution

By comparing the takings decisions to cases dealing with modern state entitlement over the last fifty years, we can see the continuing "bias" of constitutional property and call attention to new meaning for the Double Standard. The courts have said a great deal about which expectations are legitimate or "settled." They have not based that judgment on market considerations. In spite of some ideas to the contrary among those who see a theorist behind the constitutional system, John Locke is not residing in the United States Constitution. In the common law up until this century, much was made of a distinction between individual "rights," which were said to characterize the old property and "privileges" adhering in government grants. The traditional example, concerning the case of a policeman who had been fined for criticizing his chief, is cited from an opinion by Oliver Wendell Holmes, Jr., when he was a judge in Massachusetts: "The petitioner may have a constitutional right to talk politics, but he has no constitutional right to be a policeman" (*McAuliffe*, 1892: 220). The "right/privilege" distinction denied constitutional protection where a benefit or expectation arose from government grant.

The initial application of constitutional property status to public welfare benefits involved Social Security. Since the Social Security program was set up along the lines of private insurance programs, it surprised few that property interests were evaluated here. The program itself was held constitutional in 1937 against a substantive challenge to Congress's authority to create the system (*Steward Machine Co. v. Davis*, 1937). The justices subsequently addressed the entitlement issue directly in terms of the right to benefits owed to the otherwise eligible family of Ephram Nestor, who had come to the United States from Bulgaria in 1913. Nestor became eligible for Social Security in 1955, and in 1956 he was deported for having been a member of the Communist Party from 1933 to 1939 (*Flemming v. Nestor*, 1960). Focusing on the nature of an entitlement to Social Security, the Supreme Court overruled the District Court in Washington, D.C., which had held that the benefits constituted "accrued property rights" (608). Rather, according to a bare majority of the Supreme Court, the interests were a "noncontractual benefit," that could be withdrawn simply on the basis of a "rational justification" (611; see also Ackerman, 1977: 268–69). The majority opinion was written by Justice John Marshall Harlan, but dissents by Justices Black, Douglas, Brennan and Chief Justice Warren went along with the district court and indicated significant support for the property claim.

Justice Black's opinion is quite powerful. His straightforward prose lays out the nature of Nestor's right in the tradition of American rights to property rather than the evils of communism. Drawing on a continuous residency in the United States for over forty years and membership in the Communist Party when it was neither illegal nor a statutory grounds for deportation, Black saw government action taking property "without just compensation" (622) as an ex post facto law and a bill of attainder, which he understood to be part of the anticommunist hysteria in the country at the time. To Justice Black, the majority was telling contributors to the Social Security system "that despite their employer's payments[,] the Government . . . is merely giving them something for nothing and can stop doing so when it pleases" (623). Black's reading of the law, he says, was that it was Congress's intent that old people not think the government was giving them "something for nothing." He goes on to chide the majority for suggesting that "a decision requiring the Social Security system to keep faith would deprive it of flexibility" (623). He acknowledges that Congress has the power, under the act, to alter and amend and that legislators could stop covering new people or choose not to increase obligations to old contributors, but it could not disappoint "the just expectations of the contributors to the fund" (624).

Constitutional protection for new entitlements grew in the United States and in the Supreme Court during the 1960s and early 1970s. Following a decision in 1961 (*Cafeteria Workers* v. *McElroy*, which held that when public employment was terminated, there had to be an unusually important government need to outweigh the right to a prior hearing)—Charles Reich, calling the body of entitlements guaranteed in the welfare state "the New property," set off a series of developments advancing the status of this form of property. Recognition that the welfare state had altered the status of individuals—leaving them

Double Standard Practices

less capable of asserting rights in a growing body of important areas —was the basis for the milestone case of *Goldberg* v. *Kelly* (1970). Here, as we have seen, Justice Brennan invoked "realism" to support the idea that "we regard welfare entitlements as more like 'property' than a 'gratuity'" (*Goldberg*, 1970: 254). Citing Reich's view on property, Justice Brennan gave entitlements constitutional protection.

With the longstanding recognition of a property right to intangible expectations, the particular interest is the thing that is "new" about property to which people are entitled by statute as part of the social service commitment of the modern state. Social Security is a relatively recent expectation, as is Aid to Families with Dependent Children (AFDC). Licenses to run nuclear reactors are "new" in much the same way. The application of the constitutional property right, however, in historical practice grew out of licenses for economic activity and a great variety of grants from the government. These were some of the first subjects of constitutional protection as property.

The new property, having emerged under the Double Standard at a time of diminished concern for traditional economic interests and increased sensitivity to civil liberties at the Supreme Court, has made a contribution to the status of some traditional kinds of property. Justices and legal scholars have drawn on civil libertarian values to expand protection of property in land and disposable wealth (see Baker, 1986). A number of cases in the early 1980s reflected such concerns for personal or civil libertarian values in protecting the claim to a job of a handicapped shipping clerk (*Logan* v. *Zimmerman Brush Co.*, 1982), the integrity of a small apartment house owner from the big cable company (*Loretto* v. *Manhattan CATV*, 1982), and the programs of a Mennonite religious community whose land was taken for nonpayment of taxes (*Mennonite Board of Missions* v. *Adams*, 1983). In each of these cases, the property was more old than new, a common law right of action, a building, and land, but the appeal was in the tradition suggested by the Double Standard, attention to the interests of those with little power.[2] Thus, traditional civil liberties concerns have been linked to property in order to transcend the constraints imposed by a tradition of avoiding property claims. Litigation of this sort has improved its chances of success.

Yet, in spite of a civil liberties consciousness, there are important differences evident in the treatment of property questions that go beyond the distinction between "old" and "new" property. Some of these differences are largely a function of the class of wealth involved and, indirectly, the class of the property holder. The wealth or property that we know as "capital" is more fully protected than property that acknowledges the obligations of the modern state to those who work or are in need. This is a connection between property and class that is inconsistent with constitutional principles. The challenge, in the final section of this chapter, is to describe the different interests behind the jurisprudence of property and to face the political imperative for developing claims to fairness for holders of entitlements whose class status does not afford them the privileged economic and social position that has buttressed the property claims of the wealthy.

The New Double Standard

The renewed concern for the "old" property as outlined above and a new fundamentalism evident in the doctrine of original intent (Brigham, 1988) indicate movement away from the Double Standard for some. At the same time, the "new" property of a generation ago is subjected to greater scrutiny from an increasingly conservative judiciary. Perhaps as a result of the persistence of the old standard in the minds of its traditional champions, however, commentators on the Supreme Court have not adequately noted the shift in judicial attention and its implications for doctrinal discussion of property and constitutional jurisprudence. In spite of the extensive coverage given to the impact of the Court's recent decisions on the power of states to regulate property through zoning (*Morris v. Mathews*, 1986; *Lindsey v. U.S.*, 1987), most casebooks categorize new property cases under the old "substantive due process" rubric. This could be for want of a more explicit property framework given the absence of doctrinal developments over the last fifty years (Schauer, 1987). But, in any case, the appearance of the casebooks confirms that there is little attention to the jurisprudential transformation taking place.

Recent decisions of the Supreme Court portend ill for those who see the conservative swing in the judiciary as simply a reluctance on the part of the new right to extend the constitutional guarantees of the Warren Court era. In property cases, where it has been covered by the Double Standard until recently, the Lochnerizing of the modern Court has become difficult to conceal. By its 5 to 4 decision in the coastal zone case (*Nollan* v. *California Coastal Comm.*) in June of 1987, the Supreme Court overturned a state regulation that offered homeowners a deal of the sort that is the life blood of corporate transactions with government. The homeowners could have a variance if they provided an easement to the public. The easement, running parallel to the shore and permitting beachgoers direct passage between two neighboring public beaches was judged by Justice Scalia on a standard very close to "strict scrutiny." The rhetoric of the embattled property owner carried the image of minorities oppressed by a hostile state and the arrangement offered by the state was adjudged a taking. In the church property case (*First English Church* v. *County of Los Angeles*, 1987), through an opinion by the Chief Justice, the Supreme Court ruled, also in June of 1987, that property owners are entitled to compensation for government regulations that deprive them of reasonable use of their land.

In the same year, the Supreme Court extended principles of reasonableness to entitlement holders, both employers and employees (*Brock* v. *Roadway Express, Inc.*, 1987), and in private employment where there were state entitlement provisions (*Brock* v. *Roadway Express*, 1987; Rippey, 1987). The majority in the public employee case relied on *Cleveland Board of Education* v. *Loudermill*, a 1985 decision in which the Court claimed to have clarified its position relative to the power of legislative bodies to determine how much property an entitlement holder would be entitled to, the so called "bitter and the sweet" doctrine (*Arnett* v. *Kennedy*, 1974). The Chief Justice, who authored the original doctrine, dissented on public employee property. In another case, dealing with private employment, a majority of the Supreme Court upheld efforts by the State of Maine to protect its workers from plant closings. The justices allowed provisions for severance benefits for dispossessed workers to stand. Corporate interests had made a claim of unconstitutional taking and federal preemption in the area of welfare benefits and collective bargaining. The dissenters, however—Justices White, Rehnquist, O'Connor, and Scalia —were somewhat younger than the majority and may not have to brood for very long before they can write their opinions into law. While these cases show a continuing willingness to consider substantive protection for some private forms of property, public or social welfare property must struggle to be accorded due process.

Double Standard Practices

In this regard is it appropriate to clarify the distinctive character of constitutional property, especially as it operates today under a new Double Standard. Property in this area of law is different from common law property on the one hand and a liberal conception of property[3] on the other. The new constitutional standard for property sets the terms for interpretation and introduces a pernicious form of class bias into constitutional practice. The new standard leaves property in entitlements only partially fulfilled while concern about the civil liberties of traditional property expands protection in that area. Constitutional protection for entitlements is incomplete compared to the way that traditional property rights are protected. They are accorded the safeguard of due process and also the substantive protection of compensation when the property is taken.

The traditional argument for compensation is that monetary payment to one suffering a loss distributes the costs resulting from public action. A property owner whose front yard is needed for a roadway expansion is not expected to make additional economic sacrifices to subsidize the common good. Public compensation to distribute the costs of governmental takings is central to constitutional protection. By inference, then, entitlement holders with a legitimate expectation of benefits should be able to make the same claim that any losses due to such a change in policy after an expectation has been established need to be compensated, as a matter of right. This is one implication of Justice Black's discussion of "just expectations" when he dissented along with Douglas, Brennan, and Warren in *Flemming* (1960). The withdrawal of benefits was described as action taking property in Social Security benefits without compensation. In this early entitlements case, the lower court decision also revealed support for property protection of this sort of interest.

For commentators such as Professor Bruce Ackerman, the absence of constitutional protection for statutory entitlements is due to a limited conception of property protected by the Constitution as "private wealth" (1977: 269).[4] According to this theory, the basis for the protected right has been trade and the ability to transfer interests, to buy and sell the thing that is protected. Compensation seems to symbolize the higher status accorded to property when the right is associated with the market. The tradition has been to protect commercial expectation more fully than those that may be private but have no commercial potential, such as the expectation of parents with regard to benefits promised to their children (James, 1982). In *U.S. Trust Co. of N.Y.* v. *New Jersey* (1977), the Supreme Court struck down regulations impairing the claims of bond holders, while in *Atkins* v. *Parker* (1986), food stamp benefits were reduced with only general notice of a change in the regulation from the state.

In the 1986 decision in *Connolly* v. *Pension Benefit Guaranty Corp.*, Justice Bryon White discussed the takings issue in the context of statutorily created financial liability of employers for contributions to a pension plan beyond those for which they had contracted. The Court held that Congress could increase private liability in the interest of public welfare and social responsibility without being obligated to consider compensation. Protection for property grounded in market considerations, or what White termed "investment backed" expectation, supported the idea that because the field of employee pension plans was already heavily regulated, employers had adequate warning that Congress might increase their liability. This strange transposition of the Takings Clause logic suggests that the key to the interest protected by compensation is not commerce. Instead, the sovereign authority to protect the public welfare is consistently the primary consideration.

If the expectation of a particular grant is extended for a fixed period or according to certain conditions—such as Social Security survivors benefits to children until they reach eighteen or, as once was the case, twenty-two if they went to college—a cutoff prior to that time violates a legitimate expectation. Not only is the expectation of the child an issue, but so are the obligations to deceased parents, who paid into the system. After eliminating these benefits in 1982, Congress heard testimony from Alice James of Chestertown, Maryland. James's husband had died leaving four near-college-age children no longer eligible for benefits he had earned and expected while paying into the Social Security system (Joint Hearing, 1982). While her testimony spoke of betrayal and disappointment, James did not rely on the fundamental right in the American Constitution and constitutional decisions, which have protected legitimate expectation. The Double Standard, by drawing attention away from the fundamental right to property, and the limits of legal vision, which fail to see compensation issues, have conspired to preclude this powerful claim from emerging in policy debates or constitutional adjudication.

In the next generation, the insights derived from the study of institutional practices may cut through the kind of mysteries that have limited understanding in the past. The interpretive commentary on the Constitution can no longer be understood independently from the Court. Although it changes, the Constitution is, as Karl Llewellyn noted, "an institution," not a matter of words or rules but "a set of ways of living and doing" (1934: 17). Changes in the Supreme Court and the ideological basis motivating it at any given time alter how we look at the Constitution. Thus, when the "Four Horsemen" of the 1930s stood against New Deal legislation, the Constitution was referred to by the conservative jurists in static terms and the justices described themselves as operating in mechanical fashion (Belz, 1978). The attack mounted against using constitutional arguments to preserve the status quo, which was based in the political critique of the activity, became the basis for understanding the judicial activity after a group of justices willing to support New Deal policy had been appointed. As the Roosevelt Court broke out of this cocoon, the justices and the public developed a new basis for action, a "Living Constitution." The doctrinal contribution was a Double Standard structurally tied to the process based justifications for institutional power. Arguments along these lines will be discussed in the next section of this chapter.

Property and Process

Max Lerner placed the social foundations of constitutional government in "habits of mind begotten by an authoritarian Bible and a religion of submission to a higher power" that "have been carried over to an authoritarian Constitution and a philosophy of submission to a 'higher law'" (Lerner, 1937). Thus, from the political struggles of the 1930s, the foundation was set for the Supreme Court as the institutional base of constitutional authority. The criticism of the old identification with the propertied classes led to a process-based justification that would allow the Court to maintain its place as "the institutional church that incarnates the sacred document," according to Sanford Levinson (1979: 124), in an article that illuminates the interdependence of the Supreme Court and the American Constitution. The debates over New Deal policies would pit property against human rights and lay the foundation for a new constitutional authority. Criticism of the "cloak of constitutional piety" and the "constitutional negativism," by which the basic principles of government were seen as a closed system, accompanied FDR's reorganization plan and marked its most significant effect on the institution (Bradley, 1937: 92).

The shift, seen in jurisprudential terms as the Double Standard, has affected the political perspective on the institution. The view of the Supreme Court as a political body, that politics is part of the institution rather than something peripheral, is ideologically linked to the separation of property from politics. In fact, for some, "the political view" continued to mean an effort to bring attention to the Court's economic policy, as the New Deal reformers had done (Shapiro, 1964). A consequence of the distinction is what Laurence Tribe refers to as "the puzzling persistence of process-based constitutional theories" (1978). These are theories about the judicial function, specifically judicial review. They are process-based in that they justify review as keeping the democratic process open, and they are a response to the inevitable challenges to judicial review in a regime with a democratic claim to legitimacy. Thus, there is a legitimate basis for judicial concern at the constitutional level when some action "seems to obstruct political representation and accountability" (Tribe, 1978: 1063). The theories are traced to Stone's footnote and have been dominant for nearly fifty years.

The most recent proponent of the "process-based" standard for judicial review, Professor John Hart Ely, has argued that although the Warren Court appeared on the surface to be taking the "value-oriented" approach to deciding constitutional questions and where to throw its weight, it was actually an institutional jurisprudence. He wrote, "The constitutional decisions of the Warren Court evidence a deep structure significantly different from the value-oriented approach favored by the academy" (Ely, 1980: 73). Ely points to criminal procedure as a key, but brings in the Warren Court's commitment to democratic processes in a broader sense. Thus, activism in the area of freedom of expression and malapportionment came to be the 1960s expression of the *Carolene Products* footnote, at least as viewed from the next decade. This shows the significance of the institutional rationale during the Court's most recent sustained period of progressive activism. Its role was not simply an after-the-fact rationalization but rather an underlying thematic structure that appears throughout the period.

Double Standard Practices

The Court claims to be avoiding controversial judgments, but the reliance on process "determines almost nothing unless its presuppositions are specified, and its content supplemented, by a full theory of substantive rights and values" (Tribe, 1978). This is due to what Laurence Tribe sees as the substantive roots of procedural norms. There is concern for privacy embedded in the Fourth Amendment. Due process rights, especially as they are becoming evident in the administrative context, rely on a vision of what it means to be a person. Even such a classic process-based realm as voting rests on presumptions about maturity, mental competence, and sex.

Thus, process-based discussions are a legacy of the Depression struggles. They are the more recent manifestations of the greater confidence—in this, as in liberal societies, by their nature—of an ability to agree on processes as opposed to substance, particularly, of course, where the substantive call is for a redistribution of wealth. The focus suggested by Chief Justice Stone in 1938 is historically simply an "other side" of the liberal split between material and political life (Ely, 1980: 75–77). The split that results is derivative. Within the doctrinal tradition, in this jurisprudential corner, the jurist claims to be able to see process as devoid of substance. It is an inversion of the claim to see economics devoid of politics, a concatenation of ideological forms made possible by liberal democratic thought.

Ultimately, the greatest impact of process-based theories is the particularly strong claim they lay on a Constitution for judges in a democracy, or as Tribe puts it, "the impoverished relevance of the Constitution for everyone except judges" (1978: 1080). The theory would have us believe that judicial activism is an essential feature of democracy. The Double Standard, which appears on the surface to limit the scope of judicial review, actually establishes a contemporary basis for institutional legitimacy and sets the framework for pronouncements on the Constitution by the Supreme Court. Many have noted that the practice of judicial review tends to dominate all discussions of the Court, "like the death's head at a feast" (Pritchett, 1948: 72). Here we have emphasized not the tactical retreat from political forces represented by the Supreme Court, but the beliefs that give meaning to such activity. As the shift emerged, it became associated with politics as a judicial concern, while economic policy would have to be understood in other terms if it was to be understood at all.

In the struggle over authority to interpret the Constitution precipitated by the split between the majority on the Court and the political majority supporting the New Deal, the authority of the Court in relation to the Constitution became a big issue. The publication in 1938 of Professor Edward Corwin's *Court over Constitution* is a benchmark indicating the shift from the then "outmoded" doctrine of formal or static constitutionalism to the living constitutionalism of political jurisprudence. The shift of 1937 is remembered as a turn away from the bad old politics of laissez-faire constitutionalism. In accepting this description as a characterization of the institution, we have lost track of the economic policy made by this institution. Of equal significance for the institution is the turn away from the myth of mechanical jurisprudence to a new myth of political jurisprudence. It is by focusing on this view—that the Supreme Court's product is simply politics—that we lose track of the development of constitutionally significant doctrines, such as those surrounding property.

Conclusion

Thus, in judicial interpretation of the Constitution, there are now two levels of property protection: one for the wealthy, whose property gives them power, and one for the poor, whose property is symptomatic of their powerlessness. Treatment of constitutional property in the last half-century has relied on distinctions between economics and politics and between politics and law that have masked this bias in constitutional property. The recent shift toward protecting the interests of property owners and the implicit drift from the old standard would seem to require consideration of these undeveloped implications of a constitutional system. The core of such consideration would investigate the interpretive basis for judicial authority and link forms of interpretation to movement practice. The challenge for such attention today is that conservative jurisprudence is moving to supplant the deference to minorities of the past with a new doctrinal fundamentalism that is unsympathetic to entitlement rights and hostile toward the claims to an equitable standard just outlined. The judicial conservatives invoke exogenous mechanisms like "the intent of the Framers" (Wolfe, 1986) or an economic calculus to support interpretive decisions that are beginning to create a new Double Standard.

Double Standard Practices

After fifty years, we should take special note of the *Carolene Products* footnote and the many years of a civil rights jurisprudence. With it, we must reevaluate the process-based justifications and, taking the determinacy of interpretation seriously, we can begin to assess its implications for progressive rights struggles. Examining the new property from this perspective leads us to appreciate the materiality of the constitutional "word" (Silverman and Torode, 1980). Constitutional discourse is dominated by the legal profession, those judges, lawyers, and law professors who participate in professional discussions of the institutions, doctrines, and processes of the law. This is not surprising on the surface but very difficult to discern at another level because the legal community is both diverse and particularly adept at incorporation and synthesis. In addition, while the dominance of positivism in formalist jurisprudence masks the discursive force in the profession, the positivism in realist jurisprudence and interpretation assures a continuing screen. Lawyers present their activity as simply telling tales and spinning yarns, yet their community makes certain yarns particularly salient and gives certain storytellers significant advantage. Through this activity, the established institutions of the law maintain a legal order grounded in familiar practices (Fallon, 1987; Cover, 1983).

As an institutional practice, the Double Standard had implications for two key elements of constitutional policy; property was separate from and inferior to civil liberties. The ideology has not been jettisoned, but these two elements are no longer characteristic of appellate review of constitutional questions. Civil liberties and property have been linked and, for federal judges, property has again become top dog. Thus, it appears that the old standard has been turned on its head. We see this in recent Supreme Court decisions about the economy and in some provocative property cases. The new doctrine does not appear exactly like the earlier version but it bears a relation. The demise of the Double Standard has consequences for protection of all kinds of property. The character of its demise will have disproportionate effects. Given the conservative moves against entitlement protection and potential countermobilization, we should anticipate increasing instability in this area of constitutional law. As the legislative and judicial branches become more polarized, judicial opinion alone will become less adequate to justify decisions.

By focusing on what the justices should or might do with per-

Double Standard Practices

sistent attention to Supreme Court opinions, scholarship on constitutional property is limited in two respects. It is bound by a tradition that is biased. And, it is limited by the emerging coalition of justices, who reinforce that bias. Yet the Constitution is much more. Outside the Supreme Court, commentary on the property issue invites caution and a concern that developments in property protection are for the wealthy, as we will see in Chapter V. Others worry about a reliance on "legal contrivances" to produce social change (McCann, 1984), yet new conceptions of rights based on community interests (Lynd, 1984; Sparer, 1984) and strategic uses of legal form (Lazerson, 1982: 159) provide incentive for efforts to fight the new Double Standard.

There *is* a constituted "nomos" or normative sphere, with circumscriptions, worlds that are lost and new worlds that are ascending. In the field of constitutional property, this nomos has been dominated by the judiciary and mystified by the Double Standard (O'Neill, 1981; Strauber, 1983). But these interpretations are not necessarily conclusive. The perspective followed in this book is an effort from outside the lawyer's community to interpret the law with attention to its political and institutional dimensions. New jurisprudential propositions must continue to depend on interpretive communities beyond the judges, at least the federal judges. Instead, it may be state judges or legislators or communities of citizens that will ultimately overcome the intolerable bias of juridical practices and thwart the imposition of a new Double Standard in how we treat entitlements.

CHAPTER IV

Wealth Discrimination

While explaining what a society takes for granted is a legitimate enterprise for the social scientist, inquiry into the obvious is risky. If one says some people are rich and some poor, the culture protects this relation with a yawn. Professor Jennifer Hochschild, in her book *What's Fair?* (1981), spends nearly a hundred pages justifying her inquiry into the obvious, the absence of socialism in America. She does it with quantitative material on personal wealth, with interviews, and with attitude studies, and she brings to bear significant philosophical care. All that helps minimize the risks, but they can't be eliminated all together. This chapter takes some risks to illuminate an aspect of the Constitution with implications for property, the application of the promise of equal protection to deprivations based on wealth of insufficient means, in other words, an insufficiency of property.

In taking on the implications of equal protection for property in the Constitution, the greatest risk is to the sacred since it becomes necessary to question the consequences of seeing *Brown* v. *Board of Education* (1954) as an unmitigated and uncomplicated good. Of late I am not alone (Bell, 1985; Bumiller, 1987; Cruse, 1987), but the critical analysis of this extraordinarily important case is fraught with difficulties, as these colleagues can attest (Hochschild, 1989). The other risk is constitutional profanity—we speak of the promise of material equality in *Plessy* v. *Ferguson* (1896) as a lost aspiration. Without taking on the nature of the Jim Crow system, about which a very exciting contemporary debate continues (Lofgren, 1987), I suggest that modern interpretations of this case have failed to explain much of what is important about it for constitutional jurisprudence. I investigate the reach of constitutional equality or constitutional protection against discrimination in terms of the right not to be discriminated against because of the prime source of inequality in industrial societies, the disparity in wealth or material resources, the means to live.

This inquiry is not motivated by the admirable, albeit somewhat legalistic, search for a new line of reasoning on which to base a legal claim against economic inequality. This is not a brief in support of homes for the homeless. In the context of housing, the point of this inquiry leads to the claim for equality in general, and that might mean in shelter as in education or medical care. Here, the indictment of the social structure and the distribution of wealth in America is implicit rather than the focus of the inquiry. Poor people, ill housed people, are a horrible consequence of the wealth accumulated and misdirected into minks, limos, and wilderness chateaus. My discussion of the Constitution is limited to the parameters of constitutional practices, what the 1787 document and its interpretations protect. It is not limited to what the judges have said. In fact, the thesis expands analysis of the Constitution on the basis of practices rather than limiting itself to judicial interpretation. Here, I try to cast some light toward the legal and ideological underpinnings of social stratification as well. Thus, the goal is to better understand a constitutional doctrine that protects the inequalities in property. In the process, we consider the reach of constitutional rights and the effect of the expectations they generate.

Some interest in discrimination against those with insufficient property has been evident in law reviews (Clune, 1975; Nelson, 1982) and on the Supreme Court in dissents by Justices Harlan (*Shapiro* v. *Thompson*, 1969) and Marshall (*San Antonio* v. *Rodriguez*, 1973). These treatments emerge from the constitutional discourse of the 1960s. They may not have been accepted by judges or overwhelmed the legal community; but, if one acknowledges (as one of my colleagues felt compelled to remind me) that this is America, the serious interest in this question shown by those who study the Constitution is significant. In his article, Professor William Clune noted an ethical power *in the Constitution* for claims against what he called "wealth discriminations" (1975: 289). The intelligibility of such claims is part of this

Wealth Discrimination

inquiry; their significance as a subtext for the politics of entitlement is another part.

This chapter sets out a framework that might help make sense of the successes of some unexpected recipients of generous interpretations of the Equal Protection Clause by the Supreme Court. In a case from West Virginia decided in January 1989, the U.S. Supreme Court gave us one of these decisions. The case took up a situation where property tax assessments on recently purchased property were eight to thirty-five times those applied to comparable neighboring properties. The case, *Allegheny Pittsburgh Coal v. Webster County*, came out of the coal fields and was brought through the West Virginia Supreme Court of Appeals to Washington by the coal company, which argued that it was disadvantaged by traditional assessment practices. Lower courts upheld the property tax imbalance as an inevitable consequence of heavy administrative costs. In this sense, the cities couldn't be expected to reassess all property every year.

The decision by the Supreme Court in Washington, D.C. held in favor of the equal protection claim made by the company. Judgments like this link equality to property. Here, equal protection in the Constitution is a new tool of the rich, while in the recent past, the poor have failed to develop a successful jurisprudence due to the conceptual barriers erected in the Constitution against challenges to the distribution of property. Distribution, that is "who has it," may be the most important single fact about property. We approach it through the promise of equal protection of the laws. The structure of equal protection for the constitutional property right is the subject of this chapter.

The ideas about the Constitution that determine the sense in a legal claim are grounded in the life of intellectual communities, groups of people responsible for constitutional discourse. As in other chapters, we explore the traditions that comprise constitutional interpretation with an eye to sociological issues, that is, we describe real people organized and going about the business of life and in the process giving meaning to the Constitution. These are the lawyers and judges, the participants in the constitutional seminars that prepare litigators for practice, the theorists and the senior partners (Garment, 1989), and the law clerks who situate judicial argument in contemporary practice for the cognoscenti. Such communities are appropriate subjects for social research because they maintain the ideologies that underlie legal activity (Cotterrell, 1983). Where an intellectual or interpretive community knows a doctrinal tradition like equal protection, determining the nature of sensible communication becomes a sociological inquiry.

Jurisprudential Foundations

The tradition for interpreting constitutional rights is conventionally understood in positive terms. That is we see it as either formal or behavioral. This investigation of equal protection is contrasted with both "formal" or mechanical jurisprudence and the "political" jurisprudence associated with legal realism and judicial behavioralism. The approach that led to issues of sense in the first chapter, and will conclude with practices in the last, is developed a little more self-consciously in this chapter. It is "ideological" because it turns away from outcomes and is not limited by what judges will decide about discrimination against persons with inadequate means. An ideological perspective develops the premise that what people think the Constitution means and how they act on their beliefs is as important as what the judges say. This approach is taken in order to focus on the tradition of equal protection in constitutional law.

The conception of law as ideology reflects interpretive currents in contemporary constitutional scholarship (Carter, 1985). In a foreword to the *Harvard Law Review* survey of the 1982 term of the Supreme Court, Professor Robert Cover found something "there" in the traditional doctrinal materials. His "narrative jurisprudence" was sensitive to the sources, "thickness," and force behind systems of meaning in the legal sphere (see also, Cover, 1983; Fiss, 1982; Bobbitt, 1982). But rather than being linked to realism and relativism, the approach here places interpretation within a semiotic frame that takes constitutional doctrine and its implications "seriously" (Dworkin, 1977; Barber, 1984).

The American legal tradition distinguishes between law and human action. This includes the "formalist" aspiration for "a government of laws and not of men" where the law held sway over human desires and the range of possible action would be constrained. Whatever its source, according to formalism, law controls people, rather than the other way around. Traditionally, formalism suggested that when a judge made a decision, the decision really came from somewhere else. Formalism had the authority of William Blackstone's *Commentaries*, and it became the basis for claims of judicial supremacy in the nineteenth century. Formalist equal protection analysis begins after the Civil War, although formal jurisprudence received stimulus from the abolitionist struggle (Tushnet, 1981). An important modern contribution was Professor Herbert Wechsler's call for neutral principles in response to the *Brown* decision in 1954 (Wechsler, 1959).

Today the view is ridiculed in historic terminology as "mechanical" jurisprudence (Pound, 1921: 170–71) and associated with grade school civics lessons or forthright speeches by the judiciary. According to the positivist legal philosopher John Austin, the view was a "childish fiction employed by our judges, that judiciary or common law is not made by them, but is a miraculous something . . . existing . . . from eternity, and merely deduced from time to time by the judges" (Austin, 1861: 634). In fact, Supreme Court Justice Owen Roberts described his own process of deciding a case as "laying the constitution down by a statute and observing whether the latter squared with the former." Such formalism now sounds odd, but when it comes to equality and nondiscrimination, the conceptual framework derived from *Brown v. Board of Education* (1954) has an authority formalists would appreciate.

The more recent, but still traditional approach to understanding how law functions is "political." The political view achieved prominence in the 1930s. It was called "realism" in the law schools and "judicial behavioralism" in the universities. Realism and behavioralism are linked by their common skepticism about the binding authority of law. As a law professor, Felix Frankfurter once said, "People have been taught to believe that when the Supreme Court speaks, it is not they who speak but the Constitution, whereas, of course, in so many vital cases, it is they (the justices) who speak, and not the Constitution" (Frankfurter, 1967: 383). Law faculty associated with Critical Legal Studies give a contemporary cast to realism which holds that after "trashing" the law, it is possible to make up whatever one wants (Kairys, 1982). Behavioralists sharing the political orientation of legal realism operate out of political science departments where they have documented the influence of attitudes in judicial decisions to the extent that their "bloc" analysis of attitudes has become a regular feature of the *Harvard Law Review* in its November review of the Supreme Court term.

The political view has become dogma and its hegemony has diverted attention from doctrinal and interpretive considerations. An obvious instance, *The Brethren* (Woodward and Armstrong, 1979), focused almost entirely on individuals, their goals, their limitations, and their frailties. Attention to the distinctive characteristics of the Supreme Court was marginal. Doctrinal areas, like equal protection, are of course affected by the interests and agendas of the judges. The balance of power on a court may shift in response to issues as charged as racial equality has been for the last thirty years. The problem in social research on legal processes is one of balance between law *and* politics. We have known about politics in the judiciary for fifty years. Here it is incorporated into the treatment of wealth through the Equal Protection Clause. We leave the strawman of mechanical jurisprudence in favor of an ideological approach that more fully captures processes where both law and politics operate.

Some contemporary movements have reacted to realism and behavioralism, incorporating the truth in both the formal and the political viewpoints. Owen Fiss of Yale Law School describes law as "neither wholly discretionary nor a wholly mechanical activity" but dependent on an interactive process that takes place within an "interpretive community" (Fiss, 1982: 739). This is similar to the picture of legal activity in judicial "niches" discussed by Robert Cover (1983: 67). Others, critical of the turn away from law in favor of a "romance with politics," like Professor Paul Brest (1982), suggest attention to the cultural phenomena with reference to which legal choices arise. From various perspectives, legal academics are returning to the symbolic to understand judging, constitutions, and the law.

In the sociological research associated with the Law and Society movement, the limits of a disputes paradigm have led scholars to pay more attention to the culture of the law. Employing the concept of a "practice" to link the normative and empirical poles of positivist research, interpretive scholars suggest an approach to law based on ideology (Brigham, 1984a; Silbey, 1985). Some of the work has turned to the theoretical contributions of French sociologist Pierre Bourdieu, whose "theory of practice" was developed to interpret life and politics in Algeria as well as cultural forms, like taste, in France. Used in this way, exploring the manifestations of jurisprudence in social relations may be one way of responding to the "gap" orientation of traditional law and society research (Harrington, 1985b).

Similarly, in the arena of constitutional politics, we have recognized that action takes place in a world understood through language, symbols, and conventions (Brigham, 1978; O'Neill, 1981). Some of the formulations that don't make sense were introduced in Chapter I. Here, sense is about the way the constitutional tradition leads us to talk about equality. The point of the following discussion is that the attention to "nondiscrimination" or "colorblindness" is a very limited conception of equality. Because of this, the doctrines on which legal thinking relies do not simply rationalize authority. These doctrines are its conceptual basis. Where they are part of a system and have political significance, doctrines constitute an ideology maintained by lawyers and judges and evident in the coherent discourses characteristic of law. The approach is likely to be unfamiliar and appear baggage-laden. Traditional Marxists use ideology to designate ideas that are imagined and false. A more contemporary approach, such as that by Alan Hunt (1983), would treat ideologies as elements of consciousness, originating in social practice. These would be found throughout a society. In a related suggestion, a non-Marxist scholar suggests that we stop asking whether argument determines the outcome of decisions and begin to consider that when the Court hears, reads, and writes, it does so "within certain conventions" (Bobbitt, 1982: 6–7).

Legal conventions, such as those that hold statutory classifications based on race to be suspect, are beyond the control of any individual justice and beyond the reach of any single opinion. When a case comes before the Supreme Court, it is adjudicated in terms of doctrines or constitutional clauses such as Heightened Scrutiny, Equal Protection, and other unique forms of expression. These doctrines and clauses orient legal thinking. A technical language such as constitutional law not only pushes legal action toward standard practice (Schwartz, 1969: 490), it constitutes a case as subject to constitutional constraint. Without these doctrines, the uniquely legal quality of a dispute would disappear. Under the American Constitution, equal protection claims have come to rely on what modern language philosophers have called "games." These are ways of doing things steeped in professional experience. Because they are taken as given or ordinary, they limit what can be argued. Doctrines of this sort have been referred to as "artificial reason" at least since the seventeenth century jurist Edward Coke held up legal learning as a check on the King (Corwin, 1929). However, too much has been made of the "artificiality" of legal doctrine by both the formal and the political perspective. The ideological approach is more attentive to the "reason" maintained by the legal community, and when applied to equal protection doctrine, we can better understand how deprivations of a material nature, once subject to constitutional scrutiny, have nearly been eliminated from review.

Constitutional Equality

"Constitutional equality" does not mean what is conventionally understood by the phrase "to be equal." The Constitution requires that no state "deny to any person . . . the equal protection of the laws." What the justices and lawyers have extrapolated from the constitutional text is related to ordinary ideas but has its own distinct limitations. The limitations of these doctrines for claims based on insufficient property or inadequate means are the objects of this inquiry. According to conventional wisdom, distinctions between the races are suspect. Even distinguishing between the sexes raises constitutional issues. Yet, the gross economic inequalities in America seem beyond scrutiny.

Equality, although mentioned prominently in the Declaration of Independence, was not a dominant principle of the American Revolution (as it would be for the French Revolution). Later, when the Constitution was drafted, equality was compromised by measures deeply offensive to contemporary ideas of equality and to those of quite a few in the founding generation, such as the decision to count slaves when determining a state's representation in Congress but not include them as citizens. Equality as a fundamental principle of American law dates from after the Civil War, when a series of constitutional amendments attempted to institutionalize freedom for the former slaves. The Thirteenth Amendment abolished slavery, the Fifteenth Amendment guaranteed voting rights, and the Fourteenth Amendment, the cornerstone of constitutional equality and nationalization of the Constitution, provided that no state shall "deny to any person within its jurisdiction the equal protection of the laws." Inclusion of equality in the Constitution, through the Equal Protection Clause, gave significance to both judicial interpretation and the efforts to eradicate vestiges of slavery.

At first, decisions dealing with race were more often treated as commercial issues than as questions of equality (Tribe, 1978: 338). Under this rubric, the justices of the Supreme Court upheld an award to a black woman who had been removed from a railroad car reserved for "white ladies" (*Washington A and GR v. Brown*, 1873). Similarly, in *Hall v. DeCuir* (1878), the Commerce Clause was interpreted as prohibiting Louisiana from applying an antidiscrimination statute to steamboats in interstate commerce. In the *Civil Rights Cases* (1883), a step of lasting significance was taken when the Supreme Court limited the application of the Fourteenth Amendment to "state action" by striking down federal legislation prohibiting segregation in what we now call the private sector. Five years later another move setting the parameters for constitutional equal protection, the extension of Fourteenth Amendment protection to corporations, had become part of the interpretive tradition (O'Neill, 1981).

For the Civil War Amendments to establish equality of the races before the law, it became clear that the Supreme Court would have to deal with the emerging practice of Jim Crow, the segregationist social policy instituted after Reconstruction. The Court took up the first of the laws requiring separation of the races in *Louisville, New Orleans and Texas R.R. v. Mississippi* (1890). The challenge to restrictive legislation was again brought by business interests, this time against the state of Mississippi, which segregated the races in public transportation. The constitutional question arose in the context of interstate commerce, as earlier cases had, but here the justices allowed the discriminatory statute to stand since segregation did not produce a "burden" on interstate commerce. By the 1890s, business interests had begun to lose out to the architects of segregation who were reestablishing domination of the white race over the black race in the former Confederate states.

This was the context for *Plessy v. Ferguson* (1986), the opinion that set the parameters of constitutional equality. In spite of its infamous reputation (Baer, 1983: 109–111), the Supreme Court opinion in *Plessy* shifted the standard for evaluating segregated institutions from the Commerce Clause to the guarantee of equal protection, and in accommodating constitutional equality with segregation under the doctrine of "separate but equal," the justices established a framework with material, social, and political implications. Material equality applies to such things as how fast our transportation gets us where we want to go. The segregated rail cars in *Plessy* would be materially equal if they got to their destination at the same time as the cars reserved for whites. Social equality covers the value society places on different treatment. Society in the American South distinguishes between the front and the back of the bus. Political equality applies to citizenship and the right to vote or hold public office. It cannot exist independent of the material and social considerations. The framework reflects a distinction between the material, social, and ideological realms. Other approaches to this issue are legion (see Hochschild, 1981; Oppenheim, 1968).

The *Plessy* opinion protected political but not social equality. The majority, drawing on the opinion of Chief Justice Lemuel Shaw of the Supreme Judicial Court in *Roberts* v. *City of Boston* (1850), saw nothing unequal about separation in the formal, legal, sense. That is, it did not hold the law accountable for beliefs about race because it described the attitudes that made separation offensive as social and beyond the reach of the law. In some sense, this formalism was the very separation of law from society that had characterized antebellum jurisprudence (Scheiber, 1975). The concession was a guarantee of material or physical equality. The state law separated the races in railroad cars but the Constitution required that the cars be equal. Although the social consequences could not be taken into account, material conditions were implicit in the justification for separation of the races.

The legal politics of equal protection began to ferment thirty years after the *Plessy* decision. By the 1930s, the focus was on a new reading of equality in order to expunge the doctrine of separate but equal. Led by the NAACP Legal Defense Fund, the initial litigation strategy was based on *Plessy*'s promise of material equality and attempted to make it so costly to maintain segregation that the South would give it up. The plan was known as the Margold Strategy, after its proponent, Nathan Margold, a lawyer for the NAACP. The first success attributable to this claim came in 1938 in a case brought by a black applicant to law school in Missouri (*Missouri ex rel. Gaines* v. *Canada*, 1938). The result was that Missouri was ordered to admit the student to its law school or to create a new one. It was not enough, according to the Court, to simply pay Lloyd Gaines' tuition at another state law school, since this would not provide him with an equal education in Missouri. For a time, the hopes and successes of NAACP litigation were based on the failure of institutions in the South to live up to the promise of equality in *Plessy*, rather than on the evil of separation per se.

The authoritative source of modern doctrines of constitutional equality, *Brown* v. *Board of Education* (1954), eliminated separation from constitutional protection. The case was argued twice, in part because of the personnel change that brought Earl Warren to the Court as Chief Justice and because of an effort to ground the decision in a historical reading of the Fourteenth Amendment. In the end, the Fourteenth Amendment did not provide the ground, and Chief Justice Warren based the attack on separation in new psychological information that linked the law of segregation to the social reality of prejudice. By using the modern tools of the clinical psychologist, Warren's opinion accounted for what Justice Harlan had suggested in his *Plessy* dissent over 50 years before. Separate facilities had to be seen as inherently unequal in that they hurt black students.

After the decision, judicial attention shifted from the refusal to see separation as a constitutional violation to a view of separation as the primary violation of constitutional equality. The doctrine had been turned on its head from a refusal to consider social inequality to near total reliance on separation in that sphere as a measure of constitutional violations. Judicial recognition that the treatment of blacks in the South was oppressive ended the period of constitutionally acceptable segregation. The consequence was a view of equal protection that no longer included material equality. The shift may have been unintended or it may have been a reaction against the false promise in *Plessy* that had propped up segregation. In any case, the implications of this shift have been particularly significant for wealth discrimination.

An Inability to Pay

The legacy of *Brown* was scrutiny of classifications in state law, where some form of oppression or social stigma was present. Under that formula, constitutional equal protection expanded beyond race, to classifications covering paternity, citizenship, and sex. Since the *Civil Rights Cases*, interpreting the Fourteenth Amendment, the Constitution's promise has been "equal protection *of the laws*." The explicit reach of this protection has been state rather than private action, and since *Brown*, it has been hard to establish a substantive claim based simply on an absence of wealth. The three kinds of equality developed below refer to state action. Economic hardship, indigence, and the inability to pay remained peripheral, and they were considered only where they resulted in a social or political deprivation. American society would obviously look different without distinctions based on wealth, and it is not surprising that the nondiscrimination principles associated with constitutional equal protection present minimal challenge to economic stratification. Nevertheless, the community of scholars and practitioners who maintain constitutional discourse have been remarkably attentive to the implications of equal protection for those with insufficient wealth or property to purchase the basics of life.

Frank Michelman's 1969 article treated the relationship between the Fourteenth Amendment and poverty as an emerging constitutional issue. He cautioned against the position that inequality was repugnant to the Constitution, substituting instead his view that the cause of the poor would be better served by "protection against certain hazards which are endemic in an unequal society, rather than vindication of a duty to avoid complicity in unequal treatment" (Michelman, 1969). Michelman's concern at the end of the decade was to redirect the egalitarian spirit away from the material issue upon which it seemed to be impinging. As the discussion evolved, law Professor William Clune called more explicit attention to what he termed "wealth discrimination" (Clune, 1975). He was intrigued by the possibility of constitutional protection for those without the means to obtain social goods, yet he wondered how the doctrine could be limited "when all aspects of our society and government are permeated by wealth effects" (1975: 328). The concern about poverty and the power of antidiscrimination law in the mid-1970s make it a watershed for attention to equal protection for those unable to pay (see Brudno, 1976).

In the 1980s, with a very different political climate, there was very little inquiry into this question. Even where there was such attention, there was greater emphasis on the practical difficulties of following the implications of equality to wealth and the ability to pay. As Professor Scott Nelson pointed out: "If the Court ever holds that wealth is a suspect classification, the logical implication could cause alarm in many circles" (1982: 719). Similarly, Professor Michael McCann con-

Wealth Discrimination

cludes his study of what he calls "the limits of constitutional ideology for addressing inequality" with the pessimistic observation, "Any progressive ideological coup during the Reagan era (and his likely judicial legacy) . . . certainly seems doubtful" (1984: 50). Although cautious and driven by perception of political opportunity, interest in means, wealth or property discrimination is linked, conceptually at least, to constitutional equal protection doctrine.

In practice, protection for the poor, though marginal, is more fully developed for some kinds of claims than others. It is strongest when associated with political equality, including criminal due process, weaker for social equality; for claims reaching to material equality, which were possible under *Plessy*, there is little constitutional authority. A review of these cases reveals the ideological structure of discrimination on the basis of insufficient property.

Political Equality

Political equality, the most fully protected antidiscrimination principle bearing on the ability to pay, addresses the rights of citizenship. Rights in this area fall into two categories; rights of political participation, including the right to vote and run for office; and criminal due process rights, viewed here in terms of the trial, appeal, and punishment. Political participation is more fully protected for those without adequate means than any other area of social life. In the case of participation, for instance, the fact that people were being deprived of the right to vote on the basis of ability to pay led to the abolition of the poll tax, first by the Twenty-fourth Amendment at the national level and then in *Harper v. Virginia State Board* (1966) in the states. Similarly, in *Bullock v. Carter* (1972), the Supreme Court held a Texas practice of supporting primary elections through candidate filing fees to be unconstitutional and in 1989 held a property ownership requirement for service on a local commission to be in violation of the Equal Protection Clause (*Quinn v. Millsap*).

A more extensively litigated aspect of political equality involves the criminal process. The first holdings came soon after *Brown* and were followed throughout the "due process revolution" by instances where people were deprived of criminal due process rights for inability to pay some fee or court costs. Since the 1930s, indigent defendants facing capital punishment have been provided counsel, and in *Gideon* v. *Wainwright* (1964) the states were required to provide a lawyer when the defendant faced incarceration. The *Gideon* decision, based on the Sixth Amendment, acknowledges discrimination where legal representation would be denied because of the inability to pay for a lawyer. Counsel has also been provided, by the Maryland Court of Appeals, for an indigent defendant subject to incarceration in a civil contempt proceeding (*Rutherford* v. *Rutherford*, 1983) and the courts regularly order payment of witness fees and expenses, even in civil cases (*Ridgeway* v. *Baker*, 1983). As in other aspects of political equality, absolute deprivation has been the governing factor. The focus has been on the process not on the quality of representation. Claims to a lawyer with a certifiable level of competence have not been upheld, hence state supreme courts have held that representation by a law student did not deny the right to counsel.

In appellate review, the right to be protected against economic deprivation has not been as fundamental to due process as the right to trial. An appeal is considered discretionary, and the courts have not been clear about what sort of appellate rights are to be made available to those without the ability to pay. At the very least, appellants have the right to be provided with a transcript from their trial (*Griffin* v. *Illinois*, 1956). After that, what is to be available depends on how compelling a claim can be made. Counsel on appeal has been provided occasionally (*Douglas* v. *California*, 1963) but filing fees for bankruptcy (*U.S.* v. *Kras*, 1973) and for a suit challenging welfare benefits have been upheld (*Ortwein* v. *Schwab*, 1973).

Punishment is problematic when evaluated in light of means discrimination. Those without resources are more likely to face punishment, and the punishment they face is itself conditioned by the ability to pay. This is obviously true in the case of fines where proportionality is with reference to the offense rather than the ability to pay. Some constitutional limits on punishment by imprisonment as a substitute for a fine that can not be paid have been recognized (*Williams* v. *Illinois*, 1970). More recently, Danny Bearden took the state of Georgia to the Supreme Court when he was sent to prison after failing to pay a fine. In this case, Justice Sandra Day O'Connor argued that when the trial court automatically revoked Bearden's probation, it did not exercise adequate care and violated his constitutional rights (*Bearden* v. *Georgia*, 1983). As one article summarizing the developments in this

Wealth Discrimination

period said, "Few of our ideals are more venerable than is equal justice for rich and poor" (Fahringer, 1964: 394). The political sphere is particularly sensitive to discrimination because of the criminal sanction involved.

Social Equality

The modern period of constitutional equality began with the new attention toward discrimination in social life. Grounded in the doll experiments used by Kenneth Clark to demonstrate the psychological harm done by slavery and amplified in an "idea of progress" that exploded in the age of civil rights, the legacy of *Brown* was the refutation of *Plessy*, with the recognition that black people had been forced to endure a second class citizenship. The result was a standard of equal rights for racial minorities and for women, which continues to concern American courts, particularly in the states. Economic conditions play a less forceful role here than in the "political" sphere, but where the state has made legal commitments to social programs, such as those for education and medical care, means discrimination has a place.

The ideology of constitutional equality is further revealed when we take note of how the cases arising under social equality are treated. Where claims are close to the constitutional domain of political equality, such as in questions of civil procedure, they have a greater chance of success than if they involve material equality, no matter how severe a physical deprivation might be. For example, until 1971, Connecticut required a fee to file for divorce. People without adequate funds contested this infringement on the ability to end a marriage (*Boddie* v. *Connecticut,* 1971), and the state was forced to abolish the practice. Similarly, a Wisconsin remarriage statute was held to be an unconstitutional burden on the poor in *Zablocki* v. *Redhail* (1978). Consequently, where a public commitment exists, constitutional support for the claims of those who cannot pay is more likely. Issues like this have arisen around both education and abortion.

In *San Antonio School District* v. *Rodriguez* (1973), the question was whether children were being deprived of their constitutional rights because they attended a public school system funded by a tax on property that reflected the wealth of the local community. Although Texas, like most states, tried to equalize disparities between districts

Wealth Discrimination

by spreading part of its support according to need, wealthy communities could nonetheless provide a better education than poorer ones. The claimants in San Antonio argued that the *barrio* they lived in was unable to provide the same level of education as the wealthier Anglo suburbs. The Court took note of the state's efforts to equalize the differential in the quality of education between the rich and poor communities. The property tax basis of financing survived the challenge because distinctions based on wealth had been mitigated by the state and because no one was absolutely deprived of an education.

A decade after *Rodriguez*, attention to wealth discrimination with respect to schooling continued. A 1982 equal protection decision struck down a Texas statute that denied funding to schools that enrolled undocumented alien children (*Plyler* v. *Doe*, 1982). The case stimulated considerable public discussion about the equal protection rationale (Perry, 1983). In a second action that year, the Supreme Court let stand the decision of New York's highest court, which had upheld the state's school finance system (*Board of Education* v. *Nyquist*, 1983) after two lower courts had decided that reliance on the local property tax was unconstitutional.

Sexual equality has increasingly obvious implications for means discrimination (Fineman, 1983). Differentials in wealth and payment between men and women have been raised that would not likely be considered without the ingredient of sex discrimination. By living longer, women have been required to pay more for retirement systems, and by driving more safely they have paid less for car insurance. The constitutional standard forges an equality reaching to material benefits on the basis of concern about sex (see *Arizona* v. *Norris*, 1983; Brigham, 1984a: 245-46; Baer, 1983). The review of insurance classifications reveals the close relationship between economic questions and constitutional equality where there is a social issue like sex discrimination present (see Deutchman, 1985: 165).

Abortion raises compelling equal protection challenges with strong implications for discrimination based on wealth. In *Maher* v. *Roe* (1977), the Court held that a state's decision not to pay for abortions, although it paid for childbirth, did not violate the Constitution. The lower court had ruled that the right to an abortion required strict scrutiny of the distinction between abortion and childbirth. The distinction's potential for discrimination brought the case to the Court's attention, but Justice Lewis Powell, writing for the majority, held that

Wealth Discrimination

the lower court had "misconceived the nature and scope of the fundamental right recognized in *Roe*" and that past decisions do not indicate "that financial need alone identifies a suspect class for purposes of equal protection analysis." Powell argued that the Court found no "restriction on access to abortions *that was not already there*" [emphasis added]. The holding was extended in *Harris* v. *McRae* (1980), a similar public assistance case where the justices reasoned that liberty as defined in *Roe* includes the freedom of a woman to decide whether to terminate a pregnancy but does not include a public obligation to pay. The logic used by the majority harks back to *Brown*, in describing equal protection as reaching to invidious classifications but not providing a substantive right.

Although the constitutional tradition does not determine a particular outcome, in *Maher* and *Harris*, we see implications for wealth discrimination in the lines of argument initially chosen for the abortion holdings. The original abortion cases might well have been dealt with along equal protection lines. Prior to 1973, wealthier women had access to abortions that poor women did not have. For example, they could fly to other states or even other countries to obtain abortions prohibited to them where they lived, and one can imagine a sensible argument of that sort. However, the way *Roe* was decided linked abortion and privacy. Because abortion rights had been associated with privacy rather than with equal protection, the case against the denial of governmental funding for abortions, which relied heavily on equal protection logic and sentiment, was not particularly strong. Had the abortion cases been decided on equal protection grounds, with the consequent sensitivity to nondiscrimination, the expectation generated would have had an impact on the denial of public funds for abortion while the government pays for childbirth.

Comparable worth, a wage discrimination issue that has arisen where men and women who perform comparable work do not receive equal pay, is a matter of equal protection bearing on wealth through social concerns. It is an issue that would have been "meaningless to most lawyers" as recently as the mid-1970s (Bellace, 1984). That is, the claim needed the corollary developments of the women's movement and the logic of equal protection from the Constitution. Comparable worth falls within the rubric of social equality because it is associated with sex discrimination (Feldberg, 1984), that is, comparable worth measures the inequality in wages by a comparison between men and women. In addition, since the issue in law involves wages paid—usually by the government but on occasion in private actions like the strike at Yale University—and only indirectly an individual's "ability to pay," comparable worth belongs with issues of primarily social rather than material equality.

Settlements in this area have mostly come from private negotiations. But, in 1983 the Supreme Court encouraged advocates of comparable worth when it ruled that claims of sex-based discrimination in wages not covered by the 1963 Equal Pay Act, with its formula of "equal pay for equal work," could be brought under Title VII of the 1964 Civil Rights Act (*County of Washington* v. *Gunther*, 1983). One hardly expects federal courts populated by Ronald Reagan's appointees to provide leadership. Rather, it has been sex discrimination as a social aspect of constitutional equal protection that is the driving force that brings comparable worth before the public and sometimes even the courts. The ideology of sex discrimination developed with reference to the Constitution has introduced equal protection into bargaining over wages and salaries (see also McCann, 1987).

Material Equality

Involving the kinds of deprivations associated with the early challenges to segregation (see *Missouri ex rel Gaines* v. *Canada*, 1938), material equality focuses on inequities without relying on social stigma or political loss. It is hard to make sense of such a claim if one is limited to the decisions of any particular court. The claim comes from the Constitution. The previous cases turned on political and social equality. Since *Brown* v. *Board of Education* (1954), the claim of material inequality per se has been largely unsuccessful. Few cases in the appellate courts fit nicely into the category of material inequality, but Professor Phillip Bobbitt's formulation comes close. Exploring the operation of constitutional discourse, he drew on two examples from the practices of material (in)equality to demonstrate the rhetorical power of some constitutional arguments (1982: 129–31). One was Thurgood Marshall's proposition concerning the poll tax: "While a city can charge 15 cents to ride on a subway, people wouldn't want to put a dime in a turnstile to get into the voting booths" (*Harper*, 1966). The other was Archibald

Wealth Discrimination

Cox's argument in *Shapiro* v. *Thompson* (1969), where a very weak right to travel is buttressed by an equal protection claim that a twelve-month wait to qualify for welfare was unconstitutional. The opinion in *Shapiro* accepted the Cox argument and struck down the waiting period as a creation of "two classes of need resident families," indistinguishable except for the length of their stay in the state. Both cases were influenced by the nondiscrimination logic in the constitutional tradition, but they were ultimately limited by the professional discourse.

In the area of housing and residency more generally, constitutional protection against discrimination on the basis of wealth or material advantage, once considered a possible avenue of litigation, did not materialize. What success there was may have been due to the link between open-housing issues and social equality, especially when state support is involved. These issues were evident in *Warth* v. *Seldin* (1975). Warth, for low-income individuals and builders, claimed that Penfield, a suburb of Rochester, New York, had adopted a zoning ordinance that made it "economically impossible" to construct "sufficient numbers of low- and moderate-income" houses. Although racial issues were present, the litigation focused on discrimination against low-income people. Warth lost his case in the Supreme Court by a 5 to 4 decision, and equal protection claims addressing discrimination in housing due to the inability to pay, a hopeful strategy for a short time (Branfman, Cohen, and Trubek, 1973; Sager, 1969), were not successful and eventually ceased being a vibrant option for the interpretive community.

Some important decisions linked to wealth involve the effects of poverty. These cases include threats by utilities to terminate service (*Memphis Light, Gas and Water* v. *Craft*, 1977) and the sale of consumer goods for nonpayment (*Flagg Brothers* v. *Brooks*, 1978). In these cases, poor people are afforded constitutional protection when they show that they are unable to pay for some of the more elemental aspects of private life, such as utility services. The constitutional claims are not based on equal protection but on doctrines of due process and modern recognition that the poor have rights in wealth they receive from the state. Constitutional protection for those receiving statutory entitlements, such as Aid to Families with Dependent Children, existing since *Goldberg* v. *Kelly* (1970) provides a minimal due process. As applied to entitlements, constitutional protection has been extended to the poor. This is the dominant arena in the politics of constitutional property, and the protection here is only a shadow of that long accorded to wealthier property holders.

While there has been constitutional protection for the economically disadvantaged, usually something more than poverty or even indigence must be present. This was the thesis put forth by Peter Westen in his article "The Empty Idea of Equality" (1982). Westen identifies the dependence of equality on other rights and he is eager to dismiss it as altogether lacking in substance. His formulation of the notion of equality, that "people who are alike should be treated alike" (1982: 592–96) misses part of the substance of the existing constitutional tradition, protection for political and social equality. The real vacuum lies in the material realm because the promise of material equality was jettisoned with the doctrine of "separate but equal."

Conclusion

We have explored some constitutional responses to economic inequality based on equal protection doctrine. Like the property right itself, this corollary dimension of the same interests relies heavily on civil libertarian values. Like the coal company with which we began this discussion, contemporary claimants with considerable wealth wrap themselves in the protective mantle of equal protection—a mantle created for oppressed people, although never fully developed for them. There is constitutional protection from the loss of fundamental rights due to the inability to pay, and there has been recourse in the federal courts from a termination of benefits that have either become a social responsibility, such as education, or legally guaranteed, such as abortion. However, constitutional protection from material deprivation, such as substandard housing or low quality education, is seldom available.

Constitutional ideology limits the claims that can be made; it includes some things and not others. Yet, this is difficult to see from the traditional view of law with its assumptions that either a stable body of doctrine governed the decisions made by judges or that political inclination governed. Positivism in the study of law was built on this distinction and it is maintained in much of present-day jurisprudence. There are efforts to impose a new formalism (Posner, 1979) and there are efforts, ostensibly on the other side, to expand the political interpretation of the realists (Kairys, 1982). In fact, the tradition of discourse has always been influential.

Constitutional discourse is maintained by judges, lawyers, and law professors, although the dominance of positivism in contemporary jurisprudence, whether realist or formalist, makes this process hard to discern. The professional community causes certain stories to be particularly salient and important. Professionals present their activity as simply telling tales and spinning yarns, but through this activity they maintain a legal order grounded in familiar practices (Cover, 1983). Although contemporary legal academics may exhort their students "to stop circumscribing the nomos . . . to invite new worlds," the best of those students have always confused "ought" with "is," translating the world of law into a world of practice. This was discussed with great insight by Martin Shapiro (1967: 209).

Perhaps because law professors have begun to acknowledge the rhetorical and ideological dimensions of their activity, the perspective from social science can now be clarified. The best of traditional scholarship, whether in the law reviews or in political science journals, incorporates elements of the political and the legal. While the treatment by Nelson, mentioned at the beginning of the last section, implicitly considers the ideology of equality in his review of the doctrinal tradition, and the work of McCann is explicitly attentive to what he calls ideology, both scholars are limited by a traditional political view of the Constitution and of the legal profession. By focusing on what the justices should or might do, they treat the constitutional tradition as if it depends on the reigning coalition of justices for its existence. Yet, as we have seen, the Constitution is much more. For instance, the effort to amend the document itself through the political process is different because the project explicitly introduces something that is not there (see Strauber, 1983; Houseman, 1979). There is a constituted "nomos" or normative sphere, with circumscriptions, worlds that are lost, and new worlds that are ascending. Ira Strauber (1983) and Timothy O'Neill (1981) have suggested what this might look like. In fact, I think, it would be an approach like the legal ideology central to the sociology of law (Hunt, 1983).

The present inquiry into constitutional equal protection, by applying equality to material conditions, has revealed its complicity with deep-seated and oppressive classifications. Thus, classifications based on the conditions in which so many live have disappeared from the constitutional promise of equal protection. An equality that excludes material considerations and disregards the implications of wealth is characteristic of the reigning political and constitutional ideology in the economic sphere. Because one cannot say whatever one might like and make constitutional sense and because the constraints of legal discourse are imbricated in the culture and part of the way we talk about politics, transcendence requires a full appreciation of the power, manifest in ideology and an interpretive community, to set the terms and constrain action. This constitutive dimension of law makes it very hard to see the bias of constitutional property to which we now turn.

CHAPTER V

From Bias to Compensation

Debate over the Constitution's protection for property is heating up after fifty years of relative calm (Michelman, 1988; Shapiro, 1986). As a result, there is considerable fluidity to what is protected by the right (Oakes, 1981). On the one hand, individual prerogatives over property in land and commercial enterprise have grown as a function of deregulation. From assurances given by the Supreme Court that zoning variances will not be conditioned on public benefits, to the solicitude shown businesses by federal agencies like the Occupational Safety and Health Administration (Noble, 1986), traditional property owners have been empowered by the State in the last decade. On the other hand, governmental obligations to holders of statutory entitlements such as Social Security, which were only recently acknowledged as a new property right, seem to be diminishing. This is evident in what were once uncontroversial areas such as racial discrimination in the allocation of public housing[1] and in highly contested situations such as public funding for abortions.

The rights associated with traditional forms of property, while perhaps less comprehensive than they appear to the public, have always been far more generous than the rights to property associated with the welfare state. Protection for entitlements, from education to social welfare programs, though more substantial than in the distant past, is a shadow of the protection traditionally afforded to property. This chapter proposes that statutory entitlements property be given

From Bias to Compensation

full property protection, including an entitlement holder's right to just compensation under the Constitution's Takings Clause. This would be a more equitable interpretation of the constitutional property right that would eliminate the bias in favor of some forms of property.

As we have seen, property is conventionally associated with individual possession and control. Like all legal rights, however, property rights depend on the State and its governing apparatus for enforcement (as noted in Chapter I; see also Baker, 1986). The State grants a range of action to property-right holders. They can exclude others, accrue benefits, and otherwise enjoy what is theirs. The legal justification for this right is that settled or legitimate expectation deserves state protection. The tradition of constitutional guarantees for property, as we have seen, has been legally based on the due process and just compensation provisions of the Fifth and Fourteenth Amendments. Since at least 1970, with *Goldberg* v. *Kelly*, legitimate expectation with regard to statutory entitlements, such as Aid to Families with Dependent Children, has been recognized by the courts as property. But, only five years later, commitments to public assistance came under severe attack. Now, when it is hardest to generate, property rights need a comprehensive and searching attention that is more often available in charitable periods (Friedman, 1981).

This development suggests a property right that could be pivotal relative to both liberty and equality in the modern state (Cotterrell, 1986: 96). The challenge of theory explicitly taken up in an article by Professor Roger Cotterrell, is particularly relevant in the context of this chapter. For Cotterrell, "Theory should attempt to put the lawyer's analytical problems into a wider perspective by showing the nature of legal doctrine as it appears in a broader view than that which the lawyer's immediate professional concerns dictate" (1986: 85). The power of legal theory to generate strategies and expectations was discussed in Chapter I, and property, like privacy, presents vivid examples of the power of synthetic analysis as a resource in the policy context. Cotterrell also noted the vitality of debates over the interests represented by new forms of wealth

> when we move from the traditional core of property law—real property—to its expanding periphery where rights to many new, or newly recognized and debated, forms of wealth are in issue the image of property

law as a game played according to known and well-tried rules seems less appropriate (Cotterrell, 1986: 81).

The conclusion for Cotterrell, who draws on experience in England, is that contemporary conditions, such as the growth of state power benefiting corporations and various less-powerful entitlement holders, mean that the values associated with property should be security for the property owner rather than power over others. Here, "the diffusion of guaranteed entitlements to the use of resources necessary for personal welfare is recognized as the basis of genuine freedom" (1986: 96).

As it has throughout the book, the approach to entitlement policy in this chapter combines political theory, public policy analysis, and institutional jurisprudence. Law, in the form of judicial decisions interpreting the American Constitution, is a source for the examination of bias in the meaning of constitutional property. The proposal, however, is not simply a description of doctrine handed down by the justices as authoritative, nor a prediction of what future justices will decide. This is a commentary on legal protection for property as a fundamental right, which operates from the premise that the fundamental law must be impartial and nondiscriminatory in order for it to anchor a government that derives its authority from the consent of the governed.

The Constitutional Tradition

We have seen that the property right, once central to liberal theory, has been missing, since at least 1937, from various treatments of the civil liberties protected by the Constitution (Abraham, 1983). The idea that property and liberty could be separated began in the industrial revolution. Since the *Lochner* Era, reform movements attacked property as protection for the few over the many. The right was effectively expelled from the debate on constitutional principles governed by the post-1937 doctrine of the Double Standard (see Chapter III). This standard emphasized civil rather than economic liberties, and an "idea of progress" (Bickel, 1970) based in the promise of equal protection in

From Bias to Compensation

the Fourteenth Amendment. Property has remained peripheral to the canon of civil liberties in spite of the economic implications in right to counsel, equal protection, and freedom of the press. Of course, protection of property has not disappeared, as we saw in Chapter III, but its status as a civil liberty, a constitutionally protected right of every citizen, has received minimal attention.

Paradoxically, it may have been the growth of these political liberties in the last fifty years that called attention to property rights. Now, real estate and commercial interests draw support from civil liberties and two generations of activism over fundamental rights. They are also getting more protection from an increasingly conservative federal judiciary (Goldman, 1987). Yet, particularly because property is associated with the civil libertarian promise of contemporary constitutional government, the right to property cannot serve simply as protection for the rich or a shield for the wealthy. The modern constitutional system requires that rich and poor be treated the same. This look at constitutional property attacks some troubling biases in constitutional law.

When the Constitution was written in 1787, the tension between possession of property under the common law with its principle of *salus populi*, or the public good, and the Lockeian conception of property as a vested right, was particularly evident. We see, in the debates over ratification in this period, an older and more stable conception being challenged by the newer and more absolute form of property (Friedrich, 1963: 841). Mechanisms to protect economic interests appear throughout the original plan for the government. Article I establishes federal power to regulate commerce, coin money and punish pirates while limiting state power to "impair the obligation of contract" (see Wright, 1938). Article IV guarantees a republican form of government, while Article VI provides for payment of debts against the United States. We have seen that rather than rely on the term property, which is used only in the Fifth and later in the Fourteenth Amendments, and which provides that no citizen shall "be deprived of life, liberty, or property without due process of law; nor shall private property be taken for public use without just compensation," the early Supreme Court employed other provisions in the Constitution to protect economic interests. In *Fletcher v. Peck* (1810), it was the Contract Clause (Magrath, 1967). Before the Civil War, under slavery's ominous shadow, interests ranging from judicial appointments, as in

From Bias to Compensation

Marbury v. *Madison* (1803), to franchises to do business, as in *Gibbons* v. *Ogden* (1924), were the contested forms of property. After the Civil War, due process protection of property emerged and by 1937 there was a distinctive constitutional conception of property.

The Bundle of Rights

Justice Oliver Wendell Holmes, Jr., by taking up the "extent of the diminution" of property rights (413) and treating property as a "bundle" in *Pennsylvania Coal* v. *Mahon* (1922), drew attention from physical takings and to intangibles. The takings issue has now become a matter of evaluating expectation against the police power of the State. Some environmentalists have said that the compensation scale derived from the "bundle of rights" is a grant to propertied interests that unfairly limits the capacity of the state to regulate. Fred Bosselman, an influential environmental lawyer, argued for elimination of this framework in favor of holding regulations "invalid only if they fail to bear a reasonable relationship to a valid public purpose" (Bosselman, 1973: 246). Bosselman and his colleagues, who sought to strengthen the land use planning process, acknowledged that "an actual appropriation of land for public use, such as for a park, highway or reservoir, must be accompanied by compensation" (1973: 254). While the policy behind any expropriation will inevitably be ripe for dispute, where there is a substantial expropriation under the "police power," there is also a widespread expectation of compensation. As a constitutional conception for the public health and welfare authority of the state, the "police power" stands against the autonomy of the property right. Under the Constitution, the power is limited by due process and compensation. This includes the traditional requirement that property could only be taken by the government from private hands for "public use."

The 1984 case *Hawaii Housing Authority* v. *Midkiff* is particularly illustrative of modern developments in the public use standard. In that case, the state instituted a land-condemnation program to transfer property to tenants. According to Justice O'Connor, regulating oligopoly, like that of the Hawaiian landlords, and the evils associated with it was within the parameters of the traditional exercise of a state's police powers. The transfer of property to private hands did not seem to matter. Justice O'Connor's decision draws on an old maxim that there are and always have been limits on property ownership. These are the limits which Justice Jackson had characterized thirty-nine years earlier as an ordinary part of life (see Chapter I). Today there is relatively little doubt about state power over property, but controversy continues over the legitimate reach of the police power and what constitutes the settled expectation behind a property right.

Legitimate Expectation

The review of Supreme Court decisions since 1789, which is the basis for the analysis of property in this book, has established that protection of property grounded in the American Constitution is a matter of expectation that has been settled or legitimated in some fashion—as by title, grant, or the decision of a court—rather than by mere possession of tangible things (Tribe, 1978: 256). To review, with an emphasis on the application of expectation to newer entitlements, property litigation often concerns what the state must pay the property owner—what constitutes adequate compensation (Dunham, 1962: 65).

Penn. Central Trans. Co. v. City of New York (1978), illustrating one aspect of the contemporary doctrine of legitimate expectation, balanced state power over historic preservation against expected gains on land held by the company. In evaluating restrictions placed by New York City on development of historic landmarks, the Court of Appeals for New York concluded that the city had not denied due process to the corporation because the landmark regulation "permitted the same use as had been made of the Terminal for more than half a century" and "the appellant had failed to show that they could not earn a reasonable return on their investment" (121; see also Chapters 2–3). The Court held that the Penn. Central Transportation Company was not deprived of a "reasonable beneficial use of the landmark site" (at 138). Hence the regulation did not amount to a constitutional taking of property. The opinion reveals a commitment to evaluating the property right in terms of expectation.

Thus, as we have seen in various contexts, adjudication of compensation questions turns on expectation. There is no hard and fast line. There are simply ways of acknowledging the relative autonomy of particular individual (or corporate) interests within the structure of

From Bias to Compensation

constitutional authority. The relationship between the individual and the state is dealt with in the Constitution by a conceptual apparatus that triggers the Just Compensation Clause when private control and use is diminished. An effort to balance social and individual interests through principled standards has characterized evaluation of property claims under the Constitution. The principled standards, however, have not applied to all forms of expectation to the same extent. The next section examines the newer forms of expectation and considers the extent to which they can be distinguished from property in land and transferrable forms of wealth.

We have said that since *Marbury* v. *Madison* (1803), the Supreme Court recognized government created expectations. The things that were expected varied from William Marbury's judgeship to Dartmouth College's charter (1819) and monopolies such as the one held by the Charles River Bridge Company (1837). More recently, the Supreme Court, in *Fidelity Deposit* v. *Arens* (1933), described constitutional property protection as ranging over "obligations, rights, and other intangibles as well as personal things" (see Chapter 1). Now, with the rise of the welfare state and the federal regulatory apparatus, the range of expectations encompasses nearly all aspects of social life. The constitutional guarantee has held that where the expectation is legitimate or settled it will be respected by government as property. Because this modern expectation has come to be known as "new property," this terminology will be used even though the nature of the property right has not changed.

The courts have had a great deal to say about which expectation will be considered legitimate or "settled." At one time, as we have seen, much was made of a distinction between individual "rights" arising from the old property and "privileges" adhering in government grants or largesse (*McAuliffe* v. *Mayor of New Bedford*, 1892; above Chapter III). In the Supreme Court, although the Fifth Amendment was read to tie due process to "real or personal 'property,'" the extension of constitutional protection to modern forms of property has come only recently (Tribe, 1978: 509–10; Van Alstyne, 1968).

Social Security, with its private insurance framework, was held constitutional in 1937 (*Steward Machine* v. *Davis*, 1937; *Helvering* v. *Davis*, 1937), and then in *Flemming* v. *Nestor* (1960; see above, Chapter III), the Court held that entitlement to Social Security benefits did not constitute "accrued property rights" (608). The proposition from the justices at that time was that benefits were a form of interest protected only by the requirement of a rational justification. Although the outcome went against the claimant, consideration of the case by the Court, the lower court decision, and the dissents revealed support for fuller property protection of this interest. The lower court decision had struck down the provision in the Social Security Act on which denial of benefits was based, and the dissents by Black, Douglas, Brennan, and Warren indicated support for the property right.

The Modern Practice

The political climate in the 1960s brought increasing sensitivity to obligations arising from public assistance programs. In *Cafeteria Workers* v. *McElroy* (1961), the Court held that there had to be an unusually important government need to outweigh the right of the individual to have a hearing when he was being terminated. This was followed by Professor Reich's conception of "the New property" and then the 1970 case that explicitly and authoritatively recognized statutory entitlements as property, *Goldberg* v. *Kelly*. This case, described briefly already, pitted New York City and state welfare authorities against beneficiaries who had been cut off without a chance to respond. The Department of Social Services terminated a recipient because he refused to accept counseling and rehabilitation for a drug addiction that he denied having. Justice William Brennan's opinion gave the new property argument constitutional authority. Subsequent decisions held that "property interests are not created by the Constitution; rather . . . by existing rules or understandings that stem from an independent source such as state law" (*Bishop* v. *Wood,* 1976) and set up a new interpretive practice. Protection would not necessarily be afforded to any general benefit prior to its being granted by the state, although Reich mentioned a basis for his new property in the "individual's rightful share in the commonwealth" (1964: 786).

Entitlement claims have been less successful in the Supreme Court since the mid-1970's with the conservatism of the justices affecting case outcomes (see Chapter I). Between the period of the emergence of the Burger Court and the consolidation of the Reagan Court in the late 1980s, the justices of the Supreme Court generally acknowledged the new property in entitlements. The justices allowed termination of federal disability benefits without a prior hearing but granted that benefits provided by the government were a "statutorily created property interest protected by the Fifth Amendment" (*Mathews* v. *Eldridge*, 1976: 334). Other litigants were unsuccessful before the Court, but the justices at least acknowledged the new property in entitlements.

Some "new property" appeals to the Supreme Court have been successful, and we have emphasized that they exhibited a sensitivity for the powerless associated more often with civil liberties than economic issues (*Memphis Light, Gas and Water* v. *Craft*, 1977). Since protection for statutory entitlements came at a time of diminished concern for more marketable forms of property, constitutional commentary often thereafter drew from civil libertarian values to enhance protection of traditional forms of property. This phenomenon is evident in a plea by constitutional authority Gerald Gunther, who sought support for his view that the status of property be returned to "old-fashioned property" in Justice Potter Stewart's observation that "property does not have rights, people have rights" (*Lynch*, 1972). Stewart made his comment to support constitutional protection for homes and savings accounts by associating them with "established" rights to travel and to the continuation of welfare benefits. One of many cases that move part way in the direction suggested by Professor Gunther because it raises both "kinds" of property claims was decided by an 8 to 1 majority in 1981. In *Thomas* v. *Review Board*, the Supreme Court ruled that a worker who quits a job because it conflicts with religious beliefs may not be denied unemployment compensation. The case involved a Jehovah's Witness who quit a factory job after he was assigned to work on armored military vehicles. Here, religious belief constituted adequate basis for a compensable loss of work for all the justices but Rehnquist.

The Court continued to draw on civil rights to protect economic interests for a few years, and occasionally, where the rights of the powerless were particularly compelling, as in *Logan* v. *Zimmerman Brush Co.* (1982), the protection of property interests was quite expansive. In *Logan*, the protected property was a traditional common law entitlement, a cause of action in the legal terminology, provided by the Illinois Fair Employment Practices Act.[2] That is, a right to make a claim for fair treatment was held here to be a property right. The opinion reveals a modern form of enthusiasm for protection of the powerless that is very different from the view expressed by the Supreme Court 150 years ago.

Cases at the close of the 1980s being decided by an increasingly conservative Supreme Court have more than answered Gunther's appeal.[3] Since it is naive to ignore the recent conservative backlash against entitlement protection, the discussion of property that follows anticipates increasing instability in this developing area of constitutional law. As the legislative and judicial branches become more polarized, judicial doctrine alone will become inadequate to understand the nature of the fundamental right. The character of a proposed impartial right is outlined along lines emphasizing constitutional principle, the practice of policy formation and the nature of property. This proposal goes further than the elegant statement on the topic by the late Professor Robert Cover (1988), but it draws encouragement from his belief that constitutional entitlement was a bulwark against arbitrariness in the administration of Social Security. The practice of property rights must rely, ultimately, on traditional principles of obligation.

The Compensation Issue

Having identified the constitutional tradition of property with legitimate expectation and considered the modern development of constitutional property along civil liberties lines, it is now possible to examine a form of constitutional property that would *really* incorporate civil libertarian concerns. A class-neutral conception of property requires seeing entitlements as property in the full sense of the term. The transformation of entitlements into fully protected property under the Constitution remains incomplete, falling short of traditional protection for property by focusing exclusively on procedural due process protection. This provides only part of the constitutional protection accorded older forms of property.

In the traditional property calculation, rights have substance. For example, landowners who have to make way for a freeway or power line are often well compensated (Epstein, 1985). However, where expectation is altered by a change in policy—the 1983 Social Security benefit cuts, for example, there is no compensation offered. At best,

From Bias to Compensation

when faced with denial of benefits, a welfare recipient gets a hearing, but if his program is cut back, the state is not necessarily obliged by law to honor the promises we call entitlements. The following discussion of the situation of a change in policy begins with some traditional dimensions of statutory entitlements and then turns to the implications for entitlement holders of a compensation calculus.

"Taking" is the expression in constitutional law for serious injury to property by government. When a constitutional taking is deemed to have occurred, some form of compensation must result. The expression is derived from the Taking or Just Compensation Clause of the Fifth Amendment—"nor shall private property be taken for public use, without just compensation." Advocates of fundamental rights generally rely on procedural protection for entitlement holders rather than pushing for compensation (Tribe, 1978: 543). This cautious approach may be due to the fact that while the protection afforded by procedural due process is limited, it is certainly preferable to no protection at all. Images of the distinction between rights and privileges in the not-too-distant past and the judicial philosophies dominating the appellate bench in the *Lochner* Era are sobering. Before the civil rights revolution of the post–World War II period, the Supreme Court had applied the constitutional guarantees of legitimate expectation in a manner that favored entrenched interests and those who already had the upper hand. Although this judicial history and recent more conservative appointments to the federal bench cloud the future of the new property in the federal courts, that future will also be influenced by decades of sensitivity to civil rights.

According to Cotterrell, "rights as property rights" have a number of qualities in common (1986: 90). There is the right of exclusion, a right that would allow a person to remove an unwanted guest from his home or an unwanted hand from the pocket where he keeps his Social Security check. Thus, exclusion is generally related to the claims of third parties. There is also the creation of entitlements, by property, "which can be taken from the holder only if he agrees and at a price which he negotiates" (Cotterrell, 1986: 90). Finally, there are the problems of alienability.[4] Here, the market conception of property, the cost distribution rationale of compensation, and constitutional sensitivity to *ex post facto* laws comprise aspects of policy analysis in the United States that explain the nature of constitutional protection for entitlements and show the limited protection for newer kinds of property.

From Bias to Compensation

These traditional considerations have helped to define the protection of property in practice. They will be examined below to assess the costs of a more just constitutional property right.

Market Factors

As we noted in the context of what we called a new Double Standard (see Chapter III), constitutional protection for statutory entitlements is limited by a conception of property as "private wealth" (Ackerman, 1977: 269).[5] Although the basis for the protected right is said to be trade and the ability to transfer interests, this can readily be seen in some forms of statutory property, such as liquor licenses, taxi medallions, and development rights. Compensation is linked in some parts of traditional analysis to the higher status accorded to property when the right is associated with the market, and of course some statutory property is not traded, at least not directly. Although the tradition has been to protect commercial expectation more fully than an expectation that has no commercial potential, neither property rights nor the market could exist as we know it without the State.

The puzzle about market or commercial considerations as they come into play in the constitutional context is that they have little to do with hard work or creativity and everything to do with expectations made legitimate in the law. Rights associated with the old property promise to protect wealth by a standard of market opportunities. In *Penn. Central Trans. Co. v. City of New York* (1978), for instance, the decision by the Supreme Court rested, at least in part, on how much the company could reasonably expect as a return on its property. The Court's attention was on the legitimate expectation of return on corporate property when it held that the transportation company was not prevented from making substantial profits on its building because it was not absolutely precluded from altering the structure. If New York City had interfered in such a way as to preclude the company from reaping a reasonable benefit from its land and building, the city would have been required to compensate the transportation company. This protection of future benefits has been broad ever since intangible interests came under the constitutional mantle. As we proposed in the chapter discussing the new Double Standard, the logic of the

From Bias to Compensation

Takings Clause as it deals with market considerations suggests that the key to the interest protected by compensation is not commerce, but rather authority over public welfare.

Distributing Costs

One way to understand the policy of compensation is in terms of the distribution of social costs. The traditional argument for compensation is that monetary payment to one suffering a loss distributes the costs resulting from public action (*Armstrong* v. *U.S.*, 1960). That is, a property owner whose backyard is needed for a subway station is not expected to make extraordinary personal sacrifices such as giving up his opportunity for a quiet barbecue in order to subsidize the common good. Rather, the costs resulting from public action must be distributed, at least to the degree guaranteed in the Constitution. Although owners can be forced to part with their land, compensation balances the loss of peace, in the case of the subway, with some cash.

In many cases the losses are far from completely balanced. The incremental taking of land that is part of a residential site for an expanded public way often transforms the site and more substantially diminishes its use value than the compensation based on market exchanges is likely to cover. This seems more likely when the owner is a resident and the property taken has personal or sentimental value. When the property is corporately owned or involves certain kinds of easements, minimal use may be handsomely offset by financial compensation. Two cases illustrate the point. In the 1920s, an expanding Boston metropolis flooded an entire river valley in central Massachusetts to satisfy its need for water. The valley contained six towns dating to the colonial period and all the heritage and cultural significance that suggests. On the other hand, in the 1980s, Amtrak expropriated track from a railroad in Connecticut to run passenger service from Washington, D.C., to Montreal, Quebec.

Welfare recipients with a legitimate expectation of benefits, who are often disabled or raising families on what they receive, might be expected to make the same claim—that any losses due to government action affecting their expectation, like a cutback of benefits, be distributed. Historically, the public and the political response to threatened changes in benefit packages—such as those concluded in 1983, which dropped the education benefit for surviving children—has raised policy issues for legislators with regard to competing public goods and the significance of the affected groups (Block, 1987; Light, 1985; Champagne, 1984). The compensation requirement would ground the rights of entitlement holders in society's expressed commitment to the distribution of social costs. The effect would be to honor entitlements and the rights of those who claim this kind of property, just as the expectations of other kinds of property holders have traditionally been honored.

The tradition of distributing social costs has policy dimensions that go beyond what government can rationalize, beyond what White held in *Connolly* v. *Pension Benefit Guaranty Corp*. (1986; see also Chapter III), where a heavily regulated field like employee pension plans was subjected to more regulation without compensation to the employers who paid into the plan. This was a version of "the bitter and the sweet" issue, and it raises the matter of "unconstitutional conditions," both of which follow. In more explicit policy terms, it is not simply unfair to force some to bear disproportionate social burdens. In many cases, compensating an owner may lessen the resistance and discontent caused by the threat of loss. In addition, according Bruce Ackerman, in an analysis that emerges from his criticism of what he calls "ordinary" legal interpretation, when they have to consider compensation public officials will weigh the costs and benefits of alternative measures more carefully (1977: 54–56). The position emerges from what Ackerman calls "scientific" interpretation. This method relies heavily on efficiency and is meant to guarantee care in decision-making. Compensation is thus an instrument for legitimating policy choices that can have some consequences, such as lessening the political resistance of those losing entitlements; these warrant careful examination.

Retroactivity

A more technical body of legislative concerns surrounds retroactivity. Protection from bills of attainder and *ex post facto* laws are among the most settled rights in the Constitution, and they establish a presumption that legislation should be prospective. Early adjudication of constitutional property under the Contract Clause focused on when and under what conditions a legislature could change its mind. In *Fletcher* v. *Peck* (1810) and *Dartmouth College* v. *Woodward* (1819), the Court held that Article I, Section 10 limited the degree to which legislatures could rescind a prior action. Modern constitutional discussion of retroactivity draws heavily on the Due Process Clause of the Fifth Amendment (*Fort Halifax Packing* v. *Coyne*, 1987; see also *Gray*, below) rather than the Contract Clause. Consequently the range of expectation covered is broader. This has been evident in pension fund cases for some time (*Nachman Corp.* v. *Pension Benefit Guaranty Corp.*, 1979).

Justice Brennan, for a unanimous Court in *Gray* v. *Pension Benefit Guaranty Corp.* (1984), points out that the calculation of retroactivity rights in areas of socioeconomic legislation carries the constitutional burden of showing that Congress has acted arbitrarily and irrationally. The Court held that retroactivity must be examined in the context of a presumption in favor of constitutionality, but that retroactivity is a matter about which the justices must be sensitive. The analysis of state mandated pension requirements in *Gray* turns on the legitimate expectation of employers who are forced to fund the pensions. The claims of the employers for protection from what they call "retroactive legislation" fall short in the context of judicial restraint because legislative action was based on interests and expectations on the part of employees.

Those who have been promised a stipend from Social Security or a state license have legitimate expectations. If the expectation of a particular grant is extended for a fixed period, like Social Security survivor's benefits to children until they reach eighteen, then it would seem that a cutoff prior to that time would be a violation of a legitimate expectation and warrant compensation. This would not only be the present expectation of the children promised benefits, but also the expectation of the parent, now dead, who paid into the system.[6] The same consequences and obligations arise where an AFDC recipient receives a $50-per-month allocation for each of five children. The government should acknowledge the expectation of that amount for those already receiving benefits, if policymakers, for instance, tried to then limit payment to three children due to budgetary stringency. In practice, "grandfathering,"[7] while it addresses some situations of this sort, is quite often a policy based accommodation to interested parties and minimal protection in comparison to just compensation. A requirement of compensation for deprivation of statutory entitlement property would mean that changes in policy would have to honor obligations already incurred.

Entitlements, like survivor's benefits and AFDC, often involve expectation bound up with family or life plans in the most intimate way. The plea by Alice James, the widow of a teacher whose children were cut off from Social Security they expected would help support the costs of college,[8] exemplifies that intimacy. Here, policy decisions by government enter into the life plans of an entire family. At the very least, these entitlements are comparable to the relationship established between employer and employee when undertaking a pension plan. In such situations, compensation for lost property in entitlements plays a part in the fabric of social life by distributing costs and honoring obligations in a way very similar to legitimate expectations in land and commercial interests.

The first section of this chapter considered the core meaning of property and grounded the constitutional property right in legitimate expectation. In applying the just compensation provision to statutory entitlements, however, questions about the market arise along with traditional deference in constitutional law to socioeconomic legislation. Interest in distributing social costs and a concern that legislation be prospective offer the possibility of treating entitlements as property for purposes of just compensation. The following part of the chapter explores the traditional tension in politics created by contests between rights such as property and interests such as keeping the costs of government down.

The conventional understanding that statutory entitlements are created by legislation has been used to justify stipulations, limits or policy changes that condition entitlements, for instance giving financial aid but saying the amount can be reduced at any time. Some justices would hold that legislators are capable of stipulating the level of property protection that would accompany a new benefit. This claim for modern social welfare property is far greater than the historic constraints on the freedom to take property. In Anglo-American law, vested rights have stood above legislative authority. From their special position, rights structure legislative prerogatives (Tribe, 1978: 522–43). One approach has distinguished the policy dimensions of property in entitlements from "accrued property rights" on the basis

From Bias to Compensation

of the need for legislative flexibility (*Flemming* v. *Nestor*, 1960). Another exhorts the poor to take "the bitter with the sweet" (*Arnett* v. *Kennedy*, 1974; see also Chapter I) as if the inevitable price of getting protection from the State is to be put at its mercy. Both formulations turn on the relationship between rights and policies. The following section will address "the bitter and the sweet" rationale for denying just compensation protection to statutory entitlements, otherwise known as the doctrine of unconstitutional conditions (Sullivan, 1989).

"The Bitter and the Sweet"

The idea of "the bitter and the sweet" in entitlements law was articulated in *Arnett* (1974), where a federal employee had been fired after accusing his boss of bribery. The firing took place according to a federal law that denied employees any right to a hearing until after they had been dismissed. In a plurality opinion, Associate Justice Rehnquist and Warren Burger, the Chief Justice at the time, allowed the legislature to limit procedural protection in its civil service statutes. The Court held that the level of procedural due process required could vary in entitlement cases and that the decision as to how much process is "due" was for legislative bodies. The conservatives on the present Supreme Court, particularly Chief Justice Rehnquist, believe that legislatures may adjust the constitutional due process provided for any specific entitlement because they created the entitlement in the first place (Massey, 1984).

Rehnquist's position has been that when property is created by statute, the statute-makers are free to create precisely as much property as they want. In her book on Rehnquist's years as an associate justice, Professor Sue Davis (1989) makes a substantial contribution to our understanding of his views on property questions as well as his overall jurisprudence. Davis divides her analysis between nontraditional and traditional property, giving us a substantial treatment of this issue. Rehnquist's reasoning treats the policy process as if it were outside the Constitution, yet the constitutional tradition has meant that the legislature cannot create an entitlement in an arbitrary or discriminatory way (*Cleveland Board of Education* v. *Loudermill*, 1985; *Regents of the University of Michigan* v. *Ewing*, 1985). In addition, Rehnquist's formulation applies to constitutional due process protection. When it comes to traditional just compensation issues, we hear less talk of "the bitter and the sweet," and much more attention goes to legitimate expectation.

Legislative discretion, unfettered by constitutional guides, would lead to an untenable situation in which a legislature could pass a law making entitlement a totally discretionary matter, leaving the head of the welfare agency, for instance, to decide whether a benefit should continue. "The bitter and the sweet" orientation contains limited protection for entitlements. The thing that gives credibility to the orientation is a sort of contemporary Social Darwinism. Within the tradition regulating government, the tension between policy shifts and legitimate expectation is central. This tradition in the Constitution has been an object of judicial controversy since the Yazoo land deal that led to *Fletcher* v. *Peck* (1810). In general, the judiciary has been expected to defer to the legislature on the broad matters of public policy. The limits on legislative prerogative are found at the margins (Michelman, 1979). The issue of just compensation arises from one of those limits —the Fifth Amendment.

In her article, "Unconstitutional Conditions," Professor Kathleen M. Sullivan (1989) reviews the constitutional principle that legislatures lack authority to require that rights be abrogated in order to receive benefits. She finds that "the government may not do indirectly," by withholding a benefit, "what it may not do directly," ignore constitutional rights (1415). Although she believes that this position has triumphed, the debate continues in the law faculties and on the courts. Sullivan attributes the origin of the doctrine to the *Lochner* Court of the early twentieth century. Then, protection meant that although a corporation might be excluded from doing business in a state entirely, it couldn't be denied constitutional rights as a condition for incorporation (*Western Union* v. *Kansas*, 1910). More recently, the doctrine has protected public employees from being politically silenced (*Pickering* v. *Board of Education*, 1968). The contemporary doctrine is full of contradictions, but Sullivan proposes that legislative pressure of this sort unduly enhances the power of government. She argues that the politically correct position on this issue would be one that "would subject to strict review any government condition whose primary purpose or effect is to pressure recipients to alter a choice about exercise of a preferred constitutional liberty in a direction favored by government" (1499–1500).

In the context of the present discussion of entitlements, perhaps the greatest flaw in the conservative theory of "the bitter and the sweet" comes from its inconsistency with some basic tenets of traditional conservatism. One of the most important developments in conservative thought is renewed attention to social obligation. In *Beyond Entitlement*, Professor Lawrence Mead (1986) describes the main problem of the welfare state as its permissiveness and calls for the poor to work for their benefits in order to satisfy their social obligation. Mead's argument uses the economic theory of contemporary policy analysis,[9] but at the core it rests squarely on more traditional normative discourse of reciprocal obligations that forms such an important part of entitlement rights. Like the obligation behind proposals such as "workfare," these proposals require willingness to train and be placed in a job to qualify for welfare benefits (Mead, 1986; Melnick, 1986). In such a policy context, the state has an even greater duty to respect promises made to the poor in the same fashion that government has accepted obligations to the wealthy.

The Status Quo

"The bitter and the sweet" as a response to entitlement claims has led to apprehension that raising statutory entitlements to the level of compensable property would bind legislators and policymakers to the status quo. David Grais, in an influential article on entitlements, states, "If statutory entitlements and rights are equated . . . statutes that create entitlements to the continuation of a benefit also create rights to the continuation of a benefit, thereby making the benefit irrevocable" (1977). There is some truth in what he says, but the fear that full property status for statutory entitlements would chain legislators to the status quo is a caricature of constitutional property protection and the right to compensation. Under the constitutional right, compensation is simply a spreading of the cost of interfering with a property right, not an absolute prohibition on expropriation. The ways the cost can be met are varied, and they reflect the extent to which a property interest is acknowledged (Nichols, 1986). Although the historical evolution of public rights has been toward greater protection (Waters, 1985), the present composition of the federal bench obscures that progress.

In the case of the tenured professor faced with job-threatening retrenchment policies, the full property right to continued employment would define the parameters for administrative choice, but it would not eliminate choice altogether. Where that right is secure—for example, under a contract or statutory entitlement—tight budgets might inevitably force cuts in other areas, such as maintenance and plant operation, and such cuts would, of course, diminish the value of continued employment (since few people like working in a building without heat or light). This would, in turn, affect the cost of compensation.

Pressure comparable to that proposed for entitlement as a function of the compensation calculus was evident in *Boston Firefighters Union v. Boston NAACP*, decided by the Supreme Court in 1983. In the case, minority firefighters sought protection from layoffs under strict seniority, a guarantee won by the union from the state. The NAACP brought suit in the United States District Court for the Eastern District of Massachusetts, and that court ordered a modification in the seniority system to prohibit the reduction of the number of minorities in the fire department. The Court of Appeals, considering the conflict between the statutorily established seniority system and the court order as a case of two competing rights, held in favor of the minority firefighters (*Boston NAACP v. Boston Firefighters Union*, 1981). Subsequent to the decision, however, Massachusetts came up with enough money to stop the layoffs, and the Supreme Court declared the case moot. Policy was thus made around the entitlement. In subsequent cases, minorities have been more successful in establishing affirmative action rights at the local level than in the Supreme Court, and in each of these cases, conservatives have overturned policy on reverse discrimination grounds (*Firefighters Union Local No. 1784 v. Stotts*, 1984; *Wygant v. Jackson Board of Education*, 1986).

Though it is reasonable to fear vested interests whenever they threaten democratic processes, rights define the nature of American democracy and legitimate expectation is a basis for allegiance in a political system. The Constitution does not prevent the government from taking property; it protects against arbitrary takings and provides for just compensation. Because discrimination and minority rights are

From Bias to Compensation

treated under another rubric, the issue of compensation did not arise, but perhaps the seniority interests of white firefighters and teachers should have been compensated in the interest of distributing the costs and minimizing resistance to social change.

Rather than tying the hands of policymakers to the status quo, compensation would simply require that entitlement policy be made with deference to legitimate expectation. Policy must accommodate rights in a constitutional democracy. Those with power have long enjoyed respect for their expectations. The prominence of civil rights now pushes courts to recognize new protected interests in housing even where there is no statutory grant. In *Devines* v. *Maier* (1981), the Circuit Court in Chicago held that the Fifth Amendment entitled tenants to compensation for being displaced from their homes when inspectors determined that the apartments were in violation of the city's housing code. The expectations of tenants or welfare recipients are already becoming a factor in policy formation. When property takes the form of support payments or of promises of benefits, the compensation issue arises from legitimate expectation. In some programs, such as student financial aid, grants are contingent on future allocations and the property claim is diminished. Compensation, however, would at least become a consideration when policy shifts came up against the legitimate expectation of an entitlement holder.

In judicial interpretation of the Constitution there have been two levels of property protection, one for the wealthy and one for the poor. Outside the Supreme Court, commentators caution against relying on "legal contrivances" to produce social change (McCann, 1984), and there is reason to be concerned that the real gains from a revival of property rights will be for the wealthy and not the newly entitled. But, new conceptions of rights and claims for economic justice have a vital legacy (Lynd, 1984; Sparer, 1984). Given that property rights delineate fundamental guarantees, this chapter has discussed the bias that exists and has explored the implications of eliminating this injustice. While the traditional property right has never been an absolute barrier to government regulation, the property right in new entitlements should not be powerless in the face of policy shifts. Since the same government that assures the old also guarantees the new property, just compensation is necessary for entitlements to be treated as property. The right to such compensation for rich and poor alike is the only property right consistent with the Constitution.

From Bias to Compensation

To draw out the implications of the compensation issue as it has been discussed here and as a development of expropriation and eminent domain, the next chapter looks at protection for property and for the public. The approach resembles a mirror that reflects the public's interest in property to examine the politics of title to land. In pursuit of the analogy, the Takings Clause which has long been a part of property law, becomes the Giving Issue in the following inquiry.

CHAPTER VI

The Giving Issue

We have seen the community interest in property, and we have seen property linked to individual rights, particularly when determinations are being made about whether it should be taken from private hands. Here we examine the rights of the public when governments dispose of property, that is, when they transfer property from public ownership to private. Two Atlantic ports and two constitutions, one old and one new, provide a context for considering this twist on the tradition of constitutional property. The arena of economic development—where governments hope to encourage growth by providing better roads, plants, or waterfronts—often involves the transfer of property from public to private hands. This chapter, a comparative study of Canada and the United States, isolates political institutions and focuses on their role in public policy formation. Portland, Maine, and Halifax, Nova Scotia, are the sites. Economic development in both resulted in the transfer of waterfront property from public to private ownership. Yet, significant institutional differences allow for comparison of how the public welfare is handled.

While grants to the poor have traditionally received a good deal of attention in industrialized nations, there is new interest in corporate gifts and public generousity to the more well heeled. From the handling of natural resources in the American West to competition in the East for industrial development, private aggrandisement at public expense is a significant issue in the United States. With a larger nonmilitary public sector in proportion to the whole economy, Canada seems more tolerant and more generous in regard to transfers and appears to have a more developed apparatus for such policies. Arrangements appear to favor administration in Canada and courts in the United States, and this difference between the two countries provides insight into the politics of entitlement. The following comparison of the politics of entitlement in Canada and the United States refers to a transfer of property from public ownership to private as the Giving Issue.[1]

Property is linked to the courts through expropriation law. In the American Constitution, sensitivity to the private land owner requires that the costs of expropriation be spread throughout the community by payment of compensation. Under this traditional expectation, incorporated into the American Constitution by the Fifth Amendment, expropriation of private property, particularly land, is governed by the principles of the Takings Clause. The mirror image is derived from Article IV, Section 3 of the Constitution, which vests Congress with the "Power to dispose of and make all needful Rules and Regulations respecting the . . . Property belonging to the United States." Through various statutes over the years, Congress has provided for disposal of land in a manner that is "economical and efficient" (40 U.S. Code Sec. 471) as well as discounting the transfer against "any benefit which has or may accrue" (40 U.S. Code Sec. 484) from the transfer (see *Valley Forge College* v. *Americans United*, 1982). It is this second consideration that drives the comparison in this chapter—the idea that when public land is turned over to private hands, the private gain is a matter of public interest.

The Giving Issue in the United States will be associated with property rights as part of the boundary between the state and private dominion. In Canada, a country that shares a great many traditions with the U.S., administration is more characteristic and there is a more bureaucratic treatment of property transfer. The role of judges and rights is changing in Canada, and with the new constitution, we have an opportunity to add another dimension to the nature of property and the politics of entitlement.

The Comparison

The premise of this case study is that Nova Scotia and its capital city, Halifax, bear enough resemblance in culture and material conditions

The Giving Issue

to Maine, and its biggest city, Portland, so that we may attend to institutional differences. Here, development policy is considered a part of the cultures closely tied to economic or material conditions. Yet, in this comparison, determination of policy through the institutional life of the places is the primary focus of our attention.

Culture

Maine and Nova Scotia have similar traditions. Both began their Western history under colonization. Nova Scotia started out French, having been settled by the Sieur-de-Monts and Samuel de Champlain at Port Royal in 1605. It would be one hundred years before the British established sovereign authority and longer still before Halifax became a military outpost in 1749. Maine traces its European history to Sir Ferdinando Gorges, who received a grant from the Council for New England in 1622 for what is now New Hampshire and Maine. Competition between the two colonies came soon enough, so by 1690 the settlements in Massachusetts and Maine had sent a successful expedition against the French in Nova Scotia. These expeditions preceded the brutal expulsion of the French-Acadians by the English in 1755. British dominion in Nova Scotia was strengthened by the American Revolution, which brought thousands of "United Empire Loyalists" to Nova Scotia. The ties of culture and kinship between New England and the maritime region of Canada were so strong during the War of 1812 that there is said to have been an agreement between the participants on either side not to attack one another. The English and the French influences remain distinctive in Nova Scotia, but in the fishing villages and lumber towns of the province, the similarity to Maine is striking; from the lobsterman's buoy to the lumberman's jacket, these appear to be kindred cultures.

Today, Halifax, the provincial capital, is a city of 120,000 sitting with English grace and sophistication between the Atlantic and a relatively wild interior of Nova Scotia. By all appearances, the residents of Halifax are Haligonians first, with the province and the nation vying for second place in the lineage. When Nova Scotia received its name in the Royal Charter of 1621, it comprised the mainland of the present province (as well as New Brunswick), a part of the state of Maine, and part of the Gaspe Penninsula. Since then, crown lands have declined to the 27 percent that is presently held by the public. The earliest recorded grant was issued to Major General Cosby on August 24, 1731, for an acre of land on Canso Island (CCREM, 1972).

Portland, Maine, is less than half the size of Halifax. Although Maine's largest city, Portland is not the capital. It shares a beautiful setting on an important harbor with its Canadian counterpart, and a good deal of the wealth of Maine and the city has also come from the sea. For residents of Portland, Maine and America are much stronger associations than the federal government is in Halifax. This aspect of culture, the localism and regional orientations of the people, is a foundation of sovereignty. As such, the beliefs people have about their government has a bearing on institutional differences.

Material Conditions

The material conditions of life provide a clear basis for comparison. Maine and Nova Scotia are on the Atlantic coast, and Portland and Halifax, by far the largest towns in the region, are ports. Ferries leave Portland for the islands of Casco Bay and for Nova Scotia, providing a romantic transportation link. The connection to the sea sets the economic tone, but it also puts these cities on the fringe of their nations (and their continent). Both have shared hardships due to their distance from the more prosperous urban centers, down the Atlantic coast in the case of Portland and up the St. Lawrence River in the case of Halifax.

Halifax has been gaining in population over the past decades, adding one-third to its population in the last thirty years, while Portland has generally been losing people over the same period. And due to projects stimulated by the provincial Department of Development and Industrial Estates, Ltd., as well as efforts from the national government, Halifax has an attractive and reasonably prosperous waterfront and a number of new industries close by. While neighboring Lunenburgers built the famous schooner Bluenose, which appears on the Canadian dime and still work around the harbor, Halagonians are more likely to take to the sea to develop the oil reserves on the Georges Bank.

Portland lost 20 percent of its residents between 1950 and 1980 due to suburbanization, economic stagnation, and migration to American cities farther South. But Portland has recently been undergoing an economic renewal and gentrification. An influx of money and ideas brought a level of sophistication to the old port that it has not seen for some time. This study focuses on a move by a shipbuilding firm, the Bath Iron Works, to operate in the Portland harbor through a government-financed development project of major proportions.

Institutions are part of a culture and, as with any other part, they can be subjected to special scrutiny. Like the English language, which we say is the same in Canada and the United States—although we isolate phonemes (*out*) and "tag lines" (eh?) that distinguish Canadian from American English—social and political institutions manifest indigenous differences. Governmental institutions are an aspect of culture distinct enough in practice that they can be compared cross-nationally when the culture and material conditions are kept reasonably constant.

The Institutional Settings

On the South side of the international border,[2] we run into rights wherever we look, while to the north, planning and administration are the characteristic practices. The constitutional property right is distinctly and, until recently, uniquely American, although we know that in the United States, it is affected by policy to stimulate development. Development policy is more characteristic of Canadian practice, although we know it is affected by property rights rooted in the common law. The consequences, on balance, are real differences in the institutional character of state power over property in Canada and in the United States. These differences highlight the significance of institutional form while capturing the shared culture that may be making the two countries more and more alike (Moffett, 1972).

Property Rights

The circumstances of independence and relations with Great Britain help explain some characteristics of the property right. In Canada, until 1949, the supreme legal authority was the British Parliament. In the provinces, British law was the foundation on which largely independent jurisdictions operated in the Canadian confederation. Canadian constitutional law books referred to British cases for their principles for over one hundred years (Laskin, 1975). British authority in the United States was terminated more abruptly than in Canada, although influence has still been considerable. In America, the Revolution was justified in natural-law terms influenced by William Blackstone, the English jurist who personified the trend toward absolute or vested rights in property. His *Commentaries on the Laws of England* helped to transform the fact of colonial charters into the jurisprudential practice of rights (Corwin, 1929).

Property was "vested" in the United States (Pound, 1921: 103), due to its place in the Fifth Amendment to the American Constitution. The American guarantee that no person be deprived of property without due process of law, nor that it be taken without compensation, and the use of that guarantee by the judiciary to establish a tradition of rights beyond the reach of legislation is the primary legal difference between Canada and the United States. Canada did not revolt and create its own constitution. There was no Canadian Bill of Rights until 1960 and the Canadian "Constitution," until 1982, was an act of the British Parliament, a statute resting on legislative authority.

The link between property and the American Constitution, in matters of involuntary transfer, is expropriation. Here the parameters of governmental action are based on the Due Process Clause, which has held, since 1855, that the criteria for evaluating claims against the Constitution should be the document itself and "those settled usages and modes of proceeding existing in the common and statute law of England" (*Murray's Lessee*, 1856). Courts in the United States distinguish regulatory power over property from constitutionally protected expropriation. Although regulation often involves losses to property owners (prohibiting the sale and consumption of alcohol is the most dramatic example), such losses are not considered subject to compensation and are not protected by constitutional due process. Only recognized transfers of property to the public require compensation. One criteria for such transfers is that they legitimately be for the benefit of the public. Thus "public use" is required for governmental takings. Consequently, using the expropriation power to take property for the exclusive benefit of private individuals is a violation of due process in the United States. However, courts have considered privately held mills, roads, and railroads to be a public use.

The Giving Issue

After the American Civil War, jurists diminished the extent of legislative power to expropriate and enforced standards that extended the interpretation of property interests. Protection began to be accorded to loss of profits or land value that had not formerly been considered compensable. Judicial discourse on property and the Taking-Clause shifted from a presumption in favor of legislative prerogatives based on a narrow view of property to a broader view expanding the boundaries of property from things lawfully possessed to expectation of a fair return. The question became: Could the government restrict property and radically affect its expected value without compensation? Justice John Marshall Harlan said yes in *Mugler* v. *Kansas* (1887) where the state outlawed breweries, making Mugler's facility worthless. Harlan ruled that "acts done in the proper exercise of government powers, and not directly encroaching upon private property . . . do not constitute a taking." As long as the exercise is a lawful one, private property is not considered to have been infringed upon.

The changes brought by *Pennsylvania Coal* v. *Mahon* (1922) meant that property was no longer limited to land but included the money that could be made from it. In Takings Clause jurisprudence, legal tests balanced the private loss and the public gain. Because of this balancing, each case had to be examined with an eye to the positions and expectations of the particular parties. The result, for lawyers attempting to formulate rules, has been called "a crazy-quilt pattern of Supreme Court doctrine" (Dunham, 1962) that is "ethically unsatisfying" (Michelman, 1967). Nonetheless, judicial review of action affecting property has been characteristic of Fifth Amendment protection for property in the United States. Property owners in the United States may have limitless desires or expectations concerning their land (they may want to build an ice-cream stand or paint their barn purple), but their ownership may give them no such right.

Without the tradition of judicial review of legislation and an idea that law stands beyond the reach of legislatures, expropriation law is different in Canada. Since due process of law is defined as "in accordance with the common and statute law as it exists at any particular time" (*Regina* v. *Martin*, 1961), legislatures can determine due process by statute. Federal authority stems from the British North America Act and the Expropriation Act, which authorize any minister "charged with a public work" to "take, directly or through representatives, any land, real property, streams, waters and water courses necessary to build, improve, or maintain a public work." Each province also has its own statutory basis for expropriation. There are no Founding Fathers to appeal to and the founding documents are much less determinative. The lawyers and courts are relegated to questions of what the statutory provisions for expropriation are. In Quebec, failure to follow procedures invalidates the "taking," and the individual owner is free to get an injunction, petition to recover possession, or seek direct action for indemnity. Thus, the issue in Canada becomes a question of whether particular expropriations are *authorized*.

Courts fix compensation, which is provided for by statute (Todd, 1976), only when other bodies fail. Canadian courts deciding compensation issues apply the same general principles of market value as courts in the United States.[3] The goal is to put the owner in a position similar to the one occupied before the expropriation occurred. The tradition of property rights in Nova Scotia is one of strong legislative prerogatives as in the rest of Canada. A dramatic example was the expropriation of riparian rights, the rights of owners of property abutting water, by the Water Act of 1919. The legislation expropriated basic riparian rights by "vesting in the province the 'sole and exclusive right to use, divert and appropriate any and all water,' " and recourse to the courts was blocked (Nedelsky, 1979). This institutional tradition leads from legislation to the administrative process.

The Giving Issue

The modern state, whether Canadian or American, "giveth as well as taketh away," to use the discourse of an older tradition. Policies of the Reagan Administration, implemented by his first Secretary of the Interior, the infamous James Watt, led to the sale of "surplus" land in the West and spawned such local movements as the Sagebrush Rebellion by those accustomed to using these lands. In Canada, there is longstanding concern about liquidation of the public domain. In 1907, R. J. Shrimpton raised the question, "Why should any government give away lands for nothing?" (Moffett, 1972: 72). More recently, decades of development initiatives are being subjected to examination (Bickerton and Gagnon, 1984). The issues that surround public giving illuminate the operations of law in politics.

Disposal of public property, like the governmental taking that is its

The Giving Issue

analog and often a corollary, is a function of the structure of expropriation law. Embedded in this structure is sensitivity for the private land owner requiring that costs be spread throughout the community by payment of compensation. When land is taken "for public purposes," such as a highway right-of-way or a redevelopment project, the loss that the property owner is forced to accept is distributed in the form of a payment from the public treasury. By requiring the community to bear the costs, compensation is meant to assure fairness in the policy-making process (Roberts, 1977; Ackerman, 1977). An aspect of this requirement—that the public share the costs to individual landowners when land is expropriated—would be a requirement that when government land is turned over to individuals, the private gain would be limited by the public interest. This is the Giving Issue. Here, the policy rationales for compensation apply equally well to cases where public land or property is being sold or transferred to the private sector. Although the issue comes out of law in the United States, the same policy issue can be examined in the Canadian development policy.

The Giving Issue is most dramatic when disposal of public property is a consequence of government authority used to accumulate land in the first place. Hence, use of eminent domain by the government has brought much closer scrutiny of transfers to private hands than the transfer of land historically held by the public. In the case of lands managed by the Department of the Interior in the United States, recent controversies emerged from a policy context with an emphasis on the preservation of the land as well as from a sense that undue enrichment resulted for those able to use public lands. Where land had been approximated at some time or other in its history, there are constitutional issues, at least in the United States,[4] and although the public does not have a right in the same sense that an individual does, public and private interests appear throughout expropriation (Sax, 1971). Land is less often the issue in Canada, due in part to the extraordinary amount owned by Canadian governments, but the same "boundary" between the state and private dominion exists in Canada, and the issues that have been raised range from simple comparative studies of the various modes of policy implementation (Trebilcock et al., 1982) to a problem termed "the International Relations of State-Owned Enterprises" (Laux, 1983).

Protection in expropriation is understandably a concern of modern legal economists. Scholars such as Bruce Ackerman, as we saw in Chapter V, hold that compensation leads to more efficient and more responsible decision-making. By having to pay the landowner when property is taken for public use, the legislature is supposed to be deterred from enacting inefficient programs. Such logic, with its consequences for policy-making, drive the present inquiry into the transfer of property to private hands and link it to the discussion of compensation in Chapter V.

Canada and the United States differ in the institutions they rely on to handle the transfer of property. In the United States, the paradigm is reliance on law, courts, and lawyers under principles laid down in the Constitution, refined in statutory mandates, and ultimately subject to review by the judges. In Canada, the mandates laid down by the legislatures are implemented by the administrative agencies, and, at least in part due to the absence of a written textual referent, administration is rarely reviewed by the judiciary. The following sections discuss administration and litigation in both countries in order to show the relative emphasis on administration in Canada and litigation in the United States.

Administration

"Ownership" in Canada is "fee simple interest," and the right to develop rests with the government (Goldberg and Mercer, 1986). Some areas such as railroad rights of way and waterfronts mean additional public prerogatives over land. Only 9 percent of the land in Canada is privately owned (27 percent in Nova Scotia), compared to 58 percent in the United States (98 percent in Maine). This is the context for a tradition of public prerogatives in economic development in Canada that have not been evident in the United States. The key actor in this environment is the Crown Corporation.

This institution, derived from the characteristic Canadian reliance on public agencies and civil servants to carry out mandated policies, is English. Contemporary Canadian civil servants are linked with and approximate the "Whitehall tradition" (Granatstein, 1982: 1). As Michael Goldberg and John Mercer put it, "Canada demonstrates a Britannic continuity" in its "powerful and generally well-staffed bureaucracies" (1986). This tradition was discussed by Evan S. Connell (1984) in his book on Custer's defeat at the Little Bighorn. In analyzing the lax management of the American frontier, Connell recounts the vigilante murders of Indians who had traded at Fort McKenzie. They were slaughtered by the manager of the fort in the years leading up to Custer's last stand. "In Canada," according to Connell, "things were different. The Hudson's Bay Company, part of a smoothly functioning empire, understood how to live with Indians whereas the newly arrived, impatient, disorganized, aggressive American did not" (1984: 64). Thus, policies, like economic development, unfolded on quite a different terrain in Canada.

"Crown Corporation" Development

The management of basic resources in Canada has evolved from the English tradition of royal prerogatives into sophisticated public enterprises. Acting often with considerable independence, public enterprises constitute a patchwork across Canada.[5] In Manitoba, Alberta, and Saskatchewan, the telephone system is owned by the public, while in the other provinces the phone companies are privately owned and regulated by government. The patchwork is also characteristic of the capital markets that are the domain of the crown corporations and private financial institutions. Economic development in the nineteenth century put pressure on the traditional arrangements, and property rights were seen to have an antidevelopment bias (Horwitz, 1977; Nedelsky, 1979). In Canada, a way around those biases turned out to be public enterprise.[6]

The province of Nova Scotia used land in the early twentieth century to attract settlement, but by 1909 it had depleted crown resources. For the next decades, the Crown actively took back control of the land. In two 1920 cases, defendants who had violated traditional property rights pleaded license under the 1919 water legislation. The traditional right was upheld, but "the legislature responded immediately to assure the exclusive control of the cabinet and commissioners over water policy."[7] These cases, under the Power Commission Act, were characteristic of pro development legislation (Nedelsky, 1979; see also *Hanf v. Yarmouth Light and Power*, 1926).

There has been large investment by the government in Canadian industries since the 1960s. In this twenty-five-year span, the impetus has been shared between the federal government and the provinces. At the federal level, the Department of Regional Economic Expansion (DREE) has attempted to reduce regional disparities through job creation and has focused considerable attention on the maritime provinces. Between 1969 and 1979 it had built forty-five industrial parks in the Atlantic region and provided $31 million in assistance (nine of the parks were in Nova Scotia, costing $8.2 million) (DREE, 1979). The economy of the province is now driven by the offshore oil industry, a resource managed by the national government. At the provincial level, development has been carried by the Department of Development and Industrial Estates.

Industrial Estates Limited (IEL) is the Crown Corporation in the Department of Development in Nova Scotia that epitomizes the authority of the province in economic development. As a Crown Corporation, the Chief Minister is an elected official in the legislature and appointed by the Premier. The Deputy Minister is a civil servant. The corporation is the central factor in the disposal of land for purposes other than resource exploitation, and it sometimes uses eminent domain in carrying out its economic development projects. Like economic development elsewhere, the rationale for the policies of IEL is jobs. The economic clout of IEL and the large amount of land owned by the government in Canada are key variables in development policy. By 1982, IEL had loaned $270 million for industrial parks over a twenty-five year period and, through the province, it held equities worth $6.9 million. Its deficit was $1,276,900 for the year. Although amounting to millions of dollars of gifts to the private sector, the IEL projects involved relatively little taking or giving of land. The Auto Port, a development project for importing cars, involved some land "banking," although the port was built mostly on vacant land within ten miles of the center of Halifax. The Michelin tire plant was built in a rural area outside the capital in Kentville and involved some accumulation in order to provide a large industrial facility and a port, according to Steve MacDonald (1983) of the Urban Affairs Institute at Dalhousie University in Halifax.

For over a decade, Industrial Estates had been the subject of extensive evaluation and policy analysis. Perhaps because of the more professional nature of industrial development at the provincial level in Canada, the discussion was very sophisticated. The three studies that comprised the bulk of this literature were *Forced Growth* (1971)

The Giving Issue

by Philip Mathias, which compares the Nova Scotia experience with a "heavy water" plant to other development schemes throughout the country; *The Life and Times of Industrial Estates Limited* (1974) by Roy E. George, which looked at the corporation itself from its inception in 1957 until 1973; and finally, *Planning and Development* (1975), in which A. Paul Pross looked at two Nova Scotia communities, Bridgewater, the site of the tire plant and Port Hawkesbury, planned as the center of a major industrial region. The mixture of success and failure was not so different from that of the United States. However, the level of public intervention would have been unusual in the States.

American Public Administration

American administration is much weaker than Canadian. In part, this is because the United States is less grounded in a bureaucratic tradition (for reasons related to culture that we won't pursue here) and everywhere is circumscribed by the prerogatives of property and the role of the courts. But the most significant reason is the power of the private sector and the ideology of private enterprise with the consequent limitation of the public role to a regulatory one. In an American study prepared for the Bureau of Public Lands, Lloyd Rodwin at MIT argued against a statewide public development corporation in favor of local management (Rodwin, 1974). This perspective reflects different institutional expectations and, in particular, a smaller role for state management in the United States.

In Portland, requests to purchase city-owned land go first to the Planning Department for assessment of any conflicts with city projects. The recommendation of this department is considered and acted upon by the Planning Board and passed on to the City Council. If approved by the council, as most requests are (Rawlins, 1981), the proposal is sent out to bid. The Economic Development Committee, chaired by a member of the City Council, becomes involved when large parcels need to be pieced together. Most disposal of city-owned land follows private initiatives. Especially for small lots, but even for larger projects, it is the private sector that initiates requests to purchase. For small pieces, the land is usually sought by adjacent land owners. For larger parcels, the initiative for development projects also comes from private interests, simply larger ones. Only once in the last five years has the city initiated a sales campaign and made an inventory of land available for purchase. Although this resulted in disposal of approximately 40 percent of the available property, the practice did not become established.

Land disposed of in Portland takes many forms. Due to a move away from neighborhood schools in the 1960s, a number of smaller facilities became vacant. In all of these cases, notification of surplus property went first from the School Department to the city. Where no municipal need is claimed, the property is turned over to the Economic Development Committee (Knowland, 1981). The city occasionally finds itself with large parcels of military property such as a "minifort" in the harbor on George Island. These come under the economic development mandate. In these and related instances, the city has used its power to aggregate properties for development purposes. The Economic Development Committee in Portland has responsibility for joining private proposals with public programs. Through the authority of the local government and the city's capacity for initiating infrastructure improvements, the committee aides projects that promise economic benefits to the city. An interesting connection here between the issue of land disposal and economic development is that the economic development committees have in many cases emerged from the planning commissions of an earlier time.

The somewhat ad hoc approach at the local level is only slightly different at the state level, which is the parallel in Maine to Industrial Estates. The state agency overseeing industrial development in Maine is the State Development Office. With a budget of $5 million dollars and a staff of fifteen, the office is already small by Canadian standards, but its responsibilities are split between tourism, business attraction, and business assistance. The primary activity in Maine, as with other northeastern states, such as Massachusetts, is providing information and singing the praises of the state, although assistance also includes site analysis and keeping files of buildings.

Litigation

Litigating—or reliance on law by consulting lawyers, filing lawsuits, or appealing cases—is an institutional form long characteristic of efforts to protect land in the United States. We deal with it here as a form of state power rather than a cultural predisposition of the American people. Thus, we see different institutions handling the same type of development issues.

The Rights Tradition

In the United States, property questions, particularly those involving the use of public authority in eminent domain cases, will involve the courts. Reliance on courts and related legal processes is a part of the culture, a way of doing things. And with nearly one lawyer for every four hundred people, there is no country in the world that relies more heavily on these professionals than the United States. But the point here is not a cultural one. It is rather that law and courts characterize a form of governance and define the Giving Issue in Portland, Maine.

In no other institutional arrangements is the federal system more differentiated than in the law and courts of the nation. Most law governing ordinary relations is state law. Thus, the law of murder, theft, and liability is generally a product of state legislation. But the general framework and the reality in important areas is set by the Constitution and federal legislation. Thus, civil rights questions tend to be governed from Washington, D.C., and the boundaries of expropriation law are very clearly matters of constitutional concern set by the federal courts.

In the United States, land policy is governed by concepts of rights that have a distinctly individualist quality. It is quite common in the United States to speak of individual rights and to distinguish them from the interests of the community. The rights tradition amounted to a transformation of the professional mysteries of lawyers and judges into the basis for government. With rights, the language of social relations is grounded in a formal autonomy of individuals and an official respect for members of the community. Rights do not go well with generousity, gratitude, loyalty, and friendship. Rights claims are contentious and totally consistent with a process of disputation. In this context, they are an important political resource.

Unlike electoral processes, litigation is not open to the wide spectrum of participants eligible to vote. Although there are over six hundred thousand lawyers in the United States, they are not evenly distributed, and legal assistance is only a right in the criminal process. And, unlike administration, litigation is not characterized by an officialdom with expertise limited to the task at hand. The link to the authority of the State is the distinctive characteristic of lawyers. The realm of lawyers and judges is one of generalists organized by professional association and professional discourse. This is the context to which we turn to portray land policy in an American state.

The first recorded court decision involving local citizens of Portland occurred in 1640 at Saco and settled the dispute of *Cleaves* v. *Winter* (Press Herald, 1982). It was not until 1725 that a lawyer commenced practice in Maine, a Noah Emergy of Kittery. Between 1800 and 1820, the number of lawyers had jumped from fifty-four to 207. Characteristically, the legal community continued to increase and the role of law, courts, and litigation has remained important in Maine as it has in the rest of the United States.

The Bath Iron Works Litigation

The Portland *Press Herald* on May 29, 1982, in a special issue celebrating the town's 350th anniversary, described the development:

> Today the Maine State Pier sits silently. Gone are even the occasional cargo ships that took loads of paper pulp from Portland. But on this site, Bath Iron Works intends to build a $46.7 million shipyard, two thirds of it financed by taxpayers, that will have a projected annual payroll of $29.5 million by 1986. The yard is expected to create about 1,000 new jobs and spawn 3,500 other jobs throughout the Portland region.

The cost of the project was to be shared by the city ($15 million), the state ($15 million), and the company ($16.7 million). That year there was over $70 million worth of development plans for the waterfront, according to John Ferland, a reporter for the *Press Herald*, in an article published May 29, 1982. By the fall of 1984, the shipyard had been in operation for nearly a year, and it was already beginning to look as if things would not turn out entirely as had been planned.

The legal issues surrounding disposal were closely related to expropriation and matters of drafts on the public purse supplementing the disposal of land to profit-making enterprises. Historically,

The Giving Issue

government-sponsored industrial development, particularly that involving private profit-making entities, was highly suspect. It almost never passed public purpose challenges. As the public purpose concept expanded, at different times and to differing degrees in each state, often to provide an essential service (see *Laughlin v. City of Portland*, 1914 which established a coal yard), the basic proposition that industrial development may meet the public purpose test became true. Courts historically have been the final arbiters of whether public purpose requirements are in fact met when particular industrial development schemes have been challenged (Delogu, 1981: 2–4).

Two legal maneuvers had to take place before the port project could be built. The first was a transfer of title to submerged and intertidal land that had been held in public trust but had been built on by private owners. The second issue was the referendum. In 1982, Maine held a referendum on a bond issue supporting the waterfront development for Bath Iron Works. The judges initially held that the success of the referendum constituted public approval to which the judiciary would have to defer in determining whether the public interest was being served by turning the waterfront over to the shipbuilding company.

The courts in Maine favored the project at every step, yet they held up construction for nearly two years, and, along with the unusual step of a bond issue, they became the "public forum" for consideration of the development. The last effort to stop the shipyard development was an attempt to bring the authority of the law to bear. The case of *Common Cause v. Maine* was argued in the Supreme Judicial Court of Maine on September 21, 1982, and decided January 7 of the next year. The case was an appeal from a judgment of the Superior Court, Kennebec County, in favor of defendants in a suit by taxpayers alleging that agreements between state, city, and the corporation for shipyard development were in violation of state and federal constitutions.

The appellant, through their attorney Orlando E. Delogu, argued that, "governments as constituted have limited powers, they must act reasonably, and they must act within constitutional limitations." Delogu continued, "In its zeal to act, government sometimes forgets or oversteps the limitations on its power to act." A situation, he pointed out, that was frequently addressed by the courts (*Common Cause v. Maine*, 1981). For this case in particular, some of the attention was directed to action by the legislature of Maine to turn over "certain filled submerged lands" to the shipbuilding company. Delogu described the legislative limitation as "three-fold." Enactments, he said, must be " 'reasonable,' be 'for the benefit of the people,' and not be repugnant to any other provisions of the Maine or United States Constitution." In summary, Delogu proposed:

> When these principles are applied to the issues presently before us it will immediately be seen that even a governmental expenditure for schools (usually permitted) becomes impermissible if the school is a church-owned parochial school; and an expenditure for highways (also usually permissible) would also be impermissible if the proposed road were a private woods road for the exclusive use of one of Maine's forest products firms.

The challenge was unsuccessful and the opinion of the court held that although "taxpayers had standing to challenge" the agreement with the state and that any agreement would require "a public purpose for expenditure of public money and prohibiting credit of state to be directly or indirectly loaned," the "bond referendum question was not so clearly misleading as to require that referendum be set aside." This was true, according to the court because "legislative determination that the project would benefit the people of the state by reviving the commerce of the city, enhancing opportunities for employment, and improving the economy of state was not irrational."

Though unsuccessful, the litigation was more than a pro forma "day in court." In a process discussed by Professor James Willard Hurst in his treatise, *Law and Markets in United States History* (1982), the law had provided a forum for consideration of a wide range of policy issues. The legal maneuvers had taken three years and a referendum, and the fact that the last word on the project was from the bench influenced the entire development process (see also *Valley Forge College* v. *Americans United*, 1982).

Judicial Review in Canada?

Canada has not had a tradition of this sort, but there are prospects under the new Charter. Rights adjudication in Canada has been characterized by considerable deference to provincial lawmaking. Profes-

The Giving Issue

sor D. A. Schmeiser describes the property issues arising out of the Canadian Bill of Rights as ancillary to religious and communicative freedoms and freedom from discrimination. For the federal government, authority stemmed from the criminal law power (Schmeiser, 1964: 85). A basic point is that the Bill of Rights was an act of Parliament, not a constitutional amendment in the American sense. The jurisdiction of the Supreme Court has thus been a function of statutory interpretation. Professor Walter Tarnopolsky (1975: 234) tends to minimize the statutory basis while suggesting that the Canadian Charter at that time was simply not the sort of thing where the distinction between being in it or out of it was all that clear.

Application of the Bill of Rights to legislation, whether federal or provincial, would have been an exercise of judicial chutzpah not characteristically Canadian. The one case under the Bill of Rights having an application to the discussion of property was *National Capital Commission v. Laponte et al.* (1972). The case was a due process challenge to the federal Expropriation Act (RSC 70), and the court held that notwithstanding the fact that the act makes no provision for notice of expropriation and thus provides little opportunity to object or negotiate compensation, the procedures passed by Parliament, by definition, constitute due process of law. This is the statutory basis of the old Bill of Rights.

In the last few years, there has been considerable ferment in Canadian legal circles over the constitutional Charter of Rights and Freedoms. Although the right to property was not included in the new Charter, the new document may be relevant to questions about the role of litigation in the Canadian system. Property as a fundamental right had been in the Diefenbacher Bill of Rights of 1960 much as it appears in the American Constitution. The judicial experience with that clause was discussed in the treatises by Walter Tarnopolsky (1975) and D. A. Schmeiser (1964). Most of the activity, as in America at the same time, had been around protections for equality. The potential change is not only a function of having a document and a neighbor to encourage the legal community to use it. Rather, it is a function of and will be determined by the fundamental challenges to the Canadian union, which the Charter of Rights was meant to address.

Professor Peter Russell has proposed that the "main impact of the new constitutional Charter of Rights on the Canadian system of government is to increase the role of the judiciary in deciding how fundamental social and political values should be affected by public policy" (1982: 1). Evident in the switch from British to American ancillary graduate training in law, which began in the 1920s and was evident in Professor Edward McWhinney's treatise *Canadian Jurisprudence* thirty years ago (McWhinney, 1958: 11), American legal ideas have been making greater and greater headway in Canada. One of the most important is the notion that judges "can, and do, and should make law in the process of decision making." This is given for commentators who share an American orientation (Conklin, 1979). Affection for a strong judiciary and for fundamental rights as practiced in the United States has become a strong force in Canada. Both those who fear judicial policy-making and those who welcome it are influenced by the assumption that this is something the Canadians must face.

Only a few months after the Canadian Charter became law, the new Brunswick Court of Queen's Bench extended a ruling (*New Brunswick v. Fisherman's Wharf, Ltd.*, 1982). The judge employed the Charter in a dispute over property rights. The Sheriff in Fredericton had gone to court for a settlement of competing property claims arising from his having confiscated five fryers and a broiler, a stand-up cooler, a soft drink machine, and a cigarette vending machine. These items had been leased to a fast food restaurant that owed $5,850 in back taxes and interest to the town. The rental establishments that owned the property claimed that it had been unfairly taken. Having disposed of the immediate property questions brought in the Charter of Rights, the judge gave clear signals that, in some jurisdictions at least, the courts may take the introduction of a doctrinally based fundamental law as an occasion to assert power of their own.

The chapter referred to is Sec. 1, the "guarantee clause," and Sec. 7.1, which reads: "Everyone has the right to life, liberty and security of the person and the right not to be deprived thereof except in accordance with the principles of fundamental justice." The New Brunswick jurist was candid in noting that "the Charter is silent in specific reference to property rights," but he goes on to assert that "right to . . . security of the person must be construed as comprising the right to enjoyment of the ownership of property which extends to 'security of the person.'" This is a great leap, but coming when it does, the holding suggests that those who doubt that the judiciary will be strengthened from the experience with the charter are going to be surprised.

The Giving Issue

There is a paradox stemming from the American experience with due process protections of property. Knowledgeable commentators might assume that judicial protection of property would grow in Canada as it had in American law following the civil rights revolution, yet because of the backlash generated by the American experience and a time lag, the response may be the reverse, according to former Chief Justice Bora Laskin (1975: 222). Property protections in the old Bill of Rights incorporated the phrase "due process," which had "long since dropped out of Anglo-Canadian jurisprudence" (223). And the backlash was evident in the majority opinion by Chief Justice Laskin in the case of *Curr* v. *The Queen* (1972), where he discouraged Canadian jurists from following the Americans in this area other than to accept that the American Supreme Court had abandoned economic due process in 1937 because it had entered "a bog of legislative policy making in assuming to enshrine any particular theory . . . which has not been plainly expressed in the Constitution" (*Curr*, 1972: 902). Paradoxically, at least in terms of contemporary constitutional discourse, this jurisprudential position dominated the political give and take during the final drafting of the Charter of Rights in 1981.

This past is certainly prologue in this case and it may portend a future familiar to Americans. For as Professor Edward McWhinney said when the dust had barely cleared, "The seven English speaking premiers in the gang of eight who had fought to keep the constitution 'English' and to bar reception of all 'American' constitutional institutions and values, have, in losing so completely and so utterly in the end, simply speeded up the 'Americanization' (or modernization) of Canadian constitutional law" (1982: 112). This shift will no doubt elevate courts over Parliament and clothe disputations in the language of Fundamental rights.

In 1981, when Prime Minister Trudeau introduced the new constitution, property was eliminated. Here, concerns long noted by jurists like Laskin were expressed by the socialist New Democratic Party, whose support Trudeau and the Liberals needed in getting the constitution passed. The Trudeau government had been willing to include the "enjoyment of property" section from the old Bill of Rights in the Charter, but in January of 1981, support was withdrawn. This is said to have been at least partly in pursuit of backing from the New Democratic Party for the Constitution in the final days of the legislative struggle. Here, the Canadian socialist orientation reflects a fifty-year-old American view that judges are most likely to abuse their prerogatives in the interests of the propertied classes. But it also deserves note that the diversity of legal traditions in Canada, particularly the existence of the civil law system, has contributed to the belief that the law governing ordinary social relations ought to be a provincial responsibility rather than one left to either judges or legislators at the national level.

Even without explicit mention, judicial interpretation of property at all levels of government is likely to be greater under the Charter than it had been before repatriation. As Edward McWhinney said recently:

> Constitutional law is being recognized as a continuing interaction of different, sometimes directly competing social interests; constitutional law-making is becoming the resolution or synthesis of those conflicts. It is all rather American with the courts destined, as in the United States, to be at the heart of the process, whether they like it or not (McWhinney, 1982: 112).

Ultimately, however, the Giving Issue, like land policy generally, must be understood in terms of economic or market considerations. The ideological structures that make up the legal environment and the law of property in Canada and the United States affect economic choices and influence market developments at the same time that the law itself is subject to market considerations.

Conclusion

Giveaways in the western United States often take the form of desireable resources controlled by government. In Canada, such resources are also likely to be controlled by the federal government, as is the case with the oil fields off the Georges Bank. This is one area where institutional differences between the federal systems in Canada and the United States do not seem as evident. The major determinent of this sort of land sale or lease is market pressure. Here, the special responsibilities of the government as guardian of the public domain

The Giving Issue

have to be weighed against the immediate material advantage of private interests. In the most common eastern disposal situation, the government actually adds value to land and property by refurbishing buildings, providing tax advantages, or collecting parcels that as a bundle are worth more than they would be as individual parcels. Surplus property, which is often of little value, undergoes a system of government checks. With abandoned schools in Portland, Maine, the school department notifies the city. Where no municipal need is claimed, the property is turned over to the Economic Development Committee. Bureaucratic constraints stem as much from not knowing what to do with the property as from built-in protections. Larger parcels or projects with an economic interest behind them come under the economic development mandate immediately. Legal protections arise defensively in the United States and may develop in Canada with the introduction of the Charter.

Just as "takings" law was the protection government afforded to a market-centered society, "giving" is a way of looking at government policy so that market advantage does not get ignored. The relative difference in significance of the administrative section is directly parallel to the relative size of the autonomous profit-making enterprises. In this context, recognizing that individual rights are tied to private profit is simply unavoidable. In the United States, pragmatism and rights have always maintained a delicate balance. The promise of jobs is so great that institutions have been developing to meet the challenge, and for the last five years, urban development has been a measure of city and state administration. The economy has its own ideologies. The transformation of an abandoned waterfront into a private, commercial shipyard is seen not as a contribution to private wealth but rather in terms of economic development (and jobs). Still, the effort in the United States is nowhere near the scale of the Canadian provincial authority (see Table I). In part, this is because of the dominance of Washington relative to the states, although assistance from Washington is less than what we find in transportation and housing. To the extent that the experience of Maine is indicative, American institutions are moving away from conflicts over rights toward administration.

Thus, administration and litigation are exemplary institutional arrangements. In Canada, development policy is made in crown corporations. Similar institutions, such as the Port Authority of New York

TABLE I
The Atlantic Waterfront: Portland and Halifax, 1975–1985

Development	Cost to Public (in millions of $)	Land
PORTLAND		
BIW Expansion	46.7	Transfer
Pier	25.0	Eminent Domain
Ferry Terminal	0.5	—
HALIFAX		
Container Port	50.0	Nat Harbors Authorization
Waterfront Development Corporation	37.0	Purchase ($20 m)
Shipyards	14.5–51.5	NegotiatedTransfer

Sources: John Ferland, *Portland Press Herald,* May 29, 1982; Ian McAllister et al., *Projects in Search of Development* (1980), Institute of Public Affairs, Dalhousie University.

and New Jersey or Boston's Massport, are exceptional in the United States. These institutional giants are associated with transportation, an area which, along with public utilities, constitutes the special case of what supporters would like to call a public/private partnership in the United States. Yet, in Maine and most states, government involvement in economic development is largely mediative, and it is associated with courts and not planners. In a comparison of this sort, it is these differences that become interesting.

The institutional differences in government determine the outcomes, the nature of the participants, and the character of the discourse employed.[8] This is evident in the fact that Canadians rely on a public corporation comparable to a banking institution to handle development, while in the United States the development is taken directly to the people through a referendum and then to court. Maine, economically depressed for some time, has recently become frantic about the production of jobs, like much of the northeastern United States. In maritime Canada, development and employment have also been a potent policy issue. While, culture and material conditions would suggest similar patterns of response, the difference in how these issues are handled is striking. This difference is reflected in a greater role for the State in Canada and the pervasiveness of rights

The Giving Issue

claims reflecting the significance of individualism in the United States. Thus, the dynamic situation in this study has been the changing role of various institutions: the emergence of pragmatic doctrines of economic development in the United States and, more characteristic of legal ideology, the emergence in Canada of judicial review.

CHAPTER VII

Policing the Constitution

The difference between claiming a Social Security check and owning a share of stock or inherited land is the placid center of a potential policy storm. The difference is not like some other differences, such as sexual or racial ones, that we have learned to see as important for the kinds of rights we have. This one has rested nearly undisturbed while some people in America get better protection from the Constitution than others simply because they have more at stake. Recent scholarship holds that any difference between welfare payments and shares of stock will be evident in the language we use to speak and write about property. The chapter begins with judicial writing on constitutional entitlement that addresses distinctions between forms of property. There has been far more opportunity in this writing than conventional practice would suggest.

The point I hope to make as we conclude the analysis of entitlement as constitutional property is that what ordinary people can say, what they can hope to claim, is constrained or limited by interpretations of the sense in our Constitution in much the same way that I described for justices of the Supreme Court in Chapter I. Here, the ideological authority of the constitutional right for various forms of property is the foundation for an understanding of entitlement, which moves from testimony on the elimination of Social Security benefits to the level of ordinary language. Here, the politics of entitlement is traced to the practices that constitute possibilities and limit choice in

American politics. We see fundamental law in context by examining the Constitution's vernacular.

The standard against which the language of entitlement has been evaluated throughout this book is the constitutional property right derived from the Fifth Amendment.[1] By approaching this property right in terms of those who have lots of property and those who don't have much at all, we avoid the conventional focus on one or the other. That is, we resist the pull to separate research on welfare benefits from the property benefits received by the wealthy.[2] With this sort of analysis, at both the national institutions and in practice, the construction of entitlement is linked to new forms of State power. Here we see policing in the language of entitlement, the social relations of provider and client, and the specter of scarcity.

Doctrinal Opportunity

We have seen how the property right, once central to liberal theory, has been missing from conventional treatments of civil liberties (Abraham, 1982; and Chapter III above), dismissed from the debate on constitutional rights by the post-1937 Double Standard with its emphasis on civil rather than economic liberties (Funston, 1978). More recently, this distinction has been breaking down and the "idea of progress" (Bickel, 1970) has been transforming the conception of an economic liberty by including "new property" (Reich, 1964) like unemployment compensation, public assistance, and old-age insurance under the property right. Since *Goldberg* v. *Kelly* (1970), a legitimate expectation to the continuation of a statutory entitlement has been protected under the Constitution as property.[3] Property in statutory entitlements, which had only made sense for a few years, had become a protected interest according to the nation's highest court. Entitlement as property in *Perry* v. *Sindermann* (1971) amounted to the expectation of continued employment. There, Justice Potter Stewart observed that "property denotes a broad range of interests that are secured by 'existing rules or understandings.'"[4] The new right has given some modern entitlements the familiar presumption favoring the continuation that we associate with property. *Goss* v. *Lopez* (1975), involving high school students who were suspended without a hearing, reflected a "bundle of rights" scale developed by Holmes during the *Lochner* Era. According to this arrangement, property was treated as a complex of interests (*Pennsylvania Coal* v. *Mahon*, 1922), and due process varied with the competing interests. In *Goss*, the suspension amounted to a deprivation substantial enough to overcome deference to high school administrators.

Although entitlement claims have been less successful in the Supreme Court since the mid-1970's, the justices generally acknowledged property in a variety of new entitlements. They allowed termination of federal disability benefits without a prior hearing, for instance, while granting that benefits provided by the government were protected by the Fifth Amendment (*Mathews* v. *Eldridge*, 1976: 334). Property has ranged across interests as diverse as a foster family desiring to remain intact (*Smith* v. *Organ. of Foster Families*, 1977) and a medical student claiming to have been unjustly dismissed from school (*Board of Curators* v. *Horowitz*, 1978). Deference to statutory entitlements, coming at a time of diminished constitutional concern for more marketable forms of property, drew from the idea that "property does not have rights, people have rights" (*Lynch* v. *Household Finance Corp.*, 1972), thus using civil right to enhance protection of the traditional forms of property. A 1981 case in which the Supreme Court ruled in favor of unemployment compensation for a worker who quit a job because it conflicted with his religious beliefs exemplified this civil liberties dimension (*Thomas* v. *Review Board*, 1981). The enthusiasm for such protection and its foundation in concern for civil liberties was quite different from the view of entitlement expressed by the Supreme Court 150 years earlier, when it described the poor as a "moral pestilence" (*City of New York* v. *Miln*, 1837).

Yet, there are still two levels of constitutional property protection in the Supreme Court, one for the wealthy and one for the poor— the first based on right, the second on need. We have described this as a new Double Standard and it can be seen in recent discussion of entitlement by the Supreme Court. In 1987, two cases announced a day apart came down on opposite sides of the property question with little more than the class of the recipient distinguishing them. In *Nollan* v. *California Coastal Comm.*, Antonin decided June 26, Justice Antonin Scalia, writing for the majority, reviewed a ruling of the California Court of Appeals upholding the requirement of a public easement across a beachfront section of private property regulated by the California Coastal Commission. The easement was a condition for granting a permit to build a house. The Supreme Court held this easement to be a taking of private property by the state (Chapters II and III).

Scalia built his opinion on extraordinary solicitude for "James and Marilyn Nollan" who "own a beachfront lot" and "a small bungalow" (*Nollan*, 683). It's hard to feel too sorry for the Nollans, even with the specter they faced—hordes of beachgoers traipsing across their property. They wanted to build a bigger house and needed the rules to be changed. But the tone of the opinion in this case leaves no doubt about Scalia's deep concern for this couple. He asserts that requiring an easement would most certainly be an expropriation of property. The standard is that "a use restriction may constitute a 'taking' if not reasonably necessary to the effectuation of a substantial government purpose" (687; see also Chapter II).

The second case, *Bowen v. Gilliard*, announced on June 25, 1987, dealt with an injunction issued by Judge James B. McMillan of the U.S. District Court for the Western District of North Carolina. The injunction called the change in eligibility requirements mandated by Congress "a taking of property" from children receiving support payments on the basis of state law requiring child support money to be used for the exclusive benefit of the child for whom it had been obtained. A forced assignment of the support money to the state in return for AFDC benefits for the entire family constituted an expropriation of that child's private property.[5]

Justice John Paul Stevens, for the majority on the Supreme Court, addressed the property claim directly if rather unsympathetically. He began his opinion with the threat of scarcity "as part of its major effort to reduce the federal deficit" (*Bowen*, 493) before describing the Deficit Reduction Act of 1984, which authorized AFDC to require that a family's eligibility for benefits must take into account "the income of all parents, brothers and sisters living in the same home" (494). Other references to "limited Federal and State resources" set the context for discussion of the property right relative to AFDC. The argument advanced by the justice is based on the right/privilege distinction usually linked to Holmes's opinion in *MacAuliffe v. Mayor of New Bedford* (1892), although Stevens did not choose to note that connection. "Congress," he continued, "is not, by virtue of having instituted a social welfare program, bound to continue it at all, much less at the same benefit level (503)." Stevens observed that it would be "strange" if in providing benefits the state might also be said to have taken the property of some members of the family.

While there are different authors in these opinions, the tradition of institutional scholarship allows comparison of majority opinions as authoritative statements. In these opinions, the higher standard of review traditionally associated with social justice questions gives way to protection for those who would build on the wealth that they have. Thus the rights of those who would develop the coast have strong prima facie protection, and additional weight is added by the picture of the beachfront bungalow and a class-based empathy for personal rights of the higher economic kind that we have seen less of under the Double Standard of the last fifty years. The opinions reflect the strength of the upper class property owner in the eyes of justices who share positions of significant wealth. This is the basis for a more comprehensive, yet more mundane, policing in the administration of the welfare state.

The *Goldberg* decision began to develop a property right that could be pivotal relative to both liberty and equality in the modern State (Cotterrell, 1986; Friedman, 1981). Yet, for a number of reasons, some of which are evident above, we are advised to be cautious about relying on "legal contrivances" to produce social change. There is legitimate concern that the real gains from a revival of property rights will be for the wealthy and not the newly entitled (McCann, 1984; Levy, 1983; Van Alstyne, 1977). Such fears are naturally intensified by the composition of the present federal bench. But, the articulation of new rights has a legacy that draws from communities (Lynd, 1984) as well as the Supreme Court. Although most social science research relies on recent mythology concerning judges as the source for fundamental law, an older tradition draws law from social convention. Testimony before Congress reflects some of that convention, and there is much more for one who can figure out where and how to look.

Entitlement Practice

In "Property, Authority and the Criminal Law," Douglas Hay (1915) interprets the interplay between property, forms of personal dependence, and criminal law in 18th century England. Like the work of E. P. Thompson in *Whigs and Hunters* (1975), Hay looks at the "Black Acts," a set of draconian provisions for severely punishing a range of offenses against the King from minor incivilities to poaching deer in the royal forests. At this time, when law was displacing religion as the main legitimizing ideology, it was a complex practice surrounded by the elements of terror, majesty, justice, and mercy. The rhetoric of the death sentence, the ever-present sanction of the gallows, the localized and personal system by which the rural poor and occasionally the gentry were convicted—often released on technicalities or pardoned—all produced a chaotic system by which respect for property and property owners was maintained through the rule of law.

Property today surrounds us with practices equally fascinating. They operate when a suburban landowner guides his lawn mower to a certain spot and then turns back, even if there is objectively and materially more lawn to cut, and they operate to structure the exchange when a landlord and a tenant discuss conditions making it difficult for her to pay the rent. Given the practices of property, some grass gets cut and some does not, and the character of rent, with a giver and a receiver, may reveal the sex of the tenant. The character of entitlement, and lots more, is evident in these practices. Property forms the basis for the civilities of lawn cutting and arranging rent schedules. We say "it's mine" and fight on or concede to others as a function of the credibility of our property claims (see Merry, 1990: ch. 3, 5).

Those claims are also policed in terms of what talk is considered correct. For instance, in the summer of 1981, Congress voted to phase out the post secondary economic benefits administered by the Social Security Administration for an estimated total savings of $2.3 billion.[6] More than 3 million children and 750,000 widows and widowers were collecting survivors benefits in 1983 when most of the changes went into effect (Rubin, 1983: 69). The testimony of Alice James, of Chestertown, Maryland, over these cuts (Joint Hearing, 1982) shows her understanding of entitlement:

> I am the widow of a scholar who taught at Washington College for 25 years. . . . As a widowed parent I must convey to you the plight of not just my own children, but of thousands like them who may be unjustly deprived of the benefits their dead parents earned for them.

Policing the Constitution

James speaks of injustice, but her sense is that the deprivation may not strictly be illegal. In spite of benefits being denied after twenty-five years of contributions to an entitlement program, her testimony did not appeal to law nor did she or others seek legal redress for the policy change denying benefits to their children. After explaining the impact of the cuts on her four children, aged fifteen to twenty-one, and testifying about the hardships the cuts would bring, she continued:

> parents like my husband took the social security program into consideration when they examined their life insurance coverage[.] And just as they expected their insurance companies to honor their commitment to a prearranged program, so too they expected the Government of their country to honor its commitment.

The language of insurance is part of the legacy of Social Security, at least in the minds of recipients like Alice James, although it no longer has much credibility among theorists and policymakers. The more professional understanding is in terms of need and much of James' testimony is about need: "Because my husband and his employer were compelled to contribute to the social security program, he could not afford the additional life insurance that would otherwise compensate us for the loss of social security coverage." Yet there are suggestions of the depth of the entitlement, of the sense of loss and betrayal. "Congress has robbed these children of the educational opportunities their parents earned for them. It has robbed them of faith in their Government."

Similarly, a surviving child, Jacqueline Arrington of Towson State University, spoke at the same sessions of the entitlement that had been taken away from her in the following way:

> I expected to receive social security throughout my college education. My father expected it before he died. He paid into it like many men and women today and expected his daughter to be able to continue her education. . . .
>
> I just feel it is totally unfair to a student whose parents died and the parents that died who expected their children to be taken care of by the Government. . . .
>
> I did not receive any notification. I did not know about the cuts until last month.

Again, fairness rather than illegality is the language of entitlement for this former recipient. We see this also in the letter of Mary Gaudioso to the hearing, in which she asks, "Is it morally correct to dangle the carrot of higher education in front of our noses for over ten years and then yank it cruelly away without any warning?" Her "feeling" pretty obviously is one of unfairness. This is explicit in the testimony of Ginger Ackerman, "I don't think it's very fair."

Thus, in these cases the tone is one of disappointed resignation and in fact the hearings concerned impact rather than presenting any realistic hope of overturning the decision. Chair Carl D. Perkins of Kentucky, addressed the effects of the cutbacks in Social Security benefits on the student aid programs in a fashion that was characteristic of legislative "concern." The issue was policy and education for those in need, not entitlement. "We would like to know," he said, "whether needy students who would have received these benefits will be receiving benefits under the other student aid programs." Congressman Dale E. Kildee of Michigan spoke in terms of trust. He said, "I could not believe what happened to the funding of education and social programs last year. . . . I cannot believe that Congress allowed that real breach of trust." The language of right and law, the language of the new property would have made a difference here, and its absence, the lack of a legal claim of entitlement as an aspect of constitutional property deserves note. Entitlement is weak for survivors and the political numbers are less consequential. Congressman Paul Simon called a hearing on the impact of the 1983 budget cuts. There, Alice Rivlin of the Congressional Budget Office described the political considerations in the bill in the following way:

> Because the largest numbers of people are in the retirement programs, we could . . . save a relatively large amount of money with a relatively small impact per person with moderate reductions in those programs . . . [by] lowering the COLA's.

Student aid had a much larger impact on a smaller number of people, but in a rights analysis, this does not diminish the violence done to expectation in the name of economic exigency.

Evidence of widespread litigation on this issue would have suggested that the language at the hearing was atypical, that litigious Americans didn't sit back but that they fought for their rights. The ab-

Policing the Constitution

sence of such litigation attests to the fact that James's testimony was a characteristic way of reacting, at least in 1982, to the denial of entitlement as a result of policy change. The language in which this policy was addressed was weak, and politics around the issue was circumscribed even before issues of mobilization arose. This is the "policing" of constitutional property.

The idea comes from Professor Stuart Hall (1978), who used policing to describe the creation of a crisis in "law and order" while studying crime in England. His contribution was to show the involvement of various actors in stimulating the fear of mugging. Stuart Scheingold in *The Politics of Law and Order* (1984) provided a vivid image of the menacing stranger to illuminate this construction of a fear of crime. Entitlement is like mugging, in that it is an ideological construction affecting the way people act politically. In the 1980s, rather than risking outrage at the denial of settled expectations, policymakers told us that budgetary exigencies were overwhelming. The implication was that the property of the poor was vulnerable to shifts in policy.

As claimants, managers, and lawyers understand entitlement, a form of property constitutes social life. While at least a generation of research has described what happens to law in communities and in the hallways of the courthouse, most of the findings weren't presented as law. The view was that law comes from the courts, and in the community there is something else, its "impact" or reality. This perspective was limited for at least two important reasons. First, it relied on a notorious gap between law and action, which limited attention to contextual sources of law. Second, it failed to account for the significance of law in interpretive communities (Harris, 1982; O'Neill, 1981; Brigham, 1978).

To the extent that law operates from such communities, there is law "out there" (Macaulay, 1963). There is law in the practices of property in general and entitlement in particular, and it is "policed" without guns and squad cars. I saw it in my research one hot summer day in Northern California. Susan (1988), a clerk at Diamond Lumber Company, referring to a particularly attractive lake that rises out of the foothills like an oasis, described swimming as "against the law, its private property."[7] Alice (1988), a legally blind, eighty-one-year-old retired child-care worker ended a query into eligibility for Supplemental Security Income (SSI) benefits with the statement, "I probably have too much." At another point, Irv (1988), a planning professor told me, "I used to say [to planners], do whatever you want and the law can make it right. After *Nollan* I can't say that any more." These were three forms of property law in practice. In each case, language reflects understanding of what property is, or "what law does" (Lermack, 1989). Although they have different contexts and express different interests, these statements are examples of law in operation, testimony on what it is.

The data for legal practices of this sort are people's words about entitlement. I have collected them self-consciously in Chico, California; Holyoke, Massachusetts; and New York City; but I watch for examples wherever I go. This now includes social commentary ranging from the extraordinary book by the late Alfred Winslow Jones, *Life, Liberty, and Property*, a survey of working class ideas on property published in 1941, to the book by Professors Sam Bowles and Herb Gintis, *Democracy and Capitalism*, which was published in 1986. A set of field notes referred to by Professors Frances Piven and Richard Cloward in their seminal book *Regulating the Poor* (1971) demonstrated the utility of identifying practices of this sort (see also Perin, 1977; Greenberg, 1973). Whenever possible, however, recorded or documentary material has been used, although it makes people nervous. John, in Holyoke (1988), wanted me to know that his opinions were his own and not those of the Welfare Department. In fact, opinion of either sort is of less concern than the ordinary practices of the welfare department.

Landowners, social welfare recipients, managers, advocates, administrators, and jurists all discuss property. They do it in the office in sessions with clients, in courts, administrative hearings and on the street. They do it through memoranda, applications for benefits and in appeals. These linguistic practices reflect shared understandings that organize people's lives. D. (1988), a newly hired property manager with experience as an advocate for the homeless, spoke of entitlement to subsidized housing as having the same status as regular housing, she reflected a belief influenced by her work with a homeless shelter. N. (1988), a more experienced manager, describing the difficulty of evicting undesirable tenants, said: "The judge just feels that, well, if they're in subsidized housing, where else are they gonna go? You can't get rid of them." Both are testifying to what the law is.

Linguistic studies have taught that law is not just on the books or a body of rules. Professor Murray Edelman's interest in language has given support to my own. For a generation of political scientists, Edelman represented the cutting edge of social research with attention to symbols. My initial work on the language of the American Constitution was supported by his example and that of Professor Hanna Pitkin, whose *Wittgenstein and Justice* (1972) introduced American political theorists to a nonpositivist approach to symbols. In addition, Edelman placed the language of the "helping professions" (1977) in a political context and Professor Sally Merry has shown us various ways citizens with little political clout employ legal claims as an expression of their sense of justice (Merry, 1990; see also Sarat, 1989).

Law is in the knowledge and understanding of communities, those who share ways of talking about things like getting a benefit check or not getting one or getting something that is not one,—or those who know when a rented room is a tenant's to exclude the landlord and when it isn't. Law, in this sense, includes understandings about where to go to demand justice (Merry, 1990) and knowledge about what to expect that is rooted in convention (Greenhouse, 1986) Law in both senses operates linguistically as an expression of a culture and a basis for belief. Law then is ideological in the sense that action is constituted by it.

The Constitution in Social Life

The law on entitlement is particularly evident in the language of people working with the government. Law becomes their ordinary language. In this sense, language establishes "the law" in practice. Where there is class or economic conflict, the language of ownership and possession, indeed of right and wrong, is contested while stability or social peace is naturally characterized by shared ideas about property. In Akron, Ohio, in the 1930s, the subject of Jones's investigation, the struggle between capital and labor was "open, dramatic, and bitter" (Jones, 1941: 115). Union leaders who would regulate the efforts of labor in pursuit of a higher wage were treated as outlaws. Jones cites the testimony of Paul W. Litchfield, President of Goodyear, before a Senate Committee in support of the Mayor of Akron's call to "gang up for constitutional law and order in this wonderful city" and "say to those out-of-town radical leaders . . . get the hell out of here" (1941: 117).

Jones's study focused on the issue of property rights nearly fifty years ago and quoted extensively from all social classes in the rubber town of Akron. While judges and labor leaders in New York were willing to uphold the contractual obligation of the Blue Dale Dress Company to stay within a five-cent fare of the plant, storekeepers, farmers, magnates, and workers disagreed over the prerogatives of ownership (Jones, 1941: 151–53). Jones saw the development of class views on basic rights as new, comparing it to James Bryce's *American Commonwealth* (1914: 342) with its unified conception of property. We see today a remarkable return to a perspective shared by much of the public, at least on the dominant property issues. This is the consequence of the new forms of policing and a newly constructed social order. The expectation and aspiration for a universal property is sometimes the basis for transformative social theory like the "community right to industrial property" proposed by Staughton Lynd (1987). This is an effort to broaden the category of proprietarian protection in order to include industrial labor and it draws on opportunities within the conception of property. But to most Americans there is very little fluidity in the concept of property.

In the administration of an urban housing program today, the language is matter-of-fact and highly bureaucratic. N. (1988), commenting on different housing subsidies she manages, began to count, then guessed "six or seven," pointing out that a lot of paperwork is the same, "like whether it's a 707 or Sec. 8." In a Butte County, California, administrative hearing, the authority of an "all county letter" from the state welfare office was described by Wilson, a welfare worker, as "interpretation we've been going on, an interpretation that is expected to be promulgated." It turned out to be "the law" (*Rapacz v. Butte County Welfare Dept.*, 1988) in the all-important sense that this convention settled the matter.

But, it is not just officials whose vernacular amounts to legal practice. "Aid paid pending" describes a status familiar to claimants and advocates that can extend a welfare benefit allocation a month or two until there is a hearing (K. M., 1988). "Default," is a shout that rings through Housing Court when the summary docket is called. It comes most often from property owners and managers as a request for sum-

Policing the Constitution

mary judgment from the court. And, a gallon of milk, in paralegal practice, becomes a crucial indicator: "A gallon of milk weighs ten pounds. If you can't lift and carry a gallon of milk and we can get a doctor to certify it you pretty much have your disability" (C. M., 1988). Here, experience, not a law degree, is the most significant influence in interpreting how the Social Security Administration will respond to contests over entitlement that get this far.

Quite often, however, there is a distinction between managers and claimants on the kinds of things they refer to as their entitlement. For instance, in an interview at the Disabled and the Law Project in Chico, California (W., 1988), a giant man ("between four hundred and five hundred pounds") described his entitlement in terms of two very concrete aspects of his relationship to the welfare bureaucracy: the documents that he kept in a little white bank pouch and the people he knew who would handle these documents for him, interpreting them and moving them along. Already on disability, he was applying for Supplemental Security Income (SSI). He didn't read or write, but he saw his benefits "in there" (in the pouch) and he hoped that, with the case worker's help, the papers might be turned into something more negotiable. Pointing to his papers, he said: "I did all that. I goofed it up. Out of the Redding office, Norma, she's good people. See the things in there, I don't understand all the words. . . . I see the letters on different cans and boxes and I know what the box is." The client described his entitlement in terms of documents and people, not unlike the way John Marshall talked about a similar relation in the more celebrated case of *Marbury* v. *Madison* (1803). For J. (1988), a "case manager" in Holyoke, Massachusetts, entitlement was something recipients didn't understand, a complicated idea often simplified, he said, by the poorly educated or non-English-speaking claimants to pieces of paper and signatures like those the man in Chico traced to his bank pouch.

In practice, those "connected" to the government as agents also have lives and identities as clients in some other context, and those "connected" to the government as clients identify with the agents at least in some senses of a common humanity. As it blurs the authoritative barriers, this connection is integral to the policing of property at the street level. The distinctive feature of the managers is that they gain authority from the State through their positions. What they say has institutional authority, and there is a language that goes with those positions. Managers of subsidized housing and welfare workers in Holyoke, Massachusetts, who see themselves as helpers, characterize their knowledge as superior to that of the clients. Their descriptions of what recipients know in terms of "the signatures or the forms they need" (J., 1988) suggest the authority of law in a very informal practice. Superior knowledge, authoritatively asserted in distinctive linguistic forms, affirms administrative authority.

In these contexts, helping and therapeutic discourses cover the relations of power that chart the path of the law. An administrative law judge in Oroville, California, characterizes a case as "lose, lose" (*Wong Duc* v. *Butte County Welfare Dept.*, 1988), drawing on his mediation theory to indicate that he would like to do something, but can't. A few years before, "no win" would have done the same job. Language of this sort is familiar in dispute resolution practice (Harrington and Merry, 1988) but not common to the general population, yet. The language of therapy in official discourse clashes with the conditions of material deprivation as experienced by claimants. The disjunction was evident in response to a question on the intake form about "anxiety, stress or depression": "Yeah I feel it ever day in this country. I see people in the streets and all, people oughten to live that way. You see it on TV all the time." The paralegal continued, "Do you feel it because of your sickness?" The recipient answered: "I worry so much ever day. I was so much down in the dump I started talking to the people about social security, I went to the welfare department, it just gets to me." For the recipient, there were real problems, real desperation—there was no problem with his head.

When Murray Edelman (1977; 1988: 72) discussed the language of social workers, his point was that the "helping" professions are ambivalent toward those they work with, and with their help comes discipline. In shifting from power to property this ambivalence becomes an aspect of the law of entitlement. As the case worker refines an understanding of right in the interest of the client—sometimes by correction, as when K. M. (1988) instructed one of her clients over the phone that she could not refuse both school and work in order to stay with her child, and sometimes by illustration and illumination, as when C. M. (1988) instructed a claimant on the extraordinary delay in processing claims with a shrug of her shoulders—his or her interpretation of the limits imposed by the Social Security Administration becomes the law in practice, however tentative it is articulated. Sometimes the authority of therapeutic language is a resignation about "the way it is." The power gained by establishing a relationship is certainly relevant in advancing an interpretation, but in the context of law as the practice of a community, the more relevant consideration is that the nature and substance of the law is often grounded in ambiguity and helplessness.[8] That is its strength.

The language of the markets in property has its psychological dimension too. In the psychology of fear, anxiety in the market place is something to be acted on, something to be exploited. In a speech to the North Valley Property Owners Association, a representative from a new development (Donna, 1988) described property ownership as opportunity, particularly for profit. Throughout talk about property, the marketplace and scarcity are presented as realities that require adjustment in the case of the poor or that present an opportunity for profit in the case of those who are investing. The remarkable power of the policing that is done on property is evident in the extent to which the market is understood as real and the needs of welfare entitlement holders are seen as subjective. Here, the opportunity to accumulate wealth by speculation is more fully protected than the wealth that is promised to those with nothing to wager on the market.

To link these interpretations with law, to show that the practice of property is law, a relationship with the State must be made explicit. Not all knowledge of entitlement is law. Sometimes the authority of State law is laced with professional savvy, sometimes it is accompanied by class domination, and sometimes it refers explicitly to the old black letter stuff itself. But, control of the State apparatus is crucial to authority in entitlement. With administrators from Social Security, the role of the State, of official law, is a matter of institutional style (Rose, 1988). With welfare workers, the State may be an entity to be derided and its authority denied. Sometimes they present themselves as operating against the State. With lawyers, the State may be a source of authority, as references to decisions reveal, but it may also be an entity of little consequence, a way of elevating their own stature (R. D., 1988). In the case of counselors or staff in the housing project, the State is spoken of as an impediment at the same time that Housing Court is employed as a collection agency (N., 1988). Still, in each case the authority from which interpretations are made, the source of entitlement, is in some respects State authority.

At its base, this is the authority of a credible interpretation of what is required, a declaration of what will come about whether it is an imperious voice on the other end of the telephone line (in Social Security's preferred manner of communicating), a minority face blocking a window at the Welfare Office, or a sympathetic caseworker indicating with a shrug, that is just the way it is. The language of officials is shared with those "outside," but the side of the reception desk one operates from is a key to the authority of law. N. (1988) defended a new barrier placed in the rental office she ran as having been put up after she had been "slugged by an applicant" who was "screaming at Millie . . . and . . . calling people horrendous names. . . . I asked [her] to leave or she was going to get a free ride in the black and white. . . . She smacked me right in the face. . . . We had to do something." Violence had broken down the civility of the office and the physical restraints had to be reinforced.

Ordinary language reveals the law of entitlement in practice as officials and clients talk about entitlement. Where the black letter law is absent, as is the case in much legal practice, reliance is instead on knowledge of the steps to be taken and the people to be seen. Here, a distinction between officials and clients becomes pivotal, and judgments are made about the balance of interests and the appropriate responses in terms of the languages of entitlement. At another level, these distinctions are blurred and the reality of institutional power glossed over, but physical barriers may also be erected where authority is threatened and civil processes failing.

The "Is" and the "Ought"

In the discussion of entitlement before Congress, there was a reluctance on the part of participants in hearings to describe the violation they felt as a violation of the law, except in the metaphorical sense of "robbery." There was little evidence of fear, at least we saw no evidence that they desperately wanted to call their deprivation illegal rather than immoral or horrible. This is the subject of sociolegal research by anthropologists in America that takes off in a direction charted by the movement to understand the nature of disputing in America. Work by Professor Carol J. Greenhouse, such as *Praying for Justice: Faith, Order and Community* (1986), underscores the tranquility in American communities and helps us to understand its social construction.

While building on the contemporary interest in difference and disputes, Greenhouse's study of a small town takes us into the shared ideas and patterns of thought we have called, as she has, ideologies. Her town of Hopewell is pseudonymous, but it is southern and was studied in the mid-1970s and again in 1980. This is a predominately Baptist community constituted around family and faith rather than the courts. The harmonious character she finds, and attributes to religion, may be more characteristic of the culture of basic rights like property than Akron in the 1930s. This is certainly characteristic of the American legal culture as it has been described by social scientists of the last decade, where a preoccupation with issues like high school basketball had more salience than decisions of the Supreme Court (Dolbeare and Hammond, 1971). Although it is indeed a view contrary to the popular image of a litigious society, it looks very much like an accurate representation of social practice.

The world of religion constitutes for Hopewell a more significant realm than that of the law courts, just as the world of basketball had pushed litigation to the background for political scientists a decade before. In considering the ways in which entitlement claims or constitutional property rights are policed, we have been particularly attentive to the vernacular where the policing has prevented development of public understanding of the right. Following the developments associated with the Welfare Rights Movement and Charles Reich's "new property" jurisprudence, shifts in decisions of the Supreme Court had a significance far beyond what the authority of the institution requires. From the failures of liberals in the law schools to continue the developments in progressive jurisprudence in the face of limited possibilities for litigation to Reich's own much more dramatic immersion in the counter culture, the entitlement claims suggested in the late 1960s and early 1970s failed to sustain their initial aspiration. Contemporary research, like that of Greenhouse, reinforces the social and property relations that are extant without their seeming to be under the slightest pressure.

One suspects, from knowing how property is talked about, that the participants in the Senate hearing, which has become so central to this analysis, were not advised to speak of the deprivation in the terms of legal entitlement. They may or may not have thought about it in those terms themselves, indeed, its absence from the debates is more striking than evidence of a particular beneficiary being told what to say. While, our democratic conceit holds that how we think springs from within, the study of language and ideologies teaches otherwise. In the case of property, a contested concept—that is, one where politics is conducted around the potential meanings (Connolly, 1974)—what it makes sense to say is subject to the dictates of influentials. This is the sense in which property is policed in constitutional practice. In America, the meaning of law and the articulation of credible or authoritative rights has become increasingly professional. The professionals do their policing in talk about property.

A recent discussion of entitlement by law Professor William Simon shows the professional policing of the boundaries of property and a professional contest for authority over the concept (1985; see also Clune, 1975). Simon contrasts the jurisprudence of welfare entitlement developed by social workers during the New Deal with the lawyer's welfare jurisprudence of the last twenty years. He says that Reich styled the new property argument as an attack on Progressive jurisprudence. This body of thought about law and politics, according to Simon, "saw people as having no rights that couldn't be taken away to serve the public interest." The account held that "prior to 1960s welfare benefits were regarded as gratuities and recipients as incapable of rational choice and in need of supervision." The milestones for the new property movement begin with Reich's 1965 article, then the 1968 case of *King* v. *Smith* striking down the "man in the house" rules, and it concluded with *Goldberg* v. *Kelly* in 1970.

Simon points out that the advocates of new property rights included law Professors Joel Handler and Ed Sparer along with Charles Reich. Sparer (1968) argued that "social work ideology holds [that those] who have public or quasi-public power . . . should use that power to determine the place, manner, and habits of life for those who are helpless and dependent because of poverty." Handler (1960) said that "traditional social work for the poor . . . rests comfortably on the pathology theory of poverty." For Simon, the "truth" was that "social welfare jurisprudence" had already been working for change. The movement, he finds, "grew out of the Progressive critique of classical legalism (the conservative legal thought of the substantive due process era) early in this century."

Since political scientists don't do what lawyers do, the constraints on what they say operate at another level of professional authority. In the communities of political science until a little while ago, less and less was being said about the substance of law or doctrine as social research. Doctrine and decisions were the subject of teaching and public comment, but political scientists found themselves less and less able to contribute to the development of doctrines or offer research on doctrine to their community. There are some exceptions, such as Professor Timothy O'Neill's article (1981) on equality and Professor William Harris's (1982) discussion of the relation of rights to the polity. Both were published in the American Political Science Review, yet they failed to set off a movement.[9] An interest in economic questions is the basis for my fascination with the contributions of Professors Richard Funston (1975) and Martin Shapiro (1978). Funston and Shapiro transcended the perspectives of traditionalists. They were attentive early on to recent concerns expressed by Rogers Smith (1987). Quite often, however, there is a tendency in social science research to describe the new property of the decade from 1965 to 1975 as no longer viable (Nagel, 1986) or to treat the issue as primarily a matter of normative political theory (Allett, 1987; Levy, 1983). Professor Shep Melnick (1987) has begun to bridge this gap with his discussion of what he calls "programmatic rights." These are in substance very close to the new property idea, and Melnick has fashioned a realm of participation for social research that may be expanded to include research into conventional practices.

Scholars know that law is more than black letter texts and that it must include how these texts are interpreted. Law in the community is also more than what judges or legislators say it is. Law is a kind of knowledge grounded in the credibility and institutional power of governing institutions. Creative interpretation of entitlement by lawyers, counselors, administrators, and judges is lawmaking when it limits what is conventionally thought possible. To claim that this is not simply implementation or enforcement, is not to deny the institutional sources of law but only to acknowledge the significance of contextual sources for understanding entitlement in communities like Chico and Holyoke. E. P. Thompson, in a rejoinder to those who think law is simply an outgrowth of class power, described law as mediating class relations to the advantage of the rulers *and* imposing inhibitions on the rulers at the same time (Thompson, 1975). Law mystifies class rule but is more than mere sham; it constitutes the social world in which we live. Professor Boa Santos argues that the constitution of our "legal life" takes place in the "intersection of different legal orders," which are "reproduced by multiple mechanisms of acculturation and socialization" (1987: 298).

The intersection is perhaps a little too complicated, a little too European. Law at the level of the welfare office, the project, the street can be seen in talk about knowledge and the movement around what we know in talk about property. In an interview with a welfare worker in Holyoke, the clear and perceptive observation was that recipients "sometimes don't know what they are entitled to, they just know they need a signature" (J., 1988). This familiar observation is the key to the vernacular for constitutional property. It means more in the present context than it might on the street. In stating that the recipients know nothing about law and get "what they want" due to the largess of the managers, the observation is a denial of the legal foundation for a property claim.

There is a very concrete relationship between ideas and communities of interpretation, although it is sometimes overlooked due to the popularity of the interpretive turn in academic practice (Brigham and Harrington, 1989). The indeterminacy critique misses the policing function, including the role of groups and ideas in constituting social life. This must be understood through institutions and communities wielding control over what we can say with authority. We can see the manifestations of "law that constitutes" in contemporary struggles over housing. We rarely hear the homeless lament their condition as a denial of legal entitlement; their name says they do not have property. The movement for housing draws instead from sympathy for their condition. It is a charitable claim. As law professors Douglas Hay, Karl Klare, and others made clear over the last generation, this sympathy, like the grace of the gentry in the late Middle Ages, reaffirms hierarchies. Describing "Praxis" here in terms of the seeming irrationality of the legal system in the late Middle Ages, Hay tells of attempts to put the legal system on a more secure footing by making punishment sure and efficient. But Hay points out the advantage of the pardons, the grace controlled by the gentry, as an affirmation of their hegemony.

The distinction between the "homeless" and "squatters" in New York City from 1987 to 1989 has been a dramatic example of the power of conceptions of entitlement to determine aspiration and hence constitute the terrain of politics. The "homeless" are conceptually, linguistically, and politically precluded from making claims of legal entitlement. Although some of the same political terrain seems to be shared, "squatters" have a very different view of property. In the Lower East Side of New York City, the description of illegally occupied city owned buildings as "squats" is a political move that challenges the authority of the city by a claim of entitlement exercised as occupancy. This claim is understood as a radical assertion of right based on need that is only minimally mediated by the matter of title.

For the homeless, on the other hand, one sees the affirmation of title in the claim of need. Following the Listeners' Action on Homelessness and Housing, sponsored by radio station WBAI in New York City, activists proclaimed their movement a success by heralding the numbers of people who marched or were arrested,[10] the coverage and the support among lawmakers, all with clear affirmation that the homeless were without property, without entitlement, without legal rights to housing. Thus, biases reflecting the hierarchies of attitude scholarship are evident in the language of property, and the framework of the 1950s with its distrust of the citizen is reflected in the way we speak about entitlement.

Wealth and poverty are legal constructs based on entitlement. The law of property makes some people poor and some not. The wealth of those societies in which marketplace allocations prevail presents itself as an accumulation by right, its unit being an individual property right. A property right is, in this sense, a claim against the State, a legal thing that affects human action. In relation to kinds of property, the forms are the sort of things around which opinion is arrayed. Title to land, a financial aid package, or building permit, these forms are part of how we see the world, how we learn what we are entitled to. We know them as appropriate or off beat, coherent or dumb, and the politics of such things is more commonly in how they are distributed than what they are. In the end, our picture of the vernacular reveals ways of talking (and consequently thinking) about entitlement that provides a new sense of the what, where, and who and embeds politics in linguistic possibility.

Conclusion

Three points bring this inquiry to conclusion. One is methodological. It describes social research on the Constitution and recalls efforts made in this book to establish a sociological approach to legal entitlement. The effort has required attention to convention and the social obligations on which it is based. Both convention and social obligation challenge the High Court orientation in contemporary constitutional law. Another point is substantive. Turning to constitutional sense and expectation, we draw attention to the special status of gentry categories of property. Here, the property of the wealthy protects the individual prerogatives of those with a great deal of property. I suggest that these categories are wrong as a matter of the provisions in the American Constitution because they fail to account for the relevance of legitimate expectations in property law. The final point to be made for the politics of constitutional law is strategic. It addresses interpretive traditions and rights claims. There is very serious concern among many who understand the claim that legitimate and particularly settled expectation is just the sort of formulation that those with privilege are likely to seize upon. My answer here is that the leverage to be gained from a right to welfare property is not simply instrumental. The reconceptualization it should foster has much broader significance for the politics of entitlement.

Conclusion

Social Research on the Constitution

Many years ago, before the present era in social research, governing institutions were not understood by what they produced: decisions, opinions, and statutes. At least in the literature of social science, institutions were understood more by how they operated. This was the black letter institutionalism of Woodrow Wilson, the scholar of parliamentary government, and it remains healthy right up to the work of Edward Corwin, on whom I have drawn throughout this book. Scholars like Wilson and Corwin based constitutional interpretation on knowledge of how things were done in the American system. At the end of the nineteenth century, a constitutional style existed that was based on inquiry into the structures and processes of government, the governing conventions. Over the years, however, it drew more and more on the opinions of the Supreme Court.

Behavioralism, as an offshoot of realism in post–World War II political science, turned attention to the result or policy outcomes of institutions, and prediction took the place of description. Since the Constitution has come to be identified with the Supreme Court, realism focuses on inquiry into the "realities" in that institution. The more recent public choice perspective is an outgrowth of this orientation evident in Anglo-American jurisprudence and in the new analysis of property rights (Sproule-Jones, 1983). The result of all this is that in the first instance social research on the substance of constitutional rights was rarely done. Political scientists relied instead on Supreme Court opinions, which their research told them were mere rationalizations. Secondly, the research that did address substantive rights lacked confidence and was so often seen as derivative of lawyers' research that it became so.

In the last few years, some scholarship has shifted attention back to the institutions themselves with less concern about outcomes. The shift has been characterized by a portrayal of the relative autonomy of institutions and by recognition that processes that recent social science describes as "symbolic" constitute the terrain of political life (March and Olsen, 1984: 741). In contemporary social science, the processes are being recognized as institutional possibilities, routes available, and the rules of the game. They determine how the business of government is done. I began this book by discussing some aspects of the "new institutionalism" and suggest here that I have done some.

Conclusion

What I have done has drawn on political science scholarship of the last decade, which has been immersed in the practices of political life.

The effort has been to elaborate the ideological basis for choice in matters of entitlement rather than limiting the analysis to choice between given possibilities or deference to presumptions about what the Constitution protects as property. The choices generally available in the policy process are already framed ideologically. Welfare recipients are treated as if their benefits are of lesser consequence than landed property holders. But there has been little attention to constitutional property that examines the legal status of that frame. Too much institutional scholarship describes at the institutional level, but it does not interpret. The result is that the institutions are left essentially intact. There is reverence for a tradition and loyal conventional craftsmanship—but disdain for much that has been offered as a critique of the tradition. That is, the contributions to the craft of research on law and politics by a generation of scholars has not been acknowledged.

The simple fact of public law research and the implication of a new institutionalism is that politics operates through institutions in a way that public law scholars should be more adept at describing. First we need to be more rigorous in a social scientific sense and not take the political rhetoric as adequate to describe institutional life. This happens when notions of the case or the dispute condition the analysis to given or conventionally available policy choices (see Cooper, 1988: 13). We have suggested that different analytic frameworks transcend the idea that an entitlement to government "largesse" means that compensation is not a problem (see Sullivan, 1989; Ackerman, 1977). What traditional political science too often takes as unproblematic is political arguments that making a claim for poor people is somehow policymaking, while claims of a very similar nature that start from positions of great wealth have a different status. The more rigorous proposition is that the policy is *in* the entitlement and its use should not be determined by the class status of the claimant. The law that matters in an institutional sense is not what the actors pick and chose from, it is law that constitutes the environment in which political actors operate.

Another issue is the challenge of convention. We need to link action and behavior in a way that leads to interesting insights and new research questions. In using the idea of a practice as a basis for this research, I would distinguish between practices that take the form of "strategies and maxims," such as choice of a moderate justice to write

Conclusion

opinions for the Supreme Court; "conventions," such as the majority opinion and dissents in appellate courts; and "institutional practices" that have come to constitute the institution, such as perhaps judicial review in the case of the Supreme Court. The very scope of traditional public law makes it hard to go beyond explaining a decision to considering the social and political developments that the decision helps to explain (Smith, 1987: 103). In the judicial activity on desegregation, housing, and mental institutions, there are actually aspects of this sort of institutional concern. There are also the precedents and the prior struggles familiar to students of law and politics. The "most difficult task" concern and the "hard judicial choices" ideology at the heart of the enterprise constitute positivist essentials that do not penetrate or illuminate the nature of institutions. The former maintains the behavioral focus on the abnormal and consequently draws attention away from convention. The latter ideology of the tough case is a set-up for a form of analysis where complexity is there at the beginning and the end.

There is in fact much useful material in traditional institutional studies, especially where it has been developed in a way that transcends the limits of the "politics produces law" framework. Too often, those limits predominate. For instance, Phillip Cooper's treatment of the *Milliken* cases (1974, 1977), though quite traditional, is full of material that could do a great deal to delineate institutional relations and draw some comparisons. Appellate review here is dramatic from the beginning, where Judge Roth is first chastened, to the end, where his successor is overruled. This case goes twice to the Supreme Court yet this part of the process gets no special attention. The complex chain in *Milliken* makes much of the place of state and local defendants to atomize the forces for change. The agents of the government, on which Cooper relies to emphasize the "unplanned" nature of this case, might also be seen as the way the state divides and confuses the claims for redress keeping the form central and tempering the content (Cooper, 1988: 330–31).

Thus, some recent "traditional" public law scholarship, such as Cooper's study of mega cases, certainly analyzes political phenomena that are "complexly interacting." It is the very nature of the enterprise. The model of courts places them in the community where the challenge is not reading the law but applying it in a community and often against the policies of elected officials. The author is also mildly

Conclusion

critical of the propensity among students of the courts to emphasize local "triggers" at the expense of other factors—such as executive policy, including the Reagan turn away from civil rights enforcement and statutory developments. These other factors are at the national level (1988: 329), and Cooper's sensitivity to institutions in the context of culture, national and local, academic and professional, allows him to fit courts into a picture that is quite complex. This complexity analysis is also evident in Professor Susan Mezey's study of disability insurance and "nonacquiescence" to federal court orders by the Social Security Administration (1988).

In the end, I share the aspiration of the new institutionalism, to "make qualitative scholars more aware of the need to connect their claims with measured patterns" and quantitative studies "more sensitive to the complex conceptual structures and characteristics of political beliefs" (Smith, 1987: 104). But this requires a rare commitment. Given the positivism that permeates our curriculum, it has been hard to integrate the dualities. The new institutionalism, however, calls on our common sense, not the academic nonsense that there is a real world "out there" and something else in the academy. Our researchers must obviously think, but our thinkers must do more of the research than they have been doing for the last generation.

Having concluded with a more adequate account of the reach of constitutional discourse, I have called attention to forms of entitlement that are fundamental both because their subject is property and because they are part of our ordinary legal and political practice, a colloquial or vernacular constitution. As I said at the outset, very few claims will ever be subject to review by the Supreme Court, and it is not at all clear that in matters that are constitutional—that is, embedded in the ways we do things—that courts have much success with positions that are idiosyncratic and simply their own. Thus I have offered an alternative conception of constitutional property in entitlement.

Constitutional Sense and Expectations

Discourse analysis supports the discussion of the nature of sense in the Constitution. In establishing that the "sense" in Supreme Court

Conclusion

decisions is at least partly a function of the Court's past opinions, research is capable of supporting politics that can range across the membership on appellate benches and to the vernacular discourse on entitlements. The constitutional "sense" of property, in this basic respect seems to have remained stable with new forms appearing in response to changing socioeconomic and political conditions. Property rights in titles, offices, grants, and franchises, among others, have been asserted and sustained. Thus, I have proposed that it is in the same, not some new, sense that statutory entitlements are property under the American Constitution.

In describing "means discrimination," we have expanded the application to a related constitutional concept. This analysis draws from the fact that constitutional "equal protection," like property, has a technical meaning that orients legal thinking. With roots in *Plessy* v. *Ferguson* (1896) and the justification for separation of the races in schools, theaters, and other public places on the basis of a promise of material equality, it should not be too surprising that *Brown* v. *Board of Education* (1954), by eliminating separation from constitutional protection, also eliminated the constitutional promise of material equality. Here, by turning away from outcomes and looking instead at the meanings, standards and conceptual parameters that influence the application of constitutional discourse, I have been able to demonstrate discrimination against those with inadequate means.

The analysis based on sensible discourse can be applied to any of the other fundamental discursive practices that make up the Constitution. The Sixth Amendment right to a public trial and a trial by jury are good examples. The jury is under pressure in America and the other nations that share this English institution. The idea of lay decision makers is awkward enough for an increasingly expert system of government to accept, but the idea that the numbers should be substantial, that twelve lay persons should constitute the institution, is just too much for an increasingly bureaucratic system. The pressure on the jury is intense, and it is being cut back and rationalized in size, in make-up, and in the decision matrix that is expected. The Supreme Court hears claims based on the tradition. It is sensitive to some and ignores others. We can learn much by understanding the politics of the jury and due process generally in terms laid out here for property.

Sense here is essential to working with constitutional concepts as aspects of social life. When we understand the extent to which the

Conclusion

discursive practices that form the basis of our politics are inherited and the manner in which that inheritance conditions the expectations by which we live, the reciprocal nature of constitutional politics becomes more apparent and indeed may become a practice in itself. The sociological and often the ultimate political implications of intelligible discourse based in communities of interpretation is the sense of obligation those communities feel when they have conducted their life and politics on the basis of certain expectation. This is evident in the political arena, where the marshaling of forces to protect settled expectations in the civil rights field was the animus for the defeat of Robert Bork's appointment to the U.S. Supreme Court. In abortion as well, the politics of expectation is the basis for mobilization and consequently for the cautious handling of this issue.

Thus, we say of the nature of constitutional sense that it is not something that any majority of justices can change. This is true most obviously for the shifting majorities on cases that come before the court. In spite of how they are described by the national media in their headlines or miniscule bits of news, the Supreme Court does not change the Constitution with its decisions. It is also true for the more enduring relations on particular courts, like the conservative legacy of Ronald Reagan. The only level at which the claims of the fundamental in sensible discourse began to be undercut is that level which reconstitutes discursive and hence social reality over time. It is then only when we cease to have a sense that equal protection applies to the deprivations of those who have been oppressed that it loses its capacity to empower, to mobilize, and to constitute the possibilities of political action.

The Politics of Constitutional Law

In discussing wealth and material discrimination, I presented a view of the power of constitutional ideology. In *Brown* v. *Board of Education*, a line of constitutional decision served to turn a people away from issues of "material discrimination." Here, neither the focus on a limited picture of discrimination as colorblindness nor "nonseparation" has kept the constitutional implications of property claims to a minimum. Later, in presenting a picture of bias in the readings of

Conclusion

constitutional entitlement, I offered the proposition that the poor are being shortchanged on more than the quantity of property they possess. They are subjected to a Double Standard when they are denied the same rights of possession as the rich. Here, in conclusion, I want to address the implications of these claims for the politics of entitlement. Specifically, I want to answer charges that expanding the reach of constitutional property is likely to be regressive in its impact.

The greatest fear expressed by liberals on this issue is that to strengthen the claim of legitimate or settled expectations is to empower those who already have a great deal of wealth. The anxiety is at the center of liberalism. It feeds on turning away from inequities and masking them with empty promises of equal treatment, yet liberals don't believe their own proposition. They affirm the politics of interests and deny the transcendant and inspirational quality of a politics of entitlement. Here, to recognize the range of entitlement traditionally denied to the poor and conventionally ceded to the rich is to build toward transcendance in the nature of conventional practice.

To the extent that the politics of constitutional law is not simply the politics of interests but is that and an ideological politics, a politics of concepts and expectations, the formulation of an expansive, progressive concept of the property right moves in the direction of a new constitutional aspiration. To say of a benefit that it is mine in a constitutional sense is to support the claim at a level on which politics is constituted. This is to make entitlement a reciprocal relation. It is to acknowledge the deference given to the disproportionate shares of the wealth as a matter of fact, independent of policy predispositions with regard to those shares, while it demands fair treatment of the conventionally meager distribution. Rather than acquiesance to the unfairness in the distribution, that unfairness is brought to mind at every turn in the analysis.

What can't be said, or what is easy to say, sets a policy framework. The costs and limits of constitutional property will lead some decisions away from this arena to be decided on the basis of the less consequential statutory interpretation.[1] Some economic cases that are linked to the Constitution may be dealt with on grounds other than constitutional property. We didn't take up issues like the property requirement for service on a local commission in Missouri, which was struck down as a violation of equal protection (*Quinn* v. *Millsap*, 1989). In the case of constitutional property, the traditional protection for

Conclusion

legitimate expectation places the Constitution beyond the outcome in a particular case, that is, beyond interpretation. It is this status that has been absent from the claims of many entitlement holders who defer to a conventional definition of property.

Without claiming an undue affinity to the republican revival, a more enthusiastically normative movement in law, the approach suggested here does claim to make some inroads into assumptions about the limits imposed by "modern ontology and epistemology" (Fallon, 1989). Sense can be identified; it is based in what we say and how we live. In constitutional terms, sense is the bedrock, the shared practices. Compensation for withdrawal of welfare benefits makes sense according to the tradition of constitutional property. Compensation is also a strategic opportunity in the face of cynical conservative attacks because it would raise the level of debate over the vulnerability to budgetary cutbacks of those holding statutory entitlements. A sensitive analysis of constitutional property would call attention to the claims that costs be distributed for the wealthy when their property is taken in order to reaffirm the meaning of the Constitution for policy affecting the poor.

The most effective defense against the erosion of fundamental rights by those in power is the knowledgeable expression and confident articulation of alternative visions. From establishing that constitutional property amounts to legitimate expectations to suggesting the possibility of compensation for denial of an entitlement, I have offered a progressive interpretation of this policy area. But, in Chapter VII, we saw how hopes for the meaning of property have been "policed" by the experts and legitimate aspirations circumscribed. It is important to expand the idea that there are ideological constraints placed on claims to entitlement to other concepts that are being circumscribed, as well as to deepen the description presented here. We have seen it in the case of the jury, and we see it with equal protection. It is there as well and with great sophistication in the case of freedom of expression and traditional liberties enjoyed under the American Constitution.

Again, and finally, the issues to which this sort of analysis might apply are not simply those of property. In the last decade of the twentieth century, we are constantly faced with stories of erosion of constitutional expectations by the federal judiciary. The crescendo reached each year around the Fourth of July is enough to cause many to wonder about the viability of the celebration. But the truth about

Conclusion

constitutional interpretation applies as much to the celebration and the flag as it does to the doctrines of constitutional law. The meaning of constitutional right is owned by those who use (or misuse) them. The traditions of constitutional discourse, constitutional thought, and constitutional practice are matters with social meaning that may be arrayed against the interpretive claims of those occupying the seats of power.

Notes

INTRODUCTION

1. "If we are to learn anything about the constitution it is necessary first and foremost that we should learn a good deal about the land law. . . . Indeed our whole constitutional law seems at times to be but an appendix to the law of real property" (Maitland, 1908: 47).

2. The "compensation clause" is not included in the Fourteenth Amendment.

3. Several plenary sessions at the 1987 meetings of the American Political Science Association were devoted to exploring this perspective, suggesting a certain legitimacy.

4. The journal *Studies in American Political Development* from Yale shows how institutions shape political developments and are themselves influenced by social, economic, and political forces. See vol. 3 for a symposium on institutionalism.

5. There weren't any mothers, but this group has changed in the last decade.

6. In discussing the niceties of republication, Stanley Fish writes of his essays, "I could not write them today" (1980: 1). He means that the issues have changed and so has he. His arguments about texts and communities of interpretation influenced the debate on those matters, making it so he "could not write them" the same way again.

CHAPTER I

1. Excepting perhaps Karl Llewellyn (1951).
2. Almost twenty years later Justice Brennan wrote of the compassion for the "brute fact of dependence" (1988).
3. See Chapter III for discussion of these cases in the context of the Double Standard and Chapter VII for how the political implications have been circumscribed.

CHAPTER II

1. See *Allegheny Pittsburgh Coal v. Webster County* (1989) for a contemporary example.
2. Maryland, Florida, Indiana, Hawaii, Alaska, Connecticut, Oregon, New Jersey, California, and Pennsylvania.
3. Alabama, Georgia, Kansas, Louisiana, Mississippi, Tennessee, West Virginia, and Wisconsin.
4. Alabama, Arkansas, Kentucky, Louisiana, Mississippi, North Carolina, South Carolina, Tennessee, and West Virginia (Netzer, 1968: 90–91).
5. This scale shows a general trend toward the adoption of novel policies with increasing speed, a function that Savage attributed to nationalizing forces.
6. There is no evidence to indicate that the legislation changed its characteristics as the environmental movement gained momentum. Hawaii, with one of the earliest bills, included the open-space provision in 1961, and the other twelve states including this provision are distributed throughout the entire period in which this preference was institutionalized.
7. Arkansas, Arizona, Idaho, Indiana, Iowa, New Mexico, North Dakota, and Oklahoma.

CHAPTER III

1. When Judge Robert Bork was questioned before the Senate Judiciary Committee in the fall of 1987 on his nomination to the Supreme Court, he often referred to Gunther's treatise (Gunther, 1980).
2. See note 1 and the attention in the *Carolene Products* footnote to racial, religious, national or other "discrete and insular minorities."

Notes to Chapter VI

3. Margaret Jane Radin's, "The Constitution and the Liberal Conception of Property," in McCann and Houseman (1989), examines the liberal conception as it articulated in neoconservative constitutional theory, particularly Epstein (1985).

4. Little has been made of the fact that the wording of the Fifth Amendment links compensation to "private property," but the potential for issues arising from the wording remains.

CHAPTER V

1. In the 1980s, quotas for black applicants were justified as necessary to maintain a balance in the racial composition of public housing projects.

2. Ill. Rev. Stat., ch. 48, sec. 851–58.

3. We return to some of these cases in the last chapter.

4. These are issues discussed by Cotterrell in terms of "the relationship between exchange value and use value as matters for protection by property law" (1986: 90).

5. "[T]he deep methodological difficulties an Ordinary Observer encounters in conceptualizing the 'legal property' problem make even reformist judges wary of pursuing a takings analysis."

6. Although dead people don't have causes of action wills and life insurance, policies are enforced.

7. Grandfathering extends the protection of past practice beyond its authoritative life; See congressional hearings on the 1983 Social Security reforms.

8. This is developed as part of the analysis of the Double Standard in Chapter III and returned to again in the discussion of "policing."

9. For example Mead uses cost-benefit calculations, economic metaphors, and statistical models in his analysis.

CHAPTER VI

1. The conception owes a great deal to Jerry Milch, who, in a proposal for the land-use study, drafted a matrix of government land policy activities that revealed the central place of land transfer from public to private hands.

2. This comparison arises from a larger study examining distinctions between a public and a private sphere by focusing on public instruments at the boundary of that distinction.

3. "the value to the owner . . . not the value to the taker." *Cedar Rapids* v. *Lacoste* (1914).

4. For an example of protest over the delegation of eminent domain to private developers, see *Washington Post*, October 20, 1984.

5. J. Robert, S. Prichard and Michael J. Trebilcock, in Atkinson and Chandler, 1983 (see also Lipset, 1985).

6. Thus, the Nova Scotia Power Company was given the power in 1914 to divert water, to flood lands, and to expropriate (*Miller* v. *Halifax Power Co.*; see also The Crown Lands Act, 1900).

7. Section 4(2) was amended to read notwithstanding provision for previous users, the Governor-in-council may authorize any water use.

8. This has been evident for some time in law, where it is said that "the process is the punishment" (Feeley, 1979).

CHAPTER VII

1. "No person shall . . . be deprived of life, liberty, or property, without due process of law; nor shall private property be taken for public use, without just compensation."

2. A problem raised neatly at a Harvard faculty Seminar on Poverty by Theda Skocpol, who lamented the one-sided definition of the topic (recounted by Martha Minow, April 28, 1988, in Amherst, Massachusetts).

3. Stuart Scheingold (1984) provided a vivid image of the menacing stranger to illuminate this construction of a fear of crime.

4. A subsequent decision held, "Property interests are not created by the Constitution . . . [but] by existing rules or understandings that stem from an independent source such as state law (*Bishop*, 1976: 344)."

5. This formulation was remarkably similar to that by M. (1988), although this case worker was not familiar with the Supreme Court case.

6. See the Omnibus Budget Reconciliation Act of 1981 (Public Law 97-35). For a background on Social Security in light of these developments see Abbott, 1941; Stein, 1980; Witte, 1936.

7. References are to testimony listed by speaker, context, date, and place in the bibliography under "Briefs, Interviews, and Testimony."

8. Merry (1990) has provided a chronicle of the claims and aspirations of working-class New Englanders, which suggests that we substitute hopefulness for helplessness here.

9. One should also include work by Isaac Balbus (1973) and Stuart

Notes to the Conclusion

Scheingold (1974). Scheingold's conception of the 1980 American Political Science Association program reflected this new orientation and used the insights of Irving F. Lefberg to highlight "efforts to explain judicial decision-making in terms of a shared linguistic competence" and other nonpositive frameworks.

10. Flyer dated February 6, 1989, on file with the author.

CONCLUSION

1. *Mead* v. *Tilley* (1989) was an entitlement case decided as an interpretation of the Employee Retirement Income Security Act of 1974.

Bibliography

BOOKS and ARTICLES

Abbott, Grace. 1941. *From Relief to Social Security: The Development of the New Public Welfare Services and Their Administration.* Chicago: University of Chicago Press.

Abraham, Henry. 1982. *Freedom and the Court.* 4th ed. New York: Oxford University Press.

———. 1975. "'Human' Rights vs. 'Property' Rights," *Political Science Quarterly* 90:288–92.

Ackerman, Bruce. 1977. *Private Property and the Constitution.* New Haven: Yale University Press.

Allett, John. 1987. "New Liberalism and the New Property Doctrine: Welfare Rights as Property Rights." *Polity* 20:57–79.

Amherst Seminar. 1988. *Law and Society Review* 22. Special Issue: Law and Ideology.

Atkinson, Michael M., and Marsha A. Chandler, eds. 1983. *The Politics of Canadian Public Policy.* Toronto: University of Toronto Press.

Austin, John. 1861. *Lectures on Jurisprudence.* 5th ed. London: Murray.

Baer, J. A. 1983. *Equality under the Constitution: Reclaiming the Fourteenth Amendment.* Ithaca: Cornell University Press.

Baker, C. Edwin. 1986. "Property and Its Relation to Constitutionally Protected Liberty." *University of Pennsylvania Law Review* 134:741–816.

Balbus, Isaac. 1973. *The Dialectics of Legal Repression.* New York: Russell Sage.

Bibliography

Banta, John. 1980. "Operationalizing Differential Assessment for Agricultural Land." In Roberts and Brown.

Barber, S. A. 1984. *On What the Constitution Means*. Baltimore: Johns Hopkins University Press.

Barlowe, Raleigh. 1967. "Taxation of Agriculture." In Richard W. Lindholm, ed., *Property Taxation: USA*. Madison: University of Wisconsin Press.

Baum, Daniel J. 1974. *The Welfare Family and Mass Administrative Justice*. New York: Praeger.

Beard, Charles A. 1913. *An Economic Interpretation of the Constitution*. New York: Macmillan.

Becker Arthur P. 1969. "Property Tax Problems Confronting State and Local Governments." In H. T. Johnson, ed., *State and Local Tax Problems*. Knoxville: University of Tennessee Press.

Bell, Derrick. 1985. "The Supreme Court, 1984 Term—Foreword: The Civil Rights Chronicles," *Harvard Law Review* 99:4.

Bellace, J. R. 1984. "Comparable Worth: Proving Sex-Based Wage Discrimination." *Iowa Law Review* 69:655–704.

Belobaba, E. P. 1982. "National Symposium on the Charter." *Supreme Court Law Review* 4.

Belz, Herman. 1978. "Comments on the Living Constitution." Convocation for Project '87, Philadelphia.

Bickel, Alexander. 1970. *The Supreme Court and the Idea of Progress*. New York: Harper and Row.

Bickerton, James, and Alain G. Gagnon. 1984. "Regional Policy in Historical Perspective: The Federal Role in Regional Economic Development." *American Review of Canadian Studies* 14:72–88.

Block, Fred, Richard A. Cloward, Barbara Ehrenreich, and Frances Fox Piven. 1987. *The Mean Season: The Attack on the Welfare State*. New York: Pantheon.

Bobbitt, Phillip. 1982. *Constitutional Fate: Theory of the Constitution*. New York: Oxford.

Bonbright, James C. 1937. *The Valuation of Property*. New York: McGraw-Hill.

Bosselman, Fred, et al. 1973. *The Taking Issue*. Washington, D.C.: Council on Environmental Quality.

Bourdieu, Pierre. 1977. *Outline of a Theory of Practice*. Cambridge: Cambridge University Press.

Bowles, Samuel, and Herbert Gintis. 1986. *Democracy and Capitalism*. New York: Basic Books.

Bradley, Phillips. 1937. "Constitution, the Court, and the People." In Julia E. Johnsen, ed., *Reorganization of the Supreme Court*. New York: Wilson.

Bibliography

Branfman, E., B. Cohen, and David M. Trubek. 1973. "Measuring the Invisible Wall: Land Use Controls and the Residential Patterns of the Poor." *Yale Law Journal* 12:483–508.

Brennan, William J., Jr. 1988. "Reason, Passion, and 'The Progress of Law.'" *Cardozo Law Review* 10:19–22.

Brest, Paul. 1982. "Interpretation and Interest." *Stanford Law Review* 34:765–773.

Brigham, John. 1988a. "The Bias of Constitutional Property: Toward Compensation for the Elimination of Statutory Entitlements." *Journal of Law and Inequality* 5:405–29.

———. 1988b. "The Politics of Constitutional Interpretation." *Law and Society Review* 21:801–5.

———. 1987. *The Cult of the Court*. Philadelphia: Temple University Press.

———. 1984a. *Civil Liberties and American Democracy*. Washington, D.C.: CQ Press.

———. 1984b. "Property and the Supreme Court: Do the Justices Make Sense?" *Polity* 16:242–63.

———. 1978. *Constitutional Language*. Westport, Conn.: Greenwood Press.

———. 1977. *Making Public Policy: Studies in American Politics*. Lexington, Mass.: D. C. Heath and Co.

Brigham, John, and Christine B. Harrington. 1989. "Realism and Its Consequences." *International Journal of Law and Society* 17:41–62.

Brown, H. James, and Neal A. Roberts. 1978. *Land into Cities: The Land Market on the Urban Fringe*. Cambridge: Harvard University Graduate School of Design.

Brudno, B. 1976. *Poverty, Inequality, and the Law*. St. Paul, Minn.: West Publishing Co.

Bryce, James. 1914. *The American Commonwealth*. New York: Macmillan.

Bumiller, Kristin. 1987. *The Civil Rights Society: The Social Construction of Victims*. Baltimore: Johns Hopkins University.

Caldeira, Gregory. 1987. "Public Opinion and the U.S. Supreme Court: FDR's Court-packing Plan." *American Political Science Review* 81:1139–54.

Carlin, Jerome E., Jan Howard, and Sheldon L. Messinger. 1967. *Civil Justice and the Poor*. New York: Russell Sage.

Carter, Lief. 1985. *Contemporary Constitutional Lawmaking*. New York: Pergamon Press.

Census, U.S. 1977. *Statistical Abstract of the United States*. Washington, D.C.: GPO.

Bibliography

Champagne, Anthony, and Edward J. Harpham. 1984. *The Attack on the Welfare State*. Chicago: Waveland Press.

Clark, Gordon. 1985. *Judges and Cities: Interpreting Local Autonomy*. Chicago: University of Chicago Press.

Clawson, Marion. 1971. *Suburban Land Conversion in the United States*. Baltimore: Johns Hopkins University Press.

Clune, W. H., III. 1975. "The Supreme Court's Treatment of Wealth Discriminations under the Fourteenth Amendment." *The Supreme Court Review*, 289–354.

Commons, John R. 1924. *The Legal Foundations of Capitalism*. Madison: University of Wisconsin Press.

Conklin, William E. 1979. *In Defense of Fundamental Rights*. The Netherlands: Sitjthoff and Noordhoff.

Connell, Evan S. 1984. *Son of the Morning Star: Custer and the Little Bighorn*. San Francisco: North Point Press.

Connolly, William E. 1974. *The Terms of Political Discourse*. Lexington, Mass.: D. C. Heath.

Cook, Beverly B. 1978. "Women Judges: The End of Tokenism." In Winifred L. Hepperle and Laura Crites, eds., *Women in the Courts*. Williamsburg, Va.: National Center for State Courts.

Cooper, Phillip J. 1988. *Hard Judicial Choices*. New York: Oxford University Press.

Corwin, Edward S. 1938. *Court over Constitution*. Princeton: Princeton University Press.

———. 1929. *The "Higher Law" Background of America Constitutional Law*. Ithaca, New York: Cornell University Press.

Cotterrell, Roger. 1986. "The Law of Property and Legal Theory." In William Twining, ed., *Legal Theory and Common Law*. Oxford: B. Blackwell.

———. 1983. "The Sociological Concept of Law." *Journal of Law and Society* 10:241–255.

Coughlin, Robert E. 1980. "The Magnitude of the Tax Savings and Its Effect on the Land Market." In Roberts and Brown.

Council on Environmental Quality (CEQ). 1976. *Untaxing Open Space: An Evaluation of Differential Assessment of Farms and Open Space*. Washington, D.C.: GPO.

Cover, Robert M. 1988. "Social Security and Constitutional Entitlement." In Ted Marmor and Jerry Mashaw, *Social Security: Beyond the Rhetoric of Crisis*. Princeton: Princeton University Press.

———. 1986. "Violence and the Word," *Yale Law Journal* 95:1601.

Bibliography

———. 1983. "Foreword: Nomos and Narrative." *Harvard Law Review* 97:4–68.
Cruse, Harold. 1987. *Plural But Equal*. New York: William Morrow.
Davis, Sue. 1989. *Justice Rehnquist and the Constitution*. Princeton: Princeton University Press.
———. 1986. "Federalism and Property Rights: An Examination of Justice Rehnquist's Legal Positivism," *Western Political Quarterly* 39:250–64.
Deutchman, Iva E. 1985. "Women and Politics," *Polity* 18:161–66.
Dolbeare, Kenneth M., and Phillip Hammond. 1971. *The School Prayer Decisions*. Chicago: University of Chicago Press.
Donovan, C. H. 1969. "Recent Developments in Property Taxation in Florida." In Harry T. Johnson, ed., *State and Local Tax Problems*. Knoxville: University of Tennessee Press.
Dorn, James A., and Henry G. Manne, eds. 1987. *Economic Liberties and the Judiciary*. Fairfax, Va.: George Mason University Press.
Dunham, Alison. 1962. "*Griggs* v. *Allegheny County* in Perspective: 30 Years of Supreme Court Expropriation Law." *Supreme Court Review* 63:105.
Dworkin, Ronald. 1982. "Law as Interpretation," *Texas Law Review* 60:527.
———. 1977. *Taking Rights Seriously*. Cambridge: Harvard University Press.
Easterbrook, Frank. 1984. "Leading Cases of the 1983 Term," *Harvard Law Review* 98:226.
Edelman, Bernard. 1979. *Ownership of the Image: Elements for a Marxist Theory of Law*. London: Routledge and Kegan Paul.
Edelman, Murray. 1988. *Constructing the Political Spectacle*. Chicago: University of Chicago Press.
———. 1977. *Political Language*. New York: Academic Press.
Ely, John Hart. 1980. *Democracy and Distrust*. Cambridge: Harvard University Press.
Engel, N. Eugene. 1975. "Political and Economic Forces behind State and Local Approaches to Retain Prime Land," USDA Seminar on Retention of Prime Lands. Washington, D.C.: GPO.
Engle, Robert F. 1973. "De Facto Discrimination in Residential Assessments: Boston." *National Tax Journal* 28:445–51.
Epstein, Richard A. 1985. *Takings: Private Property and the Power of Eminent Domain*. Chicago: University of Chicago Press.
Fahringer, P. 1964. "Equal Protection and the Indigent Defendant: Griffin and Its Progeny," *Stanford Law Review* 16:394–415.
Fallon, Richard H., Jr. 1989. "What Is Republicanism, and Is It Worth Reviving?" *Harvard Law Review* 102:1695–1735.
———. 1987. "A Constructivist Coherence Theory of Constitutional Interpretation," *Harvard Law Review* 100:1189–1286.

Bibliography

Farrand, Max. 1913. *The Framing of the Constitution of the United States.* New Haven: Yale University Press.

Feeley, Malcolm. 1979. *The Process is the Punishment.* New York: Russell Sage Foundation.

Feldberg, R. 1984. "Comparable Worth: Toward Theory and Practice in the United States." *Signs* 10:311–28.

Feldman, Elliot, and Jerry Milch. 1987. *Land Rites and Wrongs: The Management, Regulation and Use of Land in Canada and the United States.* Cambridge, Mass.: Lincoln Institute of Land Policy.

———. 1977. "Air Transportation Infrastructures as a Problem of Public Policy." *Policy Studies Journal* 6:20.

Fellmeth, Robert C. 1973. *The Politics of Land: Nader Study Group Report on California.* New York: Grossman Publishers.

Felstiner, William, Rick Abel, and Austin Sarat. 1980. "Naming, Blaming and Claiming," *Law and Society Review* 14:631–54.

Fineman, Martha L. 1983. "Implementing Equality: Ideology, Contradiction and Social Change." *Wisconsin Law Review* 4:789–886.

Fischel, William A., ed. 1988. "Symposium: The Jurisprudence of Takings." *Columbia Law Review* 88.

Fish, Stanley. 1980. *Is There a Text in This Class? The Authority of Interpretive Communities.* Cambridge: Harvard University Press.

Fisher, Glenn W. 1976. "Property Taxation and the Political System." In Arthur D. Lynn, Jr., ed., *Property Taxation, Land Use and Public Policy.* Madison: University of Wisconsin Press.

Fiss, Owen. 1982. "Objectivity and Interpretation." *Stanford Law Review* 34:739–63.

Fleischmann, Arnold. 1989. "Politics, Administration, and Local Land-Use Regulation: Analyzing Zoning as a Policy Process." *Public Administration Review* 49:337–45.

Frankfurter, Felix. 1967. In M. Freedman, ed. *Roosevelt and Frankfurter: Their Correspondence, 1928–1945.* Boston: Little, Brown and Co.

Freeman, Alan. 1978. "Legitimizing Racial Discrimination Through Antidiscrimination Law." *Minnesota Law Review* 62:1049–1119.

Friedman, Kathi V. 1981. *Legitimation of Social Rights and the Western Welfare State: A Weberian Perspective.* Chapel Hill: University of North Carolina Press.

Friedrich, Carl J. 1963. "Rights, Liberties, Freedoms: A Reappraisal." *American Political Science Review* 62:841.

Bibliography

Frug, Gerald E. 1980. "The City as a Legal Concept," *Harvard Law Review* 93:1062–1154.
Fry, Northrop. 1953. "Letters in Canada," *University of Toronto Quarterly* 22:273.
Funston, Richard. 1978. *A Vital National Seminar: The Supreme Court in American Political Life.* Palo Alto, Calif.: Mayfield Publishing Co.
———. 1975. "The Double Standard of Constitutional Protection in the Era of the Welfare State." *Political Science Quarterly* 90:261–92.
Garment, Leonard. 1989. "The Hill Case." *New Yorker.* April 17:90–110.
Geertz, Clifford. 1973. *The Interpretation of Cultures.* New York: Basic Books.
George, Roy E. 1974. *The Life and Times of Industrial Estates Limited.* Halifax: Institute of Public Affairs, Dalhousie University.
Gloudemans, Robert T. 1974. *Use Value Farmland Assessment: Theory, Practice, Impact.* Chicago: International Association of Assessing Officers.
Goldberg, Michael, and John Mercer. 1986. *The Myth of the North American City: Continentalism Challenged.* Vancouver: University of British Columbia Press.
Goldman, Sheldon. 1987. "Reagan's Second Term Judicial Appointments: The Battle at Midway," *Judicature* 70:324–40.
———. 1981, 1986. *Constitutional Law and Supreme Court Decision-Making.* New York: Harper and Row.
Goldstein, Leslie. 1987. "The ERA and the U.S. Supreme Court," *Research in Law and Policy Studies* 1:145–61.
Gordon, Robert. 1984. "Critical Legal Histories." *Stanford Law Review* 36:57–125.
Grais, David. 1977. "Statutory Entitlement and the Concept of Property," 86 *Yale Law Journal* 709.
Gray, Virginia. 1973. "Innovation in the States: A Diffusion Study," *American Political Science Review* 62:1174–85.
Greenberg, Stanley B. 1973. *Politics and Poverty: Modernization and Response in Five Poor Neighborhoods.* New York: John Wiley.
Greenhouse, Carol J. 1986. *Praying for Justice: Faith, Order and Community.* Ithaca: Cornell University Press.
Grossman, Joel B. 1987. "Beyond the Willowbrook Wars: The Courts and Institutional Reform." *ABF Research Journal* Winter 1:249–59.
Grossman, Joel B., and Joseph Tanenhaus, eds. 1968. *The Frontiers of Judicial Research.* New York: John Wiley and Sons.
Gunther, Gerald. 1980. *Cases and Materials on Constitutional Law.* 10th Ed. Mineola, New York: Foundation Press.

Bibliography

Gustafson, Greg C., and L. T. Wallace. 1975. "Differential Assessment as Land Use Policy: The California Case," *Journal of American Institute of Planners* 41:379–89.

Hagman, Donald G. 1964. "Open Space Planning and Property Taxation—Some Suggestions." *Wisconsin Law Review* 4:628.

Hale, Dennis. 1985. "The Evolution of the Property Tax: A Study of the Relation between Public Finance and Political Theory." *Journal of Politics* 47:382–404.

Hall, Stuart et al. 1978. *Policing the Crisis: Mugging, the State and Law and Order.* London: Macmillan.

Hamilton, Walton H. 1932. "Property According to Locke," *Yale Law Journal* 41:864–80.

Handler, Joel. 1960. "Controlling Official Behavior in Welfare Administration." *California Law Review* 54:479.

Harrington, Christine B. 1985a. *Shadow Justice: The Ideology and Institutionalization of Alternatives to Court.* Westport, Conn.: Greenwood Press.

———. 1985b. "Socio-Legal Concepts in Mediation Ideology." *Legal Studies Forum* 9:33–38.

Harrington, Christine B., and Sally Merry. 1988. "Ideological Production: The Making of Community Mediation." *Law and Society Review* 22:709.

Harris, William. 1982. "Binding Word and Polity," *American Political Science Review* 76:34.

Harvard Law Review. 1962. "Inequality in Property Tax Assessments: New Cure for an Old Ill." 75:1374.

Hastings Law Journal. 1968. "Land: Unraveling the Urban Fringe." 19:421–27.

Hay, Douglas. 1975. "Property, Authority and the Criminal Law." In Hay, et al., *Albion's Fatal Tree.* New York: Free Press.

Hochschild, Jennifer. 1989. "The Politics of Victimization Makes Strange Bedfellows." *Michigan Law Review* 87:1584–98.

———. 1981. *What's Fair? American Beliefs about Distributive Justice.* Cambridge: Harvard University Press.

Holmes, Oliver Wendell, Jr. 1897. "The Path of the Law." *Harvard Law Review* 10:457–78.

Horwitz, Morton. 1977. *The Transformation of American Law: 1780–1860.* Cambridge: Harvard University Press.

Houseman, Gerald. 1979. *The Right of Mobility.* Port Washington, NY: Kennicat Press.

Hunt, Alan. 1983. "The Ideology of Law: Advances and Problems in Recent

Bibliography

Applications of the Concept of Ideology to the Analysis of Law." George Lurcey Lectures, Amherst College.

Hurst, James Willard. 1982. *Law and Markets in United States History: Different Modes of Bargaining among Interests*. Madison: University of Wisconsin Press.

———. 1980–81. "The Function of Courts in the United States: 1950–1980," *Law and Society Review* 15:456.

Jacobsohn, Gary. 1986. *The Supreme Court and the Decline of Constitutional Aspiration*. New Brunswich, N.J.: Rowman and Littlefield.

Jones, Alfred W. 1941. *Life, Liberty, and Property*. Philadelphia: J. B. Lippincott.

Jones, H. 1958. "The Rule of Law in the Welfare State." *Columbia Law Review* 58:143–56.

Kairys, David. 1982. *The Politics of Law: A Progressive Critique*. New York: Pantheon Books.

Kansas State University. 1977. "Use Value Appraisal Impact Study." Manhattan, Kans.: Department of Economics Cooperative Extension Service.

Kierans, Thomas E. 1985. "Privatization: Strengthening the Market at the Expense of the State." *Choices* (April).

Kilmer, Robert R. 1961. "Legal Requirements for Equality in Tax Assessment." *Albany Law Review* 25:203.

Klare, Karl. 1979. "Law-Making as Praxis." *Telos* 40:123–35.

Kolesar, John, and Jaye School. 1977. *Misplaced Hope, Misspent Millions: A Report on Farmland Assessments in New Jersey*. Princeton: Center for Analysis of Public Issues.

Kozinski, Alex. 1987. "Foreword: The Judiciary and the Constitution." In Dorn and Manne.

Kramer, Daniel C. 1989. "When Does a Regulation Become a Taking?" *American Business Law Journal* 26:729–82.

Ladd, Helen. 1980. "The Tax Policy Considerations Underlying Preferential Tax Treatment of Open Space and Agricultural Lands," Roberts and Brown.

Laskin, Bora. 1975. *Canadian Constitutional Law*. Toronto: Carswell Co.

Laux, Jeanne Kirk. 1983. "Expanding the State: The International Relations of State-Owned Enterprises in Canada." *Polity* 15:329.

Law, Sylvia. 1973. *The Rights of the Poor*. New York: Dutton.

Lazerson, Mark H. 1982. "In the Halls of Justice, the Only Justice Is in the Halls." In R. Abel, ed. *The Politics of Informal Justice*, vol. 1. New York: Academic Press.

Bibliography

Lermack, Paul. 1989. "What Does Law Do?" *Legal Studies Forum* 12:400–425.
Lerner, Max. 1937. "Constitutionalism and Court as Symbols." *Yale Law Journal* 46:1290.
Levinson, Sanford. 1979. "The Constitution in American Civil Religion." In Philip B. Kurland and Gerhard Casper, eds., *The Supreme Court Review*. Chicago: University of Chicago Press.
Levy, Leonard. 1957. *The Law of the Commonwealth and Chief Justice Shaw*. Cambridge: Harvard University Press.
Levy, Michael B. 1983. "Illiberal Liberalism: The New Property as Strategy," *The Review of Politics* 45:576.
Light, Paul. 1985. *Artful Work: The Politics of Social Security Reform*. New York: Random House.
Lindblom, Charles. 1979. *Politics and Markets*. New York: Basic Books.
Lindsey, Robert. 1987. "California's Open Beaches Feeling the Strain." *New York Times* (August 9):26.
Lipset, Seymour Martin. 1985. "Canada and the United States: The Cultural Dimension." In Charles F. Doran and John H. Sigler, eds., *Canada and the United States*. Englewood Cliffs, N.J.: Prentice-Hall.
Livermore, Shaw. 1939. *Early American Land Companies: Their Influence on Corporate Development*. Reprinted in 1968. New York: Octagon Books.
Llewellyn, Karl. 1951. *The Bramble Bush*. New York: Oceana Publications.
———. 1934. "The Constitution as an Institution." *Columbia Law Review* 34:1–40.
Lockhart, William B., et al. 1981. *The American Constitution*. 5th ed. St. Paul, Minn.: West Publishing Co.
Lofgren, Charles A. 1987. *The Plessy Case: A Legal, Historical Interpretation*. New York: Oxford University Press.
Los Angeles Times. 1988a. "Support for the Coast." May 11, p. 6.
———. 1988b. "Offshore Drilling Suit Settled." July 21, p. 3.
Lynd, Staunton. 1987. "Towards a Not-for-Profit Economy: Public Development Authorities for Acquisition and Use of Industrial Property." *Harvard Civil Rights-Civil Liberties Law Review* 22:13–41.
———. 1984. "Communal Rights." *Texas Law Review* 62:1417.
Macaulay, Stewart. 1963. "Non-Contractual Relations in Business: A Preliminary Study." *American Sociological Review* 28:55.
McCann, Michael. 1989. "Equal Protection and Social Inequality: Race and Class in American Constitutional Ideology." In McCann and Houseman, 1989.
———. 1987. "Challenging the Marketplace Ideology of Law: Comparable

Bibliography

Worth in the Courts." Unpublished paper, on file with the author.
———. 1984. "Resurrection and Reform: Perspectives on Property in the American Constitutional Tradition." *Politics and Society* 13:143–76.
McCann, Michael, and Gerald Houseman, eds. 1989. *Judging the Constitution: Critical Essays on Judicial Lawmaking*. New York: Little, Brown and Co.
McCloskey, Robert. 1962. "Economic Due Process and the Supreme Court: An Exhumation and Reburial." In Philip B. Kurland, ed., *The Supreme Court Review*, Chicago: University of Chicago Press.
Macpherson, C. B. 1978. *Property: Mainstream and Critical Positions*. Toronto: University of Toronto Press.
———. 1973. "A Political Theory of Property." In Macpherson, ed., *Democratic Theory: Essays in Retrieval*. Oxford: Oxford University Press.
McWhinney, Edward. 1982. *Canada and the Constitution 1979–1982: Patriation and the Charter of Rights*. Toronto: University of Toronto Press.
———. 1958. *Canadian Jurisprudence*. Toronto: Carswell.
Magrath, C. Peter. 1967. *Yazoo: Law and Politics in the New Republic*. New York: W. W. Norton.
Maine, Henry. 1883. *Popular Government*. New York: H. Holt and Company.
Maitland, Frederic W. 1908. *Constitutional History of England*. Cambridge: University Press.
March, James G., and Johan P. Olsen. 1984. "The New Institutionalism: Organizational Factors in Political Life." *American Political Science Review* 78:734–49.
Massey, S. J. 1984. "Justice Rehnquist's Theory of Property," *Yale Law Journal* 93:541–60.
Mather, Lynn, and Barbara Yngvesson. 1980. "Language, Audience and the Transformation of Disputes." *Law and Society Review* 15:775.
Mathias, Philip. 1971. *Forced Growth: Five Studies of Government Involvement in the Development of Canada*. Toronto: James Lewis and Samuel.
Maxwell, James A., and J. Richard Aronson. 1977. *Financing State and Local Governments*, 3d ed. Washington, D.C.: Brookings Institution.
Mead, Lawrence M. 1986. *Beyond Entitlement: The Social Obligations of Citizenship*. New York: Free Press.
Melnick, R. Shep. 1987. "Judicial Activism Meets the New Congress: The Growth of Programmatic Rights." Conference on the American Constitutional Experiment.
———. 1986. "The Politics of Statutory Interpretation: Congress, Courts, and Welfare Rights," Paper presented to the American Political Science Association annual meeting, Washington, D.C.

Bibliography

Merry, Sally Engle. 1990. *Getting Justice and Getting Even: Legal Consciousness among Working Class Americans.* Chicago: University of Chicago Press.
Mezey, Susan G. 1988. *No Longer Disabled: The Federal Courts and the Politics of Social Security Disability.* New York: Greenwood Press.
Michelman, Frank. 1988. "Takings," *Columbia Law Review* 88:1600–1629.
———. 1979. "Welfare Rights in a Constitutional Democracy." *Washington University Law Quarterly* 3:659–85.
———. 1969. "On Protecting the Poor through the Fourteenth Amendment." *Harvard Law Review* 83:7–39.
———. 1967. "Property, Utility, and Fairness: Comments on the Ethical Foundations of 'Just Compensation' Law," *Harvard Law Review* 80:1165.
Minow, Martha. 1987. "Interpreting Rights: An Essay for Robert Cover," *Yale Law Journal* 96:1868–1915.
Moffett, Samuel E. 1972. *The Americanization of Canada.* Toronto: University of Toronto Press.
Morgan, Richard. 1984. *Disabling America: The Rights Industry in Our Time.* New York: Basic Books.
Morris, Eugene J. 1987. "Supreme Court Land Use Decisions Uncertain in Defining a 'Taking,'" *The National Law Journal* (September 7):20.
Mosca, Gaetano. 1972. *A Short History of Political Philosophy.* New York: Crowell.
Nedelsky, Jennifer. 1979. "From Common Law to Commission: The Development of Water Law in Nova Scotia." Proceedings of the Conference on Water and Environmental Law, Dalhousie University, September 14–16.
Nelson, B. E. 1977. "Differential Assessment of Agricultural Land in Kansas." *Kansas Law Review* 25:215–45.
Nelson, J. G., et al. 1974. *Canadian Public Land Use in Perspective.* Ottawa: Social Science Research Council of Canada.
Nelson, Scott. 1982. "Wealth Classifications and Equal Protection: Quo Vadimus?" *Houston Law Review* 19:713–31.
Netzer, Dick. 1968. "Impact of the Property Tax—Effect on Housing, Urban Land Use, Local Government Finance." Committee on Urban Problems, Washington, D.C.: GPO.
Nichols, Philip. 1986. *The Law of Eminent Domain.* New York: Matthew Bender.
Noble, Charles. 1986. *Liberalism at Work.* Philadelphia: Temple University Press.
Oakes, James L. 1981. "'Property Rights' in Constitutional Analysis Today," *Washington Law Review* 56:583–626.
O'Neill, Timothy J. 1981. "The Language of Equality," *American Political Science Review* 75:626.

Bibliography

Opie, John. 1989. *The Law of the Land: Two Hundred Years of American Farmland Policy.* Lincoln: University of Nebraska Press.

Oppenheim, Felix. 1968. "The Concept of Equality." *International Encyclopedia of the Social Sciences* 5:102–8. New York: Macmillan.

Paul, Arnold. 1969. *Conservative Crisis and the Rule of Law.* New York: Peter Smith.

Paul, Diane. 1975. *The Politics of the Property Tax.* Lexington, Mass.: Lexington Books.

Paul, Ellen Frankel. 1987a. *Property Rights and Eminent Domain.* New Brunswick, N.J.: Transaction.

———. 1987b. "Public Use: A Vanishing Limitation on Governmental Takings." In Dorn and Manne.

Perin, Constance. 1977. *Everything in its Place: Social Order and Land Use in America.* Princeton: Princeton University Press.

Perry, M. J. 1983. "Equal Protection, Judicial Activism, and the Intellectual Agenda of Constitutional Theory: Reflections on, and Beyond, *Plyler* v. *Doe*." *University of Pittsburgh Law Review* 44:329–50.

Phares, Donald. 1973. *State—Local Tax Equity.* Lexington, Mass.: Lexington Books.

Pitkin, Hanna. 1972. *Wittgenstein and Justice.* Berkeley: University of California Press.

Piven, Frances Fox, and Richard Cloward. 1977. *Poor People's Movements.* New York: Pantheon.

———. 1971. *Regulating the Poor: The Functions of Public Welfare.* New York: Vintage Books.

Plotkin, Sidney. 1987. *Keep Out: The Struggle for Land Use Control.* Berkeley: University of California Press.

Posner, Richard. 1979. "Utilitarianism, Economics and Legal Theory." *Journal of Legal Studies* 8:103–40.

Pound, Roscoe. 1921. *Jurisprudence.* St. Paul, Minn.: West Publishing Co.

Press Herald. 1982. "Celebration 350." Portland, Maine (May 29).

Pritchett, C. Herman. 1948. *The Roosevelt Court: A Study in Judicial Politics and Values 1937–1947.* New York: Macmillan.

Pross, A. Paul. 1975. *Planning and Development: A Case of Two Nova Scotia Communities.* Halifax: Institute of Public Affairs, Dalhousie University.

Provine, Marie. 1986. *Judging Credentials: Nonlawyer Judges and the Politics of Professionalism.* Chicago: University of Chicago Press.

Radin, Margaret Jane. 1982. "Property and Personhood," *Stanford Law Review* 34:957.

Rakoff, T. 1987. "*Brock* v. *Roadway Express, Inc.* and the New Law of Regula-

tory Due Process," *Supreme Court Review*. Chicago: University of Chicago Press.
Reich, Charles. 1965. "Individual Rights and Social Welfare: The Emerging Legal Issues." *Yale Law Journal* 74:1245.
———. 1964. "The New Property." *Yale Law Journal* 73:733–87.
Renner, Karl. 1969. "The Institutions of Private Law." In V. Aubert, ed., *Sociology of Law*. London: Penguin Books.
Rippey, Phyllis F. 1987. "The Constitution and Community Property Rights." Presented at the American Political Science Association Annual Meeting, Chicago.
Roberts, Neal A. 1980. "The Big Giveaway Called Differential Assessment." In Roberts and Brown.
———. 1977. *The Government Land Developers*. Lexington, Mass.: Lexington Books.
Roberts, Neal A., and H. James Brown, eds. 1980. *Property Tax Preferences for Agricultural Land*. Montclair, N.J.: Allanheld, Osmun.
Rubin, Richard. 1983. *Your 1983/84 Guide to Social Security Benefits*. New York: Facts on File.
Russell, Peter H. 1982. "The Effect of a Charter of Rights on the Policy-Making Role of Canadian Courts." *Canadian Public Administration* 25:1–33.
———. 1979. "Judicial Power in Canada's Political Culture." In M. L. Friedland, ed. *Courts and Trials*. Toronto: University of Toronto Press.
Sager, Lawrence. 1969. "Tight Little Islands: Exclusionary Zoning, Equal Protection, and the Indigent." *Stanford Law Review* 21:767–800.
Sanders, Norman. 1973. *Sierra Club Bulletin* 58, no. 2, 10–13.
Santos, Boaventura deSousa. 1987. "Law: A Map of Misreading," *Journal of Law and Society* 14:279–302.
Sarat, Austin. 1989. "The Law of the Welfare Poor." Presented at the Law and Society Annual Meeting, Madison, Wisconsin.
Savage, Robert L. 1978. "Policy Innovativeness as a Trait of American States." *Journal of Politics* 40:212–24.
Sax, Joseph. 1971. "Takings, Private Property and Public Rights." *Yale Law Journal* 81:149.
Schauer, Frederick. 1987. *1987 Supplement to Constitutional Law*, 11th ed. Mineola, New York: Foundation Press.
Scheiber, Harry N. 1975. "Instrumentalism and Property Rights: A Reconsideration of American 'Styles of Judicial Reasoning' in the 19th Century," *Wisconsin Law Review* 1:1.
Scheingold, Stuart. 1984. *The Politics of Law and Order*. New York: Longman.
———. 1974. *The Politics of Rights*. New Haven: Yale University Press.

Bibliography

Schmeiser, D. A. 1964. *Civil Liberties in Canada*. London: Oxford University Press.

Schwartz, Richard D. 1969. "A Proposed Focus for Research on Judicial Behavior." In Grossman and Tanenhaus.

Scotch, Richard K. 1984. *From Goodwill to Civil Rights: Transforming Federal Disability Policy*. Philadelphia: Temple University Press.

Seligman, E. R. A. 1895. *Essays on Taxation*. New York: Macmillan.

Shannon, John. 1973. "The Property Tax: Reform or Relief?" In George Peterson, ed., *Property Tax Reform*, Washington, D.C.: Urban Institute.

Shapiro, Martin. 1986. "The Supreme Court's 'Return' to Economic Regulation." *Studies in American Political Development* 1:91–141.

———. 1978. "The Constitution and Economic Rights." In *Essays on the Constitution*, M. J. Harmon, ed. Port Washington, N.Y.: Kennikat Press.

———. 1967. *The Supreme Court and Constitutional Rights*. Glenview, Ill.: Scott, Foresman and Company.

———. 1964. *Law and Politics in the Supreme Court*. New York: Free Press.

Siegan, Bernard H. 1980. *Economic Liberties and the Constitution*. Chicago: University of Chicago Press.

———. 1977. *Planning Without Process*. Lexington, Mass.: Lexington Books.

Silbey, Susan. 1985. "Ideals and Practices in the Study of Law." *Legal Studies Forum* 9:7–22.

Silverman, David, and Brian Torode. 1980. *The Material Word: Some Theories of Language and Its Limits*. London: Routledge and Kegan Paul.

Simon, William H. 1985. "The Invention and Reinvention of Welfare Rights." *Maryland Law Review* 44:1–37.

Skocpol, Theda. 1984. *Vision and Method in Historical Sociology*. Cambridge: Cambridge University Press.

———. 1979. *States and Social Revolutions*. Cambridge: Cambridge University Press.

Skowronek, Stephen. 1982. *Building a New American State*. Cambridge: Cambridge University Press.

Smith, Rogers M. 1987. "Political Jurisprudence, the 'New Institutionalism,' and the Future of Public Law." *American Political Science Review* 82:89–108.

Sparer, Ed. 1984. "Fundamental Human Rights, Legal Entitlements, and the Social Struggle: A Friendly Critique of the Critical Legal Studies Movement." *Stanford Law Review* 36:509.

———. 1968. "The Place of Law in Social Work Education." *Buffalo Law Review*. 17:733.

Sproule-Jones, Mark. 1983. "Institutions, Constitutions, and Public Policies."

Bibliography

In Michael A. Atkinson and Marsha Chandler, eds., *The Politics of Canadian Public Policy*. Toronto: University of Toronto Press.

Stein, Bruno. 1980. *Social Security and Pensions in Transition: Understanding the American Retirement System*. New York: Free Press.

Stevens, William K. 1985. "Renaissance along the Waterfronts of Three Cities Transforms Downtowns." *New York Times*, May 26.

Stocker, Frederick D. 1976. "Property Taxation, Land Use, and Rationality in Urban Growth Policy." In Arthur D. Lynn, ed., *Property Taxation, Land Use, and Urban Policy*. Madison: University of Wisconsin Press.

Strauber, Ira L. 1983. "Transforming Political Rights into Legal Ones." *Polity* 16:72–96.

Strayer, Barry L. 1983. *Judicial Review of Legislation in Canada*. 2d ed. Toronto: University of Toronto Press.

Stumpf, Harry, Martin Shapiro, Daniel Danelski, Austin Sarat, and David O'Brien. 1983. "Whither Political Jurisprudence: A Symposium." *Western Political Quarterly* 36:533–69.

Sullivan, Kathleen M. 1989. "Unconstitutional Conditions." *Harvard Law Review* 102:1413–1506.

Symons, Lee P. 1988. "Property Rights and Local Land-Use Regulation: The Implications of *First English* and *Nollan*." *Publius* 18:81–95.

Tarnopolsky, Walter S. 1975. *The Canadian Bill of Rights*. Toronto: McClelland and Stewart.

tenBroek, Jacobus. 1964–65. "California's Dual System of Family Law: Its Origin, Development, and Present Status." *Stanford Law Review* 16–17 (three parts).

Thompson, E. P. 1975. *Whigs and Hunters*. New York: Vintage Books.

Todd, Eric C. E. 1976. *The Law of Expropriation and Compensation in Canada*. Toronto: Carswell.

Treanor, William Michael. 1985. "The Origins and Original Significance of the Just Compensation Clause of the Fifth Amendment." *Yale Law Journal* 94:694–716.

Trebilcock, M. J., et al. 1982. *The Choice of Governing Instrument*. Ottawa: Economic Council of Canada.

Tribe, Keith. 1978. *Land, Labour and Economic Discourse*. London: Routledge and Kegan Paul.

Tribe, Laurence. 1978, 1988. *American Constitutional Law*. Mineola, N.Y.: Foundation Press.

———. 1978. "The Puzzling Persistence of Process-Based Constitutional Theories." *Yale Law Journal* 89:1063.

Bibliography

Trubek, David M. 1983. "Where the Action Is: Critical Legal Studies and Empiricism." Disputes Processing Research Program, Working Papers. Madison: University of Wisconsin.
Trubek, David M., and John Esser. 1989. "'Critical Empiricism' in American Legal Studies: Paradox, Program, or Pandora's Box?" *Law and Social Inquiry* 14:3–53.
Tuebner, Gunther. 1986. *Dilemmas of Law in the Welfare State.* Berlin: Walter de Gruyter.
Tushnet, Mark. 1981. *The American Law of Slavery, 1810–1860: Considerations of Humanity and Interest.* Princeton: Princeton University Press.
Van Alstyne, William. 1977. "Cracks in the 'New Property': Adjudicative Due Process in the Administrative State," *Cornell Law Review* 62:445.
———. 1968. "The Demise of the Right-Privilege Distinction in Constitutional Law." *Harvard Law Review* 81:1439.
Vandevelde, Kenneth J. 1980. "The New Property of the Nineteenth Century: Development of the Modern Concept of Property." *Buffalo Law Review* 29:325.
Wagenseil, Harris. 1970. "Property Taxation of Agricultural and Open Space Land." *Harvard Journal on Legislation* 8:158–96.
Walker, Jack L. 1969. "The Diffusion of Innovation Among the American States." *American Political Science Review* 63:880–89.
Warren, Charles. 1922. *The Supreme Court in United States History.* Cambridge: Harvard University Press.
Waters, A. J. 1985. "Property in the Promise: A Study of the Third Party Beneficiary Rule." *Harvard Law Review* 98:1111.
Wechsler, Herbert. 1959. "Toward Neutral Principles of Constitutional Law," *Harvard Law Review* 73:1–35.
Westen, Peter. 1982. "The Empty Idea of Equality," *Harvard Law Review* 95:537–76.
White, James Boyd. 1982.l "Law as Language: Reading Law and Reading Literature." *Texas Law Review* 60:415–45.
Whyte, J. D., and W. R. Lederman. 1977. *Canadian Constitutional Law,* 2d ed. Toronto: Butterworths.
Witte, Edwin E. 1936. *Development of the Social Security Act.* Madison: University of Wisconsin.
Wolfe, Christopher. 1986. *The Rise of Modern Judicial Review.* New York: Basic Books.
Woodward, Bob, and Scott Armstrong. 1979. *The Brethren.* New York: Simon and Schuster.

Bibliography

Wright, Benjamin F., Jr. 1938. *The Contract Clause of the Constitution.* Cambridge: Harvard University Press.

Yale Law Journal. 1958. "Tax Assessment of Real Property." 68:335.

HEARINGS and GOVERNMENT DOCUMENTS

APEC. 1976. *Industrial Incentives Program in the Atlantic Region.* Halifax: Atlantic Provinces Economic Council.

CCREM. 1972. "Nova Scotia Crown Lands." In *The Administration of Crown Lands in Canada.* Council of Resource and Environment Ministers.

DREE. 1979. *Atlantic Region Industrial Parks: An Assessment of Economic Impact.* Ottawa: Department of Regional Economic Expansion.

Hearings. 1982. Task Force on Entitlements, Uncontrollables, and Indexing, Committee on the Budget, House of Representatives, 97th Congress, 2nd Session. February 22 and 26 and March 1, Washington, D.C.

Joint Hearing. 1982. Subcommittee on Postsecondary Education and Subcommittee on Elementary, Secondary and Vocational Education, of the Committee on Education and Labor, House of Representatives. 97th Congress, 2d sess. February 3, Washington, D.C.

Rodwin, Lloyd. 1974. *Economic Development and Resource Conservation: A Strategy for Maine.* Maine: Bureau of Public Lands.

Stocker, Frederick D. 1961. "How Should We Tax Farmland in the Rural Urban Fringe?" USDA, Economic Research Service, Washington, D.C.: GPO.

Summary Docket. 1988. Housing Court, Springfield, Mass. July 14.

BRIEFS, INTERVIEWS, and TESTIMONY

Alice. 1988. Normal Street, Chico, Calif., June 15.

C. M. 1988. Disabled and the Law, Chico, Calif., June 20.

D. 1988. Marken Properties, Holyoke, Mass., July 28.

D. 1988. Legal Services, Chico, Calif., June 21.

Delogu, Alexander. 1981. Reply Brief, August 31.

Donna. 1988. North Valley Property Owners, June 21.

Ferland, John. 1984. Portland *Press Herald*, Cambridge, Mass., November 23.

Irv. 1988. Planning Professor, Chico, Calif., June 10.

John. 1988. Welfare Office, Holyoke, Mass., July 28.

K. M. 1988. Welfare Rights, Chico, Calif., June 15.

Bibliography

Knowland, Ric. 1981. Portland Planning Department, November.
M. 1988. Welfare Office, Holyoke, Mass., July 28.
MacDonald, Carol. 1983. Department of Development of Nova Scotia, Halifax, Nova Scotia.
MacDonald, Steve. 1983. Urban Affairs Institute, Dalhousie University, Halifax, Nova Scotia.
MacGuire, Dan. 1984. State Development Office, Augusta, Maine.
N. 1988. Marken Properties, Holyoke, Mass., July 13.
Neily, Clark. 1982. Economic Development Director. Portland, Maine.
Rawlins, Paul. 1981. Ass. City Manager, Portland, Maine, November.
R. D. 1988. Legal Services, Holyoke, Mass., July 21.
Rose. 1988. Social Security Administration, Chico, Calif., June 14.
Susan. 1988. Diamond Lumber Co., Chico, Calif., June 21.
W. 1988. Disabled and the Law, Chico, Calif., June 20.

CASES

Allegheny Pittsburgh Coal v. Webster County, 102 L Ed 2d 688 (1989).
Allgeyer v. Louisiana, 165 U.S. 578 (1897)
Andrus v. Allard, 444 U.S. 51 (1980)
Arizona v. Norris, 463 U.S. 1073 (1983)
Armstrong v. U.S., 364 U.S. 40 (1960)
Arnett v. Kennedy, 416 U.S. 134 (1974)
Atkins v. Parker, 472 U.S. 115 (1986)
Bearden v. Georgia, 461 U.S. 660 (1983)
Bettigole v. Assessors, 178 NE 2d 10 (1961)
Bishop v. Wood, 426 U.S. 341 (1976)
Board of Curators v. Horowitz, 435 U.S. 1 (1978)
Board of Education v. Nyquist, 590 F 2d 1241 (1983)
Board of Pardons v. Allen, 482 U.S. 369 (1987)
Board of Regents v. Roth, 408 U.S. 564 (1971)
Boddie v. Connecticut, 401 U.S. 371 (1971)
Boom v. Patterson, 98 U.S. 403 (1879)
Boston Firefighters Union v. Boston NAACP, 461 U.S. 477 (1983)
Boston NAACP v. Boston Firefighters Union, 679 F 2d 965 (1981)
Bowen v. Gilliard, 107 SCt 3008 (1987)
Brock v. Roadway Express, Inc., 481 U.S. 252 (1987)
Brown v. Board of Education, 347 U.S. 483 (1954)

Bibliography

Bullock v. Carter, 405 U.S. 134 (1972)
Cafeteria Workers v. McElroy, 367 U.S. 886 (1961)
Calder v. Bull, 3 Dall. 386 (1798)
Cedar Rapids v. Lacoste, AC 569 (1914)
Charles River Bridge v. Warren Bridge, 11 Pet. 341 (1837)
Chicago, Minn. & St. Paul R.R. v. Minnesota, 134 U.S. 418 (1890)
City of New York v. Miln, 11 Pet. 102 (1837)
Civil Rights Cases, 109 U.S. 3 (1883)
Cleveland Board of Education v. Loudermill, 470 U.S. 532 (1985)
Common Cause v. Maine, 437 A 2d 597 (1981)
Connecticut Board of Pardons v. Dumschat, 452 U.S. 458 (1981)
Connolly v. Pension Benefit Guaranty Corp., 475 U.S. 211 (1986)
County of Washington v. Gunther, 452 U.S. 161 (1983)
Curr v. The Queen, SCR 889 (1972)
Dartmouth College v. Woodward, 4 Wheat. 518 (1819)
Day-Brite Lighting v. Missouri, 342 U.S. 421 (1952)
Dent v. Virginia, 129 U.S. 114 (1888)
Devines v. Maier, 665 F 2d 138 (1981)
Douglas v. California, 372 U.S. 353 (1963)
Dred Scott v. Sanford, 19 How. 393 (1857)
Euclid v. Ambler Realty Co., 272 U.S. 365 (1926)
Fall River Dyeing v. NLRB, 482 U.S. 27 (1987)
Fidelity Deposit v. Arens, 290 U.S. 66 (1933)
Firefighters Union Local No. 1784 v. Stotts, 467 U.S. 561 (1984)
First English Church v. County of Los Angeles, 107 SCt 2378 (1987).
Flagg Brothers v. Brooks, 436 U.S. 149 (1978)
Flemming v. Nestor, 363 U.S. 603 (1960)
Fletcher Paper v. City of Alpena, 125 NW 405 (1910)
Fletcher v. Peck, 6 Cranch 87 (1810)
Fort Halifax Packing Co. v. Coyne, 482 U.S. 1 (1987)
Georgia v. Brailsford, 2 Dall. 403 (1794)
Gibbons v. Ogden, 9 Wheat. 1 (1824)
Gideon v. Wainwright, 373 U.S. 335 (1964)
Glass v. Sloop Betsy, 3 Dall. 6 (1794)
Goldberg v. Kelly, 397 U.S. 254 (1970)
Goss v. Lopez, 419 U.S. 565 (1975)
Gray v. Pension Benefit Guaranty Corp., 467 U.S. 717 (1984)
Green v. Biddle, 8 Wheat. 1 (1823)
Greene v. Louisville, 244 U.S. 499 (1917)

Bibliography

Griffin v. *Illinois*, 351 U.S. 12 (1956)
Halifax Industries, Ltd. v. *Director of Assessment*, 55 NSR 2d 285 (1982)
Hall v. *DeCuir*, 95 U.S. 485 (1878)
Hamm v. *State*, 95 NW 2d 649 (1959)
Hanf v. *Yarmouth Light and Power*, 58 NSR 430 (1926)
Harper v. *Virginia State Board*, 383 U.S. 663 (1966)
Harris v. *McRae*, 448 U.S. 297 (1980)
Hawaii Housing Authority v. *Midkiff*, 467 U.S. 229 (1984)
Hellerstein v. *Assessor of Islip*, 332 NE 2d 279 (1975)
Helvering v. *Davis*, 301 U.S. 619 (1937)
Hewitt v. *Helms*, 459 U.S. 460 (1983)
Jackson v. *Lampshire*, 3 Pet. 280 (1830)
Jones v. *Mayer*, 392 U.S. 409 (1968)
Kentucky Department of Corrections v. *Thompson*, 104 L. Ed. 2d 506 (1989)
Kohl v. *U.S.*, 91 U.S. 367 (1875)
Laughlin v. *City of Portland*, 90 A. 318 (1914)
Lindsey v. *U.S.*, 108 SCt. 310 (1987)
Lochner v. *New York*, 198 U.S. 45 (1905)
Logan v. *Zimmerman Brush Co.*, 455 U.S. 422 (1982)
Loretto v. *Manhattan CATV*, 458 U.S. 419 (1982)
Louisville New Orleans and Texas R.R. v. *Mississippi*, 133 U.S. 587 (1890)
Lynch v. *Household Finance Corp.*, 405 U.S. 538 (1972)
MacAuliffe v. *Mayor of New Bedford*, 155 Mass. 216 (1892)
Maher v. *Roe*, 432 U.S. 464 (1977)
Marbury v. *Madison*, 1 Cranch 137 (1803)
Martin v. *Hunter's Lessee*, 1 Wheat. 304 (1816)
Mathews v. *Eldridge*, 424 U.S. 319 (1976)
Meachum v. *Fano*, 427 U.S. 215 (1976)
Mead v. *Tilley*, 104 L. Ed. 2d 796 (1989)
Memphis Light, Gas and Water v. *Craft*, 436 U.S. 1 (1977)
Mennonite Board of Missions v. *Adams*, 462 U.S. 791 (1983)
Miller v. *Halifax Power Co.*, 13 ELR 394 (1914)
Milliken v. *Bradley*, 433 U.S. 267 (1977)
Milliken v. *Bradley*, 418 U.S. 717 (1974)
Missouri ex rel. Gaines v. *Canada*, 305 U.S. 337 (1938)
Mitchell v. *U.S.*, 267 U.S. 341 (1924)
Monogahela v. *U.S.*, 148 U.S. 312 (1893)
Morris v. *Mathews*, 475 U.S. 237 (1986)
Mugler v. *Kansas*, 123 U.S. 623 (1887)

Bibliography

Mullane v. Central Hanover Bank and Trust Co., 339 U.S. 306 (1950)
Munn v. Illinois, 4 Otto 8 (1876)
Murray's Lessee v. Hoboken Land, 18 How. 272 (1856)
Nachman Corp. v. Pension Benefit Guaranty Corp., 592 F 2d 947 (1979)
National Capital Commission v. Laponte et al., RSC 70 (1972)
New Brunswick v. Fisherman's Wharf Ltd., 135 DLR 3rd 307 (1982)
Nollan v. California Coastal Comm., 107 SCt 3141 (1987)
Ogden v. Saunders, 12 Wheat. 213 (1827)
Ortwein v. Schwab, 410 U.S. 656 (1973)
Penn. Central Trans. Co. v. New York City, 438 U.S. 104 (1978)
Pennsylvania Coal v. Mahon, 260 U.S. 393 (1922)
Perry v. Sindermann, 408 U.S. 593 (1971)
Pickering v. Board of Education, 391 U.S. 563 (1968)
Plessy v. Ferguson, 163 U.S. 537 (1896)
Plyler v. Doe, 457 U.S. 202 (1982)
Providence Bank v. Billings, 4 Pet. 514 (1830)
Pruneyard Shopping Center v. Robins, 447 U.S. 74 (1980)
Quinn v. Millsap, 105 L. Ed. 2d 796 (1989)
Rapacz v. Butte County Welfare Dept., Oroville, California, June 24, 1988.
Regents of the University of Michigan v. Ewing, 474 U.S. 214 (1985)
Regina v. Martin, 35 W.W.R. 285 (1961)
Ridgeway v. Baker, 52 LW 2372 (1983)
Roberts v. City of Boston, 59 Mass. (5 Cush.) 198 (1850)
Roe v. Wade, 410 U.S. 113 (1973)
Ruckelshaus v. Monsanto Co., 467 U.S. 986 (1984)
Russman v. Luckett, 391 SW 2d 694 (1965)
Rutherford v. Rutherford, 52 LW 2130 (1983)
San Antonio School District v. Rodriguez, 411 U.S. 1 (1973)
San Diego Gas & Electric v. San Diego, 450 U.S. 621 (1981)
Satterlee v. Matthewson, 2 Pet. 627 (1829)
Serrano v. Priest, 487 P. 2d 1241 (Cal. 1971)
Shapiro v. Thompson, 394 U.S. 618 (1969)
Slaughter House Cases, 16 Wall. 36 (1873)
Smith v. Organ. of Foster Families, 431 U.S. 816 (1977)
Societe Internationale v. Rogers, 357 U.S. 197 (1958)
Steward Machine Co. v. Davis, 301 U.S. 548 (1937)
Strauder v. West Virginia, 100 U.S. 303 (1880)
Sturgis v. Crownshield, 4 Wheat. 122 (1819)
Sudbury v. Comm. of Corps. and Taxation, 321 NE 2d 641 (1973)

Bibliography

Switz v. Kingsley, 182 A 2d 841 (1962)
Terrett v. Taylor, 9 Cranch 43 (1815)
Thomas v. Review Board, 450 U.S. 707 (1981)
U.S. ex rel TVA v. Powelson, 319 U.S. 266 (1942)
U.S. Trust Co. of N.Y. v. New Jersey, 431 U.S. 1 (1977)
U.S. v. Arredonda, 6 Pet. 691 (1832)
U.S. v. Carolene Products Co., 304 U.S. 144 (1938)
U.S. v. Commodities Corp., 339 U.S. 121 (1950)
U.S. v. Fisher, 2 Cranch 3 (1805)
U.S. v. Kras, 409 U.S. 434 (1973)
U.S. v. Petty Motor Co., 327 U.S. 372 (1945)
U.S. v. River Rouge Imp. Co., 269 U.S. 411 (1925)
U.S. v. Willow River Power Co., 324 U.S. 499 (1944)
Valley Forge College v. Americans United, 454 U.S. 464 (1982)
Ware v. Hylton, 3 Dall. 199 (1796)
Warth v. Seldin, 422 U.S. 490 (1975)
Washington A and GR v. Brown, 84 U.S. 445 (1873)
West Coast Hotel v. Parrish, 300 U.S. 379 (1937)
Western Union v. Kansas, 216 U.S. 1 (1910)
West River Bridge Co. v. Dix, 6 How. 507 (1848)
Wilkinson v. Leland, 2 Pet. 627 (1829)
Williams v. Illinois, 399 U.S. 235 (1970)
Williamson v. Lee Optical, 348 U.S. 483 (1955)
Wong Duc v. Butte County Welfare Dept., Oroville, California, June 24, 1988.
Wygant v. Jackson Board of Education, 476 U.S. 267 (1986)
Zablocki v. Redhail, 434 U.S. 374 (1978)

Index

Abortion, 102–3, 109
Abraham, Henry, 67, 71
Ackerman, Bruce, 79, 122, 139
Agenda setting, 49
Aid to Families with Dependent Children (AFDC), 76, 105, 110, 160; compensation issues, 123
Arnett v. *Kennedy*, 20, 78, 125
Article I, 71
Article IV, 71
Article VI, 71
Assessment lag, 43

Balbus, Isaac, 11, 192n.9
Bath Iron Works, 135, 146
Beard, Charles A., 6, 23
Behavioralism, 11, 19, 91, 180
Bickel, Alexander, 158
Bill of Rights, 6, 67
Bills of attainder, 75, 122
Bitter and the sweet. *See* Rehnquist, William
Black, Hugo, 33, 75, 79
Blackmun, Harry, 37–38, 63
Bork, Robert, 185, 190n.1

Bosselman, Fred, 113
Boston Firefighters Union v. *Boston NAACP*, 128
Bourdieu, Pierre, 92
Bowen v. *Gilliard*, 19, 62, 160
Bowles, Sam, 166
Brennan, William, 34, 35, 63, 75–76, 79, 123, 190n.2; on police power, 63
Brown v. *Board of Education*, 13–14, 21, 87, 91, 97, 101, 103–4, 184
Bumiller, Kristin, 11
"Bundle of rights," 33, 34, 72, 113, 159
Butte County, California, 168

California Coastal Commission, 41, 53, 54, 57; creation, 58; development permit, 62; final plan, 61; regional commissions, 58
Canada, 132; administrative agencies, 140; Bill of Rights, 149; Charter of Rights and Freedoms, 149; constitutional law, 136; Department of Regional Economic Expansion (DREE), 142; language, 135; management style, 141; maritime region, 133

219

Index

Carolene Products footnote, 65, 68, 82, 85
Chico, California, 169
Choice theory, 10
Civil War, 23, 28, 31, 72, 91, 137; Civil War Amendments, 29, 95; and equality, 94; as transition, 112–13
Clune, William, 88, 98
Coastal Zone Management Act, 57, 61
Coke, Edward, 93–94
Commerce Clause, 95, 112
Common Cause v. *Maine*, 147
Commons, John R., 5, 22, 28, 30, 32
Communities of interpretation, 70, 165
Community property right, 14–15
Comparable worth, 11, 103–4
Compensation, 15–16, 24, 30–34, 72, 79, 115; displaced from housing, 129; distribution of costs, 122, 132
Conservatives: on the bench, 20, 38, 125; bias, 20; constitutional theories, 7
Constitution, U.S., 81, 88; erosion of local power, 55; as a language, 4, 93; 1937, 5, 84, 111, 158; vernacular, 158. *See also* Article I, Article IV, Article VI, Bill of Rights, Fifteenth Amendment, Fifth Amendment, Fourteenth Amendment, Sixth Amendment, Thirteenth Amendment
Constitutional Convention, 23
Constitutional Language, 4
Contract cases, 26–28, 71, 112, 123
Cooper, Phillip, 182
Corwin, Edward, 84, 180
Cotterrell, Roger, 110, 119
Council on Environmental Quality, 51
Cover, Robert, 90, 92, 118
"Critical empiricism," 12
Critical Legal Studies Movement, 6, 10, 91

Dartmouth College v. *Woodward*, 26, 115, 123
Davis, Sue, 125
Debts, 23, 24

Department of Regional Economic Expansion (DREE). *See* Canada.
Double Standard, 5, 13, 15, 65–86, 111; changes, 66, 161; delineating the boundary, 66; as institutional practice, 69; new class bias, 74, 79, 120, 157, 159; process justifications, 83
Dred Scott v. *Sanford*, 21, 29, 40

Easterbrook, Frank, 73
Economic development, 31, 131; private/public partnerships, 154
Edelman, Murray, 167, 170
Entitlement, politics of, 4, 12
Epstein, Richard, 12; *enfant terrible*, 7; "takings" theory, 7, 16
Equality: political, social, material, 95–96, 99–106; sexual, 102. *See also* Equal protection
Equal protection, 12, 89–90, 92, 94, 97
Expectations, 29, 34–35, 38, 72–73, 76, 79, 114; investment backed, 80; legitimate, 31, 41; settled, 29, 31
Ex post facto laws, 24, 119

Farmland: assessment lag, 43, 44; loss of, 43; sensitivity to, 48, 50
Farrand, Max, 6
Federalist Papers: #81, 6
Feminism, 11
Field, Stephen, 32
Fifteenth Amendment, 94
Fifth Amendment, 21, 30, 33, 62, 70–71, 110; defined, 5–6; due process, 3, 38, 123; expectations, 34, 72–73; impact, 28; practices, 6; protecting statutory interest, 37, 159; standard for entitlement, 158
Flemming v. *Nestor*, 35, 74–75, 79, 115
Fletcher v. *Peck*, 26
Formalism, 90–91, 96, 107

Index

Fourteenth Amendment, 6, 28, 31, 34, 46, 72, 94, 97–98; state action, 95, 110
Frankfurter, Felix, 33, 91

Gideon v. *Wainwright*, 100
"Giving Issue," 138, 152
Goldberg v. *Kelly*, 7, 19, 35, 105, 110, 116; milestone, 76, 174; protection for expectation, 158
Goldman, Sheldon, 23, 71
Gordon, Robert, 10
Goss v. *Lopez*, 19, 158–59
Grandfathering, 191n.7
Greenhouse, Carol, 172–73
Grossman, Joel, 10
Gunther, Gerald, 36, 67, 71, 190n.1

Halifax (Nova Scotia), 14, 131, 132; Auto Port, 142; population, 133
Hall, Stuart, 165
Hamilton, Alexander, 25
Harlan, John Marshall, 30, 33, 75, 88, 97, 137
Harrington, Christine B., 170
Hawaii Housing Authority v. *Midkiff*, 113
Hay, Douglas, 161–62, 176
Hochschild, Jennifer, 87
Holmes, Oliver Wendell, Jr., 32, 72, 74, 113, 159
Homeless, 176–77
Horwitz, Morton, 21, 22, 24
Hunt, Alan, 93
Hurst, James Willard, 68, 148

Industrial Estates Limited. *See* Nova Scotia
Inequality, economic, 88
Initiative process, 58

Jackson, Robert, 114
James, Alice, 80, 124, 162–63
Jones, Alfred Winslow, 166

Judiciary, federal: increasing conservatism, 112
Jurisprudence: ideological, 90; mechanical, 90–91; political, 90

Klare, Karl, 176

Land titles, 4, 13, 23, 157
Land-use planning, 42–43, 52–54, 55–56
Laskin, Bora, 136, 151
Law and Economics movement, 16
Law and Society movement, 92
Lawn mowing, 162
Legal realism, 19
Lerner, Max, 81
Levinson, Sanford, 81
Liberalism: militant, 6; post-World War II, 15; social science type, 7; traditional, 17
Litigation, 45, 145
Llewellyn, Karl, 81, 190n.1
Lochner v. *New York*, 66, 111, 159
Locke, John, 8, 19, 39, 74, 112
Lynd, Staunton, 14–15, 129

McCann, Michael, 11, 98–99, 104, 107, 191n.3
McCloskey, Robert, 68
Macpherson, C. B., 22
Magna Carta, 5
Maine, Sir Henry, 22
Maine (state of): first settlements, 133; referendum, 147; State Development Office, 144
Mandarin discourse, 15
Marbury v. *Madison*, 24, 34, 72, 113, 115
March, James, 9
Margold, Nathan, 96
Marshall, John, 23, 24–25, 26, 71
Marshall, Thurgood, 63, 88, 104
Marx, Karl, 9, 20, 39, 93
Marxism. *See* Marx, Karl
Mead, Lawrence, 127, 191n.9

Index

Meese, Edwin, 66
Merry, Sally, 4, 167, 192n.8
Michelman, Frank, 98, 109
Minow, Martha, 192n.2
Mosca, Gaetano, 5
Munn v. Illinois, 30

NAACP, 96
Nedelsky, Jennifer, 138, 141
"New institutionalism," 9, 11, 180
"New property," 6, 16, 19, 115; development, 74–76; not new, 35, 39; recent successes, 117
Nollan v. California Coastal Commission, 19, 61–64, 78, 159
Nova Scotia, 131, 132; and the American Revolution, 133; Industrial Estates Limited, 142. *See also* Halifax (Nova Scotia)

O'Connor, Sandra Day, 37–38, 100, 113
Old Age Survivors Disability, 4
Olsen, Johan, 9
Opie, John, 3

Partial valuation, 44
Paul, Ellen Frankel, 16
Penn. Central v. Trans. Co. of New York City, 34, 73, 114, 120
Pennsylvania Coal v. Mahon, 32, 72, 113, 137
Piven, Frances Fox, 166
Plant closings, 15, 78
Plessy v. Ferguson, 13, 21, 87, 99, 101, 184; kinds of equality, 95–97; legacy in *Brown*, 101; property claim, 29
Police power, 63, 113
Poor people's movements, 69
Portland (Maine), 14, 131, 133; Economic Development Committee, 143; population, 134
Positivism, 9–10, 85, 91–92, 106–7
Practices, 20, 92, 157

Preferential assessment, 42, 48; ad hoc informal, 46; limitations, 52; in Massachusetts, 47; as tax reform, 46; as use value, 49, 50
Pritchett, C. Herman, 11
Progressive Movement, 58
Property: accrued rights, 124; as boundary, 132, 139; comparison, 136; definition, 22; due process, 113; exchange value, 30; as government promises, 39; growth as civil liberty, 112, 158; legal construction, 3; precapitalist, 20; private, 191n.4, 192n.1; from state law, 36; as substantive predicate, 38; in tenure, 36, 128; use value, 30
Property tax, 41, 49, 64, 89, 102; administration, 45; de facto preferences, 43, 45; equal protection, 89; full valuation, 46; market value, 45, 46; relic of the Middle Ages, 42
Public ownership, 140

Reagan administration: influence on judiciary, 99, 185; on offshore drilling, 61
Rehnquist, William, 37, 78; "the bitter and the sweet," 20, 38, 78, 125
Reich, Charles, 19, 22, 35, 75–76, 116, 173–74
Renner, Karl, 20
Republican property, 67
Roberts, Owen, 67, 91
Roe v. Wade, 103
Russell, Peter, 149–50

Sagebrush Rebellion, 138
San Antonio School District v. Rodriguez, 45, 101
Santos, Boaventura deSousa, 176
Scalia, Antonin, 12, 16, 78; in *Nollan*, 62–63, 78, 159
Scheingold, Stuart, 11, 165, 192n.3, 192n.9
Schwartz, Richard D., 11, 19

Index

Sense, 4, 12, 20, 39, 40, 157, 183–85
Shapiro, Martin, 67, 107, 109, 175
Siegan, Bernard H., 16
Sixth Amendment, 100
Skocpol, Theda, 9, 192n.2
Skowronek, Stephen, 9
Slavery, 25, 29, 40, 72, 94, 112
Smith, Rogers, 9
Social Security, 4, 14, 35, 74–76, 80, 192n.6; diminishing protection, 109; distinguished, 157; held constitutional, 115; James plea, 124; 1983 reforms, 118, 162, 191n.7; nonacquiescence, 183; office practices, 172; withdrawal of benefits, 79
Squatters, 176–77
Steel mills, 15
Stone, Harlan Fiske, 65, 68, 82–83
Strauss, Leo, 16
Sullivan, Kathleen, 125
Supplemental Security Income (SSI), 165, 169
Supreme Court: shifting on entitlement, 20, 22, 77, 159, 161

"Takings," 3, 30–34, 72–74, 110, 132, 137; in California, 62; developments under Double Standard, 70; as injury to property, 119; and markets, 121; for public purposes, 139; use restrictions as, 63
Thirteenth Amendment, 94
Thompson, E. P., 162, 175
Tribe, Laurence, 14, 31, 72, 82–83
Trudeau, Pierre, 151

"Unconstitutional Conditions," 126
United States, 132; Bureau of Public Lands, 143; reliance on law, 140
U.S. Constitution. *See* Constitution, U.S.

Vested rights, 128, 136

Warren, Earl, 97
Wealth: discrimination, 84, 88, 97–98; equal protection, 45; redistribution, 44, 83
Weber, Max, 9
Welfare: benefits, 35, 36, 39, 74, 78, 121, 158; Welfare Rights Movement, 173
White, Byron, 80
Williamson Act, 48, 52

Yazoo land deal, 126

Zoning, 42, 54, 56, 60, 63, 105–9; domination by experts, 64